THE RADICAL VISION
OF SAUL ALINSKY

P. David Finks

PAULIST PRESS
New York ◆ Ramsey

For My Parents
Frances Gillard Finks
Perry David Finks

Saul's Kind of Radicals

Library of Congress
Catalog Card Number: 83-62390

ISBN: 0-8091-2608-7

Published by Paulist Press
545 Island Road, Ramsey, N.J. 07446

Printed and bound in the
United States of America

CONTENTS

Acknowledgments iv

Sources v

Introduction vii

1. The Making of an Organizer 1

2. An Itinerant Organizer 19

3. Surviving the Fifties 51

4. Back to Chicago 109

5. The Golden Years 132

6. Alinsky in Smugtown 176

7. New Directions 229

8. The Professional Organizer 250

Notes 276

Index 293

ACKNOWLEDGEMENTS

A number of individuals and institutions contributed to this book. To them I owe a debt of gratitude.

The Ford Foundation, through Mitchell Sviridoff and Robert Schrank, provided a travel-study grant. The grant enabled me to crisscross the United States to interview Saul Alinsky's friends and co-workers and to search out the written records of his thirty-five-year organizing career.

My wife Christy C. Bulkeley supported, encouraged and put up with me during the long process.

Chicago's Msgr. John J. Egan encouraged my Alinsky research and writing at every step.

Edward T. Chambers, the executive director of the Industrial Areas Foundation Alinsky Institute, opened to me Saul's files and IAF's hospitality.

Those men and women who knew Saul best contributed from their fund of Alinsky memories, stories and correspondence in personal interviews with the author: Irene McGinnis Alinsky, Jean Graham Alinsky, Edward T. Chambers, Cesar Chavez, Father Robert T. Dunn, Julius C.C. Edelstein, Msgr. John J. Egan, Father Martin Farrell, Minister Franklyn D.R. Florence, Tom Gaudette, Bryant George, Richard Harmon, Ralph Helstein, Lester Hunt, Charles T. Leber, Peter Martinez, Bishop Lawrence McNamara, Joseph B. Meegan, D. Barry Menuez, Mike Miller, David Ramage, Peggy Roach, Fred Ross, Sr., George N. Shuster, Douglas M. Still, Margery Tabankin, Marc Tanenbaum, Carl Tjerandsen, Nicholas von Hoffman, Lucius Walker, Herbert D. and Jessica Fernandez White, Marvin and Estelle Wurth.

Good friends gave assistance and encouragement, answered questions, and gave me helpful criticism: Thomas Blackburn, Gabrielle Burton, Michael P. Connolly, Msgr. Lawrence Corcoran, Joseph and Sally Cunneen, Charles E. Curran, Jay Dolan, John and Maureen Sullivan Drury, John Ehmann, Msgr. George G. Higgins, William T. Liu, Patricia McNeal, James J. Young.

Robert J. Heyer was my editor at Paulist Press.

The typists were Betty Veith, Edie Hesser, and Diana Powell. Karolyn Strassner helped with the Alinsky files. Special services were provided by Edward C. Hegeler III and William S. Morgan. Librarians from coast to coast were generous with assistance, especially in the public libraries of Danville, Ill., Rochester, N.Y. and Saratoga Springs, N.Y.

SOURCES

The basic collection of Alinsky's letters and papers are kept at the Industrial Areas Foundation Alinsky Institute in Huntington, New York. At last report the papers remain uncollated and uncatalogued. The collection is not as yet open to the public.

In 1966 Alinsky gave several boxes of his papers to the Library of the University of Illinois, Chicago Campus. This collection is available to researchers. It remains, however, fragmentary because the main collection is at the IAF Alinsky Institute.

The papers of Msgr. John O'Grady have been given recently by the National Conference of Catholic Charities to the Library of the Catholic University of America in Washington, D.C. The papers remain largely uncollated and uncatalogued.

The Clifford R. Shaw Papers (Institute for Juvenile Research) are in the collection of the Chicago Historical Society.

The complete set of the annual reports of the Industrial Areas Foundation disappeared and were never recovered after Alinsky's California home and Chicago office were broken into and robbed in 1967. Copies of some of these reports are in the possession of individual IAF trustees.

All but a few of the personal letters written by Saul to Jean Graham Alinsky have been destroyed.

An excellent (now somewhat dated) bibliography of Alinsky-style community organization was published by the Institute on the Church in Urban-Industrial Society in Chicago: "Community Organization Bibliography" by Mary J. Kirklin and Lyle E. Franzen (Chicago: ICUIS, 1973).

My dearest Saul . . . [*Rules for Radicals*] brings to us the fruit of your experience as an incomparable creative organizer—an experience which is both indomitable generosity and magnanimous sadness with regard to human nature, and which proceeds from the life-long dedication of the greatest man of action in our modern age.

Jacques Maritain

When Saul talked to me the first time, it was like coming in contact with my father, my mother, where I came from, how I felt inside. . . . All my life I'd been trying to figure out what I'm supposed to do. That's frustration. I think when Saul was talking about middle class people in his last years, that's what he was talking about: They're beautiful people; they're frustrated. What do you want me to do? . . . Tell me what I can do with my power, my talents, and my abilities. But nobody would ever give me a good answer. Then Saul came along and said, "Gaudette, you son of a bitch, if you want to organize Northwest Chicago, then quit your job, and I'll help you do it."

Tom Gaudette

We must believe in man's struggle for an even better world; that man is moving toward a world of more beauty, love, laughter, and creation. That is the vision of man.

Saul D. Alinsky

Introduction

On a cold April evening in 1939, in Chicago's Packingtown, Saul Alinsky knew he had found his life's work. The tall, solidly built crime researcher and prison sociologist sat in the corner of the room; he smiled to himself as he witnessed the first stirrings of the Back of the Yards Neighborhood Council. A steering committee of local leaders was making plans for their first neighborhood convention.

For months Alinsky had tried every trick he knew to bring together in this room a tough, red-baiting Slovak Catholic priest and an equally outspoken, cigar-smoking Communist labor leader. Between them, these two men had the largest following of residents in the Back of the Yards area. Without their cooperation, Alinsky knew, there would be no neighborhood council, and what was worse, if the Church and the union didn't get together soon, there would be violence in the stockyards and the neighborhood.

But Alinsky was smiling now because he had just won his first organizing victory. After months of cajoling and arguing with the two stubborn men, the pastor and the labor leader had shaken hands and were sitting side-by-side on the committee that was going to organize the poor, stinking, crime-ridden stockyards neighborhood into a strong, well-run community.

For the next thirty-three years, Saul Alinsky traveled from coast to coast, like a political Johnny Appleseed, organizing dozens of powerless urban neighborhoods into the kind of active self-help communities he believed were the essential components of the American democratic enterprise.

Later, when he had time to think about it, Alinsky described himself as an American radical—just one more in a long parade that stretched back to the Founding Fathers. Sam Adams, Tom Paine, Thomas Jefferson and James Madison were his heroes. From them he took his political philosophy. Alinsky's job, as he saw it, was to do what he could so that all Americans would get a chance to participate in the democratic process, even the "little guys" who usually get pushed around.

It was not an easy road. Everywhere Alinsky went, his organizing approach made him a center of controversy and community conflict. Helping the little guys get their share of the American pie proved to be an exciting and dangerous business. As his reputation grew, he became as welcome in most American cities as would Ghengis Khan.

In Kansas City, the local police chief had him picked up as soon as he stepped off the train from Chicago. Alinsky said that he wrote a lot of his first book during long weekends in the Kansas City jail.

A big city mayor tried to restrain a neighborhood organization's activities by raising the price of milk served to local schoolchildren. Alinsky then organized the children to offer daily Mass and public prayers to bring the mayor to repentance. The mayor did repent, but, in turn, condemned Alinsky as a dangerous agitator.

In Omaha Alinsky was charged with Communist subversion when he organized the working class neighborhoods of that city.

Californians called him a Trotskyite because he sponsored voter registration drives and citizenship classes for the state's Mexican-American adults.

In the 1950's Protestant church leaders charged that Alinsky was an undercover agent for the Catholic Church. They said his organizing of Chicago's neighborhoods was a way to turn the city over to the Catholic Church.

In Rochester, New York, Alinsky was charged with anti-semitism for organizing poor blacks to take on inner city slum landlords.

Alinsky laughed at these attacks. Organizing communities

had its tedious aspects, he admitted, but when he saw people stand up and fight for their share of the American enterprise it was worth all the effort. Alinsky never let society reform dull his sense of humor: "The establishment can accept being screwed, but not being laughed at. What bugs them most about me is that unlike humorless radicals, I have a hell of a time doing what I'm doing."[1]

Like the New Deal and the CIO, Saul Alinsky's community organization was a product of the Great Depression. He started out as a crime researcher and spent the 1930's walking the crowded streets of Chicago's immigrant neighborhoods. From a street corner sociologist's vantage point he witnessed American citizens suffering the effects of a national economic breakdown. He saw the silent factories, soup lines in the cities, the anguish of millions of unemployed people in a land of plenty. For the masses of Americans the Depression was proof that the system was not working for them.[2]

By the mid-1930's, however, things started slowly to change. A new spirit appeared in the cities; people began to awaken with a kind of feistiness, a new readiness to get together to change things. Roosevelt's New Deal legislation began to take hold; the radical organizers of the Congress of Industrial Organizations led the steel, rubber and auto workers to victories over powerful industrial giants; a new solidarity was felt in working class neighborhoods and in the factories. The nation's citizens began to come together to share the common enterprise.

In that "wondrous experience" of human solidarity and readiness to fight for survival Alinsky saw the potential for mass citizen's organizations in America's urban neighborhoods. With the skills he learned moonlighting with the CIO organizers in the Chicago stockyards, Alinsky set out on the mean streets of Chicago's Back of the Yards district to reorganize America from the bottom up.

It is now ten years since Alinsky's death. In many ways, however, he is as current as today's headlines about Polish workers in Gdansk and Mexican-Americans in Texas. Hard times, the worst since the Great Depression, have returned to crush millions of Americans. The nation's economy is limping badly, political leaders and corporate tycoons are unpopular with most Americans, our cities are deteriorating and debt-ridden, the unemployed are once again being forced to migrate in search of jobs, the prisons are overflowing, and most people are disaffected and disgruntled.

As more Americans start to hurt, they are turning in large numbers to Alinsky's brand of urban populist organizations. Almost unnoticed by the news media, new, Alinsky-style mass organizations are building all over the country. These voluntary organizations are drawing together moderates, liberals and conservatives—ordinary American citizens who are trying to reassert a measure of control over their neighborhoods, their cities and towns and their jobs.

♦ In New York City the Queens Citizen Organization is fighting professional arsonists who have already burned down the Bronx. They are demanding that Mayor Edward Koch pay serious attention to the concerns of the working class neighborhoods of Queens.

♦ In San Antonio, Communities Organized for Public Service (COPS) has been running voter registration drives among the city's large Mexican-American population. The organization has built up the power to get its share of municipal resources.

♦ For six years the Oakland Community Organizations (OCO) has been fighting a city-wide campaign to gain control of the neighborhoods. OCO has reduced truancy in the city schools, developed jobs for unemployed youth, controlled prostitution in residential areas and set up neighborhood citizen-police cooperation.

♦ The United Neighborhood Organizations (UNO) in East Los Angeles turns out more than five thousand voting delegates at its annual convention. The organization waged a victorious campaign to change discriminatory automobile insurance rates for East Los Angeles residents.

♦ Former Alinsky organizer Cesar Chavez leads the United
Farm Workers of America. The union has brought collective
bargaining to the laborers in California's agricultural industry.

These and many other organizations make use of the services of trained organizers, like Alinsky, to build up mass-
organized, politically active local communities. One observer
calls this phenomenon a "Backyard Revolution" and claims
that some twenty million Americans now belong to voluntary
neighborhood-based organizations.[3]
Organizations begin with basic community issues: municipal services, jobs, health care, housing finance, parent-school
problems, consumer action, insurance rates, police protection—all the things that touch people where they live.
Each victory strengthens people's hope and helps build up
the organization's membership. Gradually they develop the
power and skills needed to deal collectively with a variety of
local needs and problems. When the organization is strong
enough, the members move beyond simple local concerns, and
they form networks with other organized communities to work
on issues on a larger scale. According to Alinsky, the bottom-
up approach to democratic process is precisely the way Founding Fathers Jefferson and Madison intended the U.S. system to
work.
Saul Alinsky organized communities as a means of building up people's pride and dignity. He said that government or
social agencies cannot give citizens what they need to live a full
life. Social change happens only when ordinary people working together possess the power to make it happen. That was the
gist of the democratic process as far as Alinsky was concerned:
when citizens can negotiate with the powers that be instead of
begging, only then can they create the situation in which there
is dignity, freedom and independence.
Saul Alinsky's goal of reorganizing America from the bottom-up has not been reached. The results of his thirty-three
years of organizing were, to say the least, uneven. Altogether
he organized about two million people. Sometimes he failed to
produce a viable organization. Many times he had to turn

down a community invitation to organize because he didn't have the manpower or because he feared the odds against it were too great. He never did get around to building the regional and national networks of people's organizations he described in the pages of *Reveille for Radicals*.[4]

The Industrial Areas Foundation he established to bankroll his organizing was chronically underfunded. During his whole career, Alinsky was able to recruit and train no more than a half-dozen first-class organizers. Even these few organizers were paid so poorly and worked so hard that most of them burned out after a few years on the job.

The most difficult part of organizing, however, was the fragile nature of even the most successful of Alinsky's local organizations. The problem of continuity, Alinsky found, was something built into the democratic system. When there was a crisis in a community, or serious neighborhood problems, people rushed to join the organization, eager to take on City Hall or a giant corporation, if that's what it took to change things. But afterward, when the immediate battle was won, popular interest and participation dropped off, local leaders turned to more conservative pursuits, organizational arteries hardened and organizations sometimes died. Afterward, it often seemed that nothing remained of the brave experiment in democratic citizen participation.

To the end of his life, however, Alinsky kept organizing because he was convinced that if the United States was to survive as a free democratic nation, it had to have active citizens organized into local "communities of interest." So he continued to teach people how to organize their communities even if those organizations didn't always last.

Alinsky was not easily discouraged. It was important for him to be able to teach people how to organize, choose their own leaders and policies and be able to change both whenever necessary. "That's the way a democratic process works," he said—"a few steps forward, maybe only one back, if you're lucky."[5]

Like his mentor, Thomas Jefferson, Alinsky remained convinced that the American Revolution had to be a permanent state of affairs. Before he died, Alinsky established a training school for future organizers. He wanted a new generation of organizers to be better prepared to carry on the reorganizing of America.

Alinsky believed, with Alexis de Tocqueville, that the American Republic would be in grave danger if its citizens became apathetic and grew too dependent on public authority to solve their problems. External enemies, he said, were less a threat to the nation than the "enemy within us—that hidden and malignant inertia that foreshadows more certain destruction to our life and future than any nuclear warhead." For Saul Alinsky there could be "no more devastating tragedy than the death of man's faith in himself and in his power to direct his future."[6]

1.

The Making of an Organizer

Immigrant Son

In the winter there is a freezing wind the old-timers call the "Hawk." It roars in from Lake Michigan and sweeps across the Near West Side of Chicago. On such a night in the winter of 1909, a son was born to an immigrant Jewish couple, Sarah and Benjamin Alinsky. They named the boy Saul David.

Years later, when an angry heckler demanded of Saul Alinsky: "Go back where you came from," he laughed at the heckler and answered: "I would, but that corner of 13th and Racine is now a public housing project, and my income is too high to qualify."[1]

On January 30, 1909, however, his parents were glad to have their tiny ground-floor flat in the old three-story tenement. Benjamin and Sarah had both come from Russia, part of the flood of fifty thousand Eastern European Jews who came to Chicago around the turn of the century. They came west to escape the crush of the overcrowded immigrant neighborhoods in New York City. They chose, instead, to settle in the sprawling new city the immigrants called the "Klondike of America." Chicago was the heart of America in 1909, a giant rail center with four hundred trains a day chugging into its rail terminals.

Sarah Tannenbaum Alinsky was barely seventeen when Saul was born. She and her parents had moved in with her older brothers and sisters when they arrived in Chicago five years before. Sarah's sister found her a job as a seamstress in a small garment shop owned by Benjamin Alinsky. The shop

1

was one of hundreds which did piece work for Chicago's large clothing firms. Alinsky said later that his father ran a "sweat-shop"—paid his workers low wages and forced them to work long hours in a crowded, poorly ventilated room.

With her lovely oval face and sunny disposition, the young girl soon caught the eye of the recently divorced Benjamin. They married and settled down in the tiny ground floor flat, separated by only a curtain from the noisy tailor shop. All his life Saul would remember his mother banging on the bathroom door, routing him out to make way for a customer or a shop girl.

When it came time for the boy to attend school, he was sent by his Orthodox parents to the local "heder," the neighborhood Jewish parochial school. The young Alinsky dutifully droned the Hebrew alphabet with his classmates and learned to read the Scriptures. But Sarah's quietly nurtured hope that her intelligent, studious son would eventualy become a rabbi was short-lived. One day his reading skill won him the rabbi's favor in the practical form of a penny reward. The next time Saul read well he held out his hand for another penny; this act warranted him a slap and a visit from the rabbi who complained to the Alinskys about their son's disrespect. Shortly thereafter he was allowed to attend the neighborhood public school.

Saul loved his bright and lively mother. He had no such feelings for his father, a stern disciplinarian. Benjamin Alinsky was an ambitious, hard-working, small businessman, determined to be an American-style success. He had little time or affection for his only son. When Saul was ten, he defied his father over some small matter and refused to back down, even after receiving a beating. That small victory, according to Alinsky, was the beginning of his lifelong readiness to tangle with any "duly constituted authority."

Saul's other childhood memory of his father was of collecting missiles—stones, chunks of metal and bits of broken glass—whenever he and his dad walked through the neighborhood. Saul's father insisted they be prepared to defend their home should marauding mobs of their Polish neighbors decide to invade the Jewish ghetto, bent on an Old World-style pogrom.

The elder Alinsky's fear of street mobs in Chicago was not unfounded. In the years before and after World War I, the city's largest Jewish neighborhood was an enclave on the Near West Side, surrounded entirely by unfriendly neighbors. A few years before Saul was born, social worker Jane Addams, who founded the famous Hull-House settlement house a few blocks to the north of the Alinsky home, described the Near West Side of Chicago as an unlovely, crowded conglomeration of immigrant slums. "Between Halstead Street and the river," she wrote, "live about ten thousand Italians—Neopolitans, Sicilians, Calabrians, with an occasional Lombard or Venetian. To the South on Twelfth Street are many Germans, and side streets are given over entirely to Polish and Russian Jews."[2] By the time Alinsky was going to school the Poles had grown to outnumber all the other ethnic groups on the Near West Side. Saul called the Jewish neighborhood a "slum within a slum."

Gangs of young toughs terrorized the West Side streets. As late as 1921, mobs attacked Jewish neighborhoods. Chicago's "melting pot" was often a boiling cauldron of street crime and bloody gang fights.

There were Jewish gangs in Alinsky's neighborhood, the most notorious of which was the "Boundary Gang." These kids were real hoodlums. Gang fights often erupted into riots. By the time he was eleven, Saul was hanging around the gang's headquarters on 12th Street. Belonging to the gang meant acceptance, adventure and, more importantly, protection from other gangs. "If any of us crossed 16th Street," Alinsky said, "we got the shit beaten out of us. And we did the same to the Poles if we caught them in our neighborhood."

One afternoon Saul came home from school with a big bruise on his forehead and his clothes torn and dirty. He made the mistake of bragging to his mother about fighting with some Polish kids who wandered into the Jewish "turf." Sarah saw her worst fears realized: her wonderful boy was turning into a street ruffian like all the rest. She grabbed him by the collar and marched him off to the rabbi.

Never one to back down easily, Saul defended his fighting

by quoting to the rabbi the biblical passage about the taking of "an eye for an eye and a tooth for a tooth," adding: "That's the way things are settled in America."

The rabbi liked the precocious boy. He spoke quietly to him about what is involved in becoming a "mensch," a real man. He gave Saul a maxim of the great Rabbi Hillel: "Where there are no men, be thou a man." Alinsky never forgot it.[3]

Some of the West Side Jewish kids of Alinsky's day grew up to be real criminals like Jake "Greasy Thumb" Gerzik, a key member of the Capone gang, and Jack Ruby (Rubenstein), the murderer of Lee Harvey Oswald. There were others like Alinsky, however, who moved on to better things: Benjamin "Benny" Goodman, the celebrated "King of Swing," Supreme Court Justice Arthur Goldberg, CBS Chairman William S. Paley, Admiral Hyman Rickover, and Chicago sociologist Philip Hauser. All these men grew up in the Chicago ghetto within a few blocks of Alinsky's home.

The young Alinsky knew how to fight, but he learned early to talk his way out of tight spots. His mother managed to keep him out of the gang's criminal activities by watching over him day and night. Sarah wanted a better life for her only son. As Saul approached his teens, she begged Benjamin to let them move to a better neighborhood, away from the gangs and the crime.

When Benjamin finally decided to move from the house on 13th and Racine, he did not take his wife and son. One day Benjamin Alinsky packed up his tailor shop and moved to California. A few months after Saul's parents were divorced, Sarah remarried. Her new husband took her and her son to a new house, away from the old neighborhood.

According to the terms of the Alinskys' divorce settlement, Saul's parents agreed that the boy would spend part of each year with his father. Benjamin soon got married again— this time to a woman with three children. When Saul arrived for his first visit to Los Angeles, he was told he could not stay in his father's home. Benjamin told his son that he would be living in a nearby boarding house. Benjamin paid Saul's board and room and gave him spending money, but that was all. He told his son he was not to call him unless he became sick.

Alinsky spent the next four years shuttling between Los Angeles and Chicago. His loneliness on the West Coast was offset, to some degree, by the warmth of his mother's care in Chicago, but it was surely an unusual adolescence.

Between his summertime travels and moves by his mother in Chicago, Alinsky attended a number of high schools, but he did well in his studies. He learned to play tennis by working as a clubhouse attendant at the swank Hollywood Tennis Club. Sometime during his stay on the West Coast he had an affair with an "older woman" of twenty-two. During his high school years he injured his back in a schoolyard football game, and he was forced to take it easy for many months. He became an avid reader.

By the time he graduated from Hollywood High in 1925, Alinsky had a spirit of independence well beyond his seventeen years. He had learned to take care of himself and to get along with all sorts of people. This independence, together with his love of travel, would mark his later "lone wolf" style of itinerant organizing.

Saul's father did agree to pay his college expenses, but only on the condition that he would have no further responsibility for his son. Saul was happy to trade the annual visit to Los Angeles for the university. He chose to attend the great American university which was within walking distance of his home on Chicago's South Side.

Urban Sociology

The University of Chicago was a whole new world to the Jewish kid who grew up in the Near West Side ghetto. Alinsky walked in to register for classes with a show of worldly assurance. He refused to ask for help in signing up for classes. As a result he made some mistakes. An aviation buff at that time, Alinsky wanted to earn his pilot's license. He signed up for a course in aeronautical engineering. That turned out to be a mistake. He followed a pretty girl into another line and registered for a course in equitation. It sounded like something having to do with flying. It was, in a way. He persevered through one semester, but ever afterward Alinsky avoided horses, even from the relative safety of the two dollar window. His one good move, that first day, was to sign up for the campus ROTC; it provided much needed spending money.

Alinsky chose archaeology as his major. It was a good choice. He worked on the excavations of Winnebago Indian burial sites near Chicago and spent two of his summer vacations laboring in the hot sun on American Indian digs in the Southwest.

Alinsky also took an interest in sociology. Fortunately for him, the University of Chicago's sociology department (the "Chicago School" of urban sociology) in the 1920's was probably the best place in the world to study the sociology of the city. Professor Robert Ezra Park, the Chicago School's leading light, became Alinsky's favorite professor.

The crusty Park was a practical man, a newspaper reporter-turned sociologist, who talked about cities in terms Alinsky understood. Of his background, Park wrote: "I expect that I have actually covered more ground, tramping about in cities in different parts of the world, than any living man. Out of all this I gained, among other things, a conception of the city, the community, and the region, not as a geographical phenomenon merely, but as a kind of social organism."[4] The city became for Park's students more than a haphazard collection of neighborhoods, police precincts, churches, schools, business, clubs and taverns. The city was the sum of these parts, but it had also a life of its own, with discernible patterns of growth, expansion, decline and death. This "urban ecology" could be studied and the data used to help people plan more effective, better organized communities in which to live.

From Park's colleague, Ernest K. Burgess, Alinsky learned the art of field study. He moved out with his notebook to observe what he could of Chicago's streets and neighborhoods. Alinsky became adept at blending into the neighborhood background where he could watch carefully all that was going on and write it down in his reports to Burgess. This information about the neighborhoods was fed by Burgess' students into a great map of Chicago that produced a working diagram of Chicago's life and operation.

In the 1920's Chicago was a perfect laboratory for a sociologist. The city had grown to phenomenal size in less than a hundred years. It was the city of Jane Addams, Al Capone and Mother Cabrini. Alinsky loved Chicago's variety. What he enjoyed about sociology was the chance it gave him to escape the classroom and to roam the city's streets and neighborhoods. He soon became a talented street corner observer and social analyst.

In the course of an assignment for Burgess, Alinsky reported on the operation of the public dance halls which were then the rage of Chicago's younger set. One evening, in the course of an assignment at the Dreamland Ballroom, Alinsky interviewed a young woman named Opal—"of pleasant face and splendid physical development." After dancing with her all evening, Alinsky offered to drive her to her home on the city's North Side. His careful report included a side trip to a nearby park where he continued his interview. Alinsky was never guilty of "ivory tower" sociology.[5]

In the University of Chicago's 1930 yearbook, *Cap and Gown*, Alinsky's picture shows him to be a serious-looking, bespectacled youth, with a mop of curly dark hair. The yearbook entry makes no mention of his belonging to a fraternity or any student clubs. Alinsky was a loner.

After graduation he could not find a job. The Depression was on, and archeology was as dead as the long-buried Winnebago Indians. Later he recalled, "By that time the Depression was setting in and the only digging jobs were with the W.P.A."

His mother had no money, and his father, now a successful dealer in Los Angeles real estate, refused Saul's request for a loan. For months Alinsky hung around the university, running errands for faculty members and cadging meals wherever he could.

Finally someone in the sociology department took a hand in his fate, and Alinsky was awarded a social science fellowship for graduate study. The grant provided tuition, room and board. Saul's survival was assured for a couple of years.

Alinsky chose to concentrate on the study of criminology, and in particular on the study of organized crime in Chicago. In those days organized crime was the Capone gang, a major economic and social institution in the city. It took Alinsky three months to work his way into the mob's good graces. He did it by hanging around the Lexington Hotel, the mob's South Side headquarters. When the gangsters finally noticed him and wanted to know what he was doing, Alinsky told them that he was a university student who wanted to study the gang's operations. He avoided getting in the way and made himself useful as a "gofer"—fetching coffee and listening to the mobsters tell their "war stories." Once or twice he drove a couple of the gang members home after a drunken party. Eventually he got to know a couple of Capone's lieutenants, "Big Ed" Stash and the mob's "Enforcer," Frank Nitti.

Nitti was in charge of the day-to-day operations at this time because Capone was in prison. The gang leader took a liking to the intelligent "college boy." Once Nitti took him under his protection, Alinsky was "in." He became a fixture at mob headquarters and was allowed to come and go as he pleased. He went along to gangster parties at Chicago's underworld hotspots. The easy-going twenty-three year old sociologist talked to all of them: bosses, "soldiers," girlfriends, hangers-on and the lawyers, judges and politicians on Capone's payroll. Alinsky wrote it all down in his notebook.

For nearly two years Alinsky enjoyed an insider's spot—a criminologist's dream. He said it was better than the movies— tough guys, beautiful girls, free booze, fast cars and a chance to see underworld power at work.

In his heyday, Capone, far from being hated by the man-in-the-street, was seen by many Chicagoans as an urban Robin Hood. He ran a kind of public utility for a city population suffering from economic depression and Prohibition. Capone supplied what people wanted—girls, booze, gambling. The Chicago underworld was a part of the real world in Chicago.

Alinsky also learned about the darker side of the mob's empire—extortion, beatings, terror, brutality, murder. One day Frank Nitti explained to the young "professor" why the mob hired out-of-town killers for local jobs. It was one thing to shoot a stranger, Nitti explained, but much tougher when he had to kill a guy he knew, a man from the old neighborhood whom you saw at ballgames and parties—a guy with a wife and kids. Saul said that Capone's mobsters taught him a valuable lesson about the "terrific importance of personal relation- ships."[6]

Partway through the second year, however, Alinsky grew restless. He was bored with graduate school, with the endless lectures about social pathology and the etiology of juvenile delinquency. He was also tired of hanging around with mob- sters. Anyway, all of a sudden society seemed to be catching up with them; more and more of Capone's hoods were being sent to jail.

The main cause of his growing indifference to graduate school, however, was a young woman he met at the university. Saul was deeply in love with Helene Simon. The young couple wanted to get married. What Alinsky needed now was a real job.

Juvenile Delinquency Researcher

One day after class, Professor Burgess introduced Alinsky to Clifford R. Shaw. Word had gotten around about Alinsky's working his way inside the Capone gang. Crime researcher Shaw asked to meet the budding criminologist. Clifford Shaw, a protégé of Burgess, was the director of the Chicago-based Institute for Juvenile Research. Originally IJR was set up to provide diagnostic studies of delinquents brought before the city's juvenile court. IJR had continued to grow until, in Alinsky's time, it was a division of the Illinois Division of Criminology.

Two weeks after the conversation in Burgess' office, Shaw offered Alinsky a job as an IJR field researcher. Without a moment's hesitation, Saul picked up his books and walked out of graduate school. He never did write his dissertation on the Capone gang. For the next eight years he worked with Shaw and his IJR colleagues who were producing basic empirical studies on juvenile delinquency in the United States.

The research at IJR was patterned on R.E. Park's urban ecology model. Shaw dispatched his researchers into Chicago's streets to study the zones or areas of the city where crime was

rampant. On the basis of the data collected by the field workers, a detailed analysis of each high-crime area was prepared.
Chicago's high-crime areas were found to form a great gray arc
of poor neighborhoods surrounding the city's central business
district. Alinsky and his fellow researchers then moved into the
individual neighborhoods and interviewed young delinquents
and their families. Alinsky worked with a dozen of these boys,
helping them write their life histories. Data from these life
histories and neighborhood interviews showed that kids become involved in criminal activities as a normal part of their
social development in poor, disorganized communities. Alinsky
was encouraged by Shaw's practical approach to delinquency
research.

For his first assignment Alinsky went to "Little Italy," the
Italian slum, on the Near West Side, a few blocks from his
boyhood home. Because of his success in gaining entry to the
Capone gang, Shaw decided that Alinsky would be able to
crack Little Italy's notorious "42 Gang."

A few years earlier in an extensive study of street-corner
youth gangs in Chicago, sociologist Fredrich M. Thrasher
counted 1,313 active gangs in the city's slum neighborhoods.
Among the toughest of them was the 42 Gang, known as "the
farm team" for the Capone gang. One IJR researcher described
the gang as a "daring fearless lot at open warfare with the
police and society." The trademark of the "42's" was a wide-
brimmed white felt hat, worn at a rakish angle by the gang
members.[7] Their specialty was automobiles—stealing, strip-
ping and selling the parts. In their lighter moods they engaged
in window-smashing burglaries of Chicago stores, "under the
energetic leadership of one of their numbers nicknamed 'Babe
Ruth,' not a ballplayer."[8]

One graduate of the 42 Gang was Momo Salvatore "Sam"
Giancana, described by Robert Kennedy as the "chief gunman
for the group that succeeded the Capone mob."[9]

The 42 Gang ignored Alinsky. The young hoodlums
would not talk to him. Saul continued to hang around the
neighborhood, hoping for an opportunity to gain the gang's
trust.

One night, one of the gang leaders, a kid called "Little

Dumas" Massina, was killed during a holdup. Alinsky went to the kid's home to see what he could do for the family. Mrs. Massina was crying and telling everyone who came in that she didn't even have a picture with which to remember her dead son.

Alinsky disappeared. The next morning he brought the boy's picture to the mother. The night before, after he had left the boy's house, Alinsky had gone to the morgue with a photographer. They took a picture of the kid, and the photographer touched it up to look as natural as possible.

Little Dumas' mother was overjoyed with the photograph. Word of Alinsky's kindness spread quickly through the "Little Italy" grapevine. At last Alinsky had found an entree to the 42 Gang.[10]

For the next two years Alinsky was in almost daily contact with the gang members, their families and friends. Fifteen delinquents wrote their life histories with Saul's help. In an article Alinsky wrote for the American Prison Association, he explained the interview techniques he used with the 42 Gang members.[11]

Clifford Shaw was delighted with Alinsky's reports. In fact, Shaw was so impressed with Alinsky's interviews that he suggested they co-author a book on the 42 Gang. A couple of months later Shaw rewarded the twenty-four year old criminologist by getting him assigned to a newly created job as prison sociologist at the Illinois State Penitentiary at Joliet.[12]

For three years Alinsky served on the prison classification board at Joliet. He interviewed each new arrival at the prison and made a detailed evaluation of each prisoner, based on his background and criminal record. The board's recommendations were intended to assist the prison authorities in developing individualized rehabilitation programs for the inmates. Within a couple of months Alinsky realized that these evaluations were used by the warden and guards for purposes other than rehabilitation. He became convinced at Joliet that, whatever other social functions prisons serve, they do not rehabilitate criminals.

Because Alinsky maintained good relations with Chicago's underworld, he was trusted, to some extent, by the Joliet inmates. As far as the prison officials were concerned, Alinsky kept all the rules. He interceded for prisoners at times, but in a clearly professional manner. Alinsky did not want to lose his job. Later he did help find jobs on the outside for inmates due for parole. Many years later, one of these Joliet "graduates," a powerful Midwest labor leader, offered to send some "muscle" to help Alinsky in a battle he was having with Chicago city officials.

What Joliet taught Alinsky was that most of the inmates were no more than petty criminals who were unfortunate enough to grow up in high-crime, slum neighborhoods where it was virtually impossible to avoid trouble with the police. Once these delinquents were sent to prison, they usually became career criminals.

The professional criminologists, Alinsky decided, did little or nothing to help these youthful criminals. The experts knew that the chief causes of crime were the economic and social conditions—bad living conditions, lack of jobs, poverty. But to avoid controversy, Alinsky said that the criminologists prescribed for the youthful delinquents a variety of recreational programs and "something mysterious called 'character building.'"[13]

In 1935, the twenty-six year old Alinsky was an up-and-coming criminologist. Clifford Shaw recommended him warmly for a position as director of the municipal probation department in Philadelphia. He wrote a letter on Saul's behalf to Philadelphia Judge Theodore Rosen, in which he praised Alinsky's work in the Chicago neighborhoods and at Joliet.[14]

Rosen worked hard to get Alinsky to take the position. Saul was tempted; for his wife Helene it meant moving back to her home town and family. But Alinsky hesitated. He and Rosen spent long hours discussing how they would reform the probation department. Rosen increased the pressure. In addition to a large increase in salary, the job offer now included a lectureship at the University of Pennsylvania and a regular column in a Philadelphia newspaper. In the end, however, Alinsky turned down the job.

Later, Saul said that he was tempted by the Philadelphia position—the good salary, security for his family, a chance to teach and work closely with Judge Rosen. But it meant buying further into the system, and he was already looking for a more active role in combating juvenile delinquency.[15]

Although Alinsky wasn't aware of it at the time, his refusal of the Philadelphia job was a turning point in his career. At the end of his three year term at Joliet, he had returned to his job at the Institute for Juvenile Research. Sometime later Clifford Shaw sent him to a West Side neighborhood called the Back of the Yards, a foul-smelling, crime-ridden slum, downwind of Chicago's Union Stockyards. Shaw's instructions to Alinsky were to get to know the neighborhood, to search out the local leaders and, with them, to organize a community program to combat juvenile delinquency.

Reorganizing a Neighborhood

When Saul Alinsky arrived in the Back of the Yards, he was ready for something different. His work with the gangs and at the penitentiary made him aware of the influence of neighborhood conditions on young criminals. The Depression was continuing, however, and he needed a steady job.

He did his best to carry out his assignment to organize a unit of Shaw's Chicago Area Project (CAP) in the stockyards area. CAP was the current brainchild of Shaw and University of Chicago professor Ernest K. Burgess. Unlike the usual settlement house program, Shaw insisted that the CAP was to be run by the neighborhood residents. IJR provided the neighborhood residents with start-up funds and a trained delinquency worker like Alinsky to help them organize and run the project. The program offered by the CAP, however, was entirely traditional—the usual mixture of recreational activities, counseling for troubled kids, and talking school dropouts into going back to school or finding them jobs.[16]

What Alinsky liked about CAP was IJR's insistence that local residents—parents, teachers, police and clergy—were to run the program. Saul agreed with Shaw's theory that an organized community could do more than "outside" experts to keep most kids out of places like Joliet.

The Back of the Yards section was a sad place. It was a notorious slum at the turn-of-the-century, when Upton Sinclair used it as the locale for his muckraking novel *The Jungle*. In stark Dickensian terms, Sinclair told the story of poor immigrant families, Poles, Slovaks and Lithuanians, who lived, worked and died in the bloody, stinking stockyards and the nearby community.[17] Thirty years later, when Alinsky arrived, he said that the neighborhood was still "a byword for disease, delinquency, deterioration, dirt and dependency."[18]

For months Alinsky did what he knew best: he picked his way carefully through the neighborhood streets and haunts, observing what was going on, listening to what people talked about in taverns and on streetcorners, meeting the local "influentials" (parish priests, saloon keepers, ward politicians, funeral directors)—those individuals who knew everyone and everything in the neighborhood. Working over his notes at night, Alinsky often wondered how on earth this run-down, disaster of a neighborhood worked as well as it did for its ninety thousand residents. No one in the Back of the Yards paid any attention to him; as far as they were concerned he was another university student, doing another worthless study of juvenile delinquency.

But this time the residents were wrong. This researcher came along just as a fierce labor battle was raging in the Chicago stockyards and overflowing into the residential community. John L. Lewis, the president of the recently formed Congress of Industrial Organizations (CIO), had sent a crack team of labor organizers to "organize the unorganized" workers in Chicago's meat packing industry. The Chicago campaign was the kickoff of a national CIO effort to organize the meat industry. In 1938, Chicago was still the "Hog Butcher for the World."[19] The "Big Four" meat packing companies (Swift, Armour, Wilson and Cudahy) were prepared to crush this new union threat as they had crushed three earlier union drives in Chicago's stockyards.

The union organizers Alinsky found working in the Back of the Yards were professional radicals. Their specific assignment from CIO president Lewis was to organize Chicago's packinghouse workers. To accomplish this, they entered into the lives of the stockyard workers. For these professionals, organizing was a full time job. It involved agitation—convincing people that their problems were not unique, but connected with the problems of poor, exploited people everywhere. They preached unity, solidarity, action, and reform. Alinsky went to the CIO's mass meetings in the Back of the Yards. The organizers fascinated him. The mass meetings the CIO organizers held in the Back of the Yards, Alinsky noticed, dealt with more issues than the packinghouse union. The organizers were involved in all the important social and political issues of the day: legal funds for blacks imprisoned in the South, the sufferings of the Dust Bowl migrants, the Spanish Civil War, government relief programs, jobs for the unemployed, anti-fascist organizations, rent strikes, all kinds of local community problems.[20]

Discouraged as he was with criminologists who seemed unable to do anything but study about poverty and crime, Alinsky was greatly impressed by these union activists who were committed to organizing people to attack and change the conditions that kept them poor and downtrodden. These men were professional organizers, and they were good at the job.

During this period Alinsky was being paid to organize the Chicago Area Project. At least that's what IJR's Clifford Shaw thought. The weekly reports Alinsky was sending to him were full of descriptions of meetings held, issues discussed, contacts made—lots of activity. The radicalization of Saul Alinsky was proceeding but had not yet advanced to the point where he was willing to give up his weekly paycheck from IJR. However Shaw's talented delinquency researcher was really moonlighting as a CIO volunteer.

For months Alinsky spent most of his time with the CIO organizers. They were teaching the street-corner sociologist the skills of mass organization. He learned how to organize mass meetings, to focus attention on the issues that really bothered people, to direct an action, to raise money, and to recruit members. In the process Alinsky witnessed something unique in Depression-bound Chicago. Slum dwellers, people who had nothing, were coming together by the hundreds, ready to fight for control of their own lives and hopes. Life in the Back of the Yards was exciting. It was at that point that Alinsky came up with a plan to help the CIO organizers overcome a major obstacle to a packinghouse union.

In early 1939, the CIO organizers were stalled in their drive to build the packinghouse union because of opposition from the pastors of the Catholic churches in the Back of the Yards. From their Sunday pulpits the priests attacked the CIO union as a Communist plot to win over the local workers, ninety percent of whom were Catholics. The stockyard workers were confused by the priests' opposition to the union. They wanted the union, but they didn't want to lose the Church. The meat packing bosses, on the other hand, were delighted with the Church's anti-union stand. They played up the Communist threat for all it was worth.

As a last resort, the union organizers had decided to call a mass strike in the stockyards to force the companies to accept the union. But no one in the Back of the Yards really wanted a strike. Union leader Herb March knew how the workers and their friends feared a stockyards strike: "Men who make their living with knives," he said, "are not peaceful strikers."[21]

In the course of Alinsky's neighborhood wanderings, he had met Joseph Meegan, a young high school teacher and a part-time director at Davis Square Park, a playground in the middle of the Back of the Yards. Alinsky recognized in Meegan a key neighborhood contact. Joe and his wife were Catholics, and they knew everyone in the area. Meegan's brother was a Chicago priest.

The Meegans agreed to invite a few of their friends to meet with Alinsky. The group who came to the Meegan house included teachers, store clerks, stockyard workers and a couple of young priests from neighborhood parishes. The group began meeting weekly to talk about the problems of the neighborhood.

What came out of these discussions was a plan to organize, not IJR's youth program, but the whole Back of the Yards neighborhood. Alinsky and the group of young residents decided on a neighborhood council, patterned after the CIO's union organization. The council, made up of local residents, would have the power to deal with the flood of neighborhood problems. Alinsky told his recruits that a neighborhood council could remove the CIO's big organizing obstacle: if they could get the churches and the union working together on issues of the local community, priests and organizers would work out their differences over the union.

With Meegan's help, Alinsky made an appointment to talk to Bishop Bernard J. "Bennie" Sheil. Bishop Sheil was the Archdiocese of Chicago's senior auxiliary bishop and the top aide to Cardinal George W. Mundelein. He was also the founder of the Catholic Youth Organization (CYO), now a national Church-funded program. A long-time supporter of the union movement, Sheil saw no reason for priests to fear the involvement of Communists within the CIO. "Communism," he often said, "presents no threat to a society where justice and charity prevail." Sheil agreed to accompany Alinsky on a visit to each of the Back of the Yards pastors. They got most of the pastors to promise support for the neighborhood council, and all but one priest agreed to stop condemning the packinghouse organizers.

All during that spring and early summer, Alinsky, Meegan and a committee of residents worked to build the new organization. They knocked on doors, talked up the council before local groups, held house meetings, argued over issues, and made plans for their first community convention. Alinsky convinced them that the organization would be stronger if it were an organization made up of existing local organizations rather than just a collection of individuals. The steering committee signed up every group they could find in the Back of the Yards: church societies, union locals, ethnic clubs, bowling leagues, a businessmen's association, card clubs, even the American Legion.

On the evening of July 14, 1939, the Back of the Yards Neighborhood Council held its constitutional convention in the recreation building at Davis Square Park. In a marathon session that lasted until after 2:00 A.M., more than 350 voting delegates, representing 109 local organizations, agreed on a constitution for the new council and approved a one-year reorganization plan for the neighborhood. The hall resounded with cheers and applause when the delegates voted full support for the CIO Packinghouse Workers Union. Saul was overjoyed.

Two nights later, the Back of the Yards Neighborhood Council marched with a large delegation of Back of the Yards residents to the CIO's rally at the Chicago Coliseum. On the stage, Bishop Sheil sat next to CIO President John L. Lewis.

Up to the last hour meat packing company officials and their hired goons did everything they could to stop the rally. Union leader Herbert March, a newly elected director of the Back of the Yards Council, was shot and slightly wounded near Davis Square Park. A series of telephone calls warned Bishop Sheil to stay away from the Coliseum. Sheil and Alinsky were shot at in separate incidents; both men escaped injury. On the night of the rally a squad of Chicago police escorted Sheil from his office to the Coliseum. Thirty thousand people packed the hall and overflowed into the streets.

After the rally, only hours before the promised strike, the meat packers capitulated. The rally convinced the companies that they could not hold out against this coalition of neighborhood churches, residents and workers. In backing the victorious union, the Back of the Yards Council gained its own first victory. *Time* magazine praised the unique partnership of church, union and community that brought peace to Chicago's stockyards.[22]

Alinsky, now a successful community organizer, was delighted. For the first time in fifty years, the Back of the Yards residents stood shoulder-to-shoulder in a common cause. Lithuanians, Poles, Czechs, Slovaks, Germans, Irish and Mexicans; Catholics, Protestants and Jews; the Chamber of Commerce and the CIO, housewives and school teachers, whites and blacks—all stood up and spoke out with a single voice and won a great community victory.

Back at IJR's office, Clifford Shaw read the newspaper accounts of how Saul Alinsky organized the Back of the Yards Council. He threw the newspaper into the wastebasket. Saul's days at IJR were numbered.

2.

An Itinerant Organizer

Neighborhood Power

Two days after Clifford Shaw fired Alinsky for organizing the Back of the Yards Council, the neighborhood organization shot back an ultimatum: "Keep Alinsky or stay out of the Back of the Yards." Shaw backed down, and Alinsky kept his job at the Institute for Juvenile Research.[1]

Alinsky knew, however, that Shaw would wait until the furor died down and fire him on some trumped-up charge. He began looking for another job.

Despite his excellent record during the eight years he worked at IJR, Alinsky's leaving was marked by bitterness. Shaw refused to complete his part of the book on the 42 Gang, and it was never published.[2] Years later, Alinsky praised Shaw's "delinquency areas" research, calling it an "outstanding contribution to the understanding of juvenile crime." But he said that the research was also Shaw's undoing: "His needle got stuck in the same groove and kept playing the same tune."[3]

The years Alinsky spent at the Institute for Juvenile Research were an important part of his training as an organizer. In terms of his family, IJR gave him a steady job and a generous paycheck all during the Depression. The research job gave him time and opportunity to concentrate his attention on Chicago's poorest and most disorganized neighborhoods.

As a social researcher Alinsky showed himself to be a superb observer and analyst of city life. From Robert Ezra Park he had learned that to understand a neighborhood, its people and what made it function demanded more of the

19

researcher than filling his notebook with a jumble of facts. When Shaw sent him in to the Back of the Yards, Alinsky began his study by hanging around the neighborhood at all hours. It took him many months to build up his data on the Back of the Yards and its residents. The social profile he drew was based on daily observation, conversations, interviews, and tavern gossip drawn together by him with sympathy and appreciation for the neighborhood people and their problems.

The split with Clifford Shaw and IJR came because he was tired of just doing research. One day Alinsky realized that he had to do something more to help the powerless residents and the juvenile delinquents he met in the Back of the Yards. The Chicago Area Project Shaw proposed for the neighborhood's problems was too tame and one-dimensional—a "cosmetic touch on the ugly face of the city."[4] So Alinsky became an activist and decided to reorganize the whole neighborhood so that its kids could grow up and someday move out, if they wished, without becoming criminals. Shaw got rid of Alinsky, then, because the student had surpassed his mentor, and had become a hero in the process.[5]

After the Back of the Yards convention, Joseph Meegan was hired as the organization's executive secretary. His job was to run the day-to-day business of the Back of the Yards Neighborhood Council. Alinsky moved gradually into the background as an unpaid "technical advisor" to the Council's leaders. He was free now to use the organization as a laboratory to develop his organizing method and test strategy and tactics for future urban campaigning.

At the end of the Depression Chicago's Back of the Yards was suffering all the problems of a big-city slum. Its two- and three-story frame houses had been thrown up at the turn of the century by speculators for the newly-arrived European immigrants. Forty years later, the houses were overcrowded and falling apart. Sometimes as many as twelve families lived in a single family dwelling. Bathtubs were a luxury; residents used the public showers at Davis Square Park for their weekly bath. The city administration did its best to ignore the stockyards area—side streets were unpaved, uncollected garbage clogged its alleyways, vacant houses were left to the vandals. Fires were a frequent and deadly occurrence. Polluted air from the packing plants hung like a pall over the neighborhood. Health conditions were deplorable: ten percent of neighborhood babies did not live beyond infancy.

The Back of the Yards Council spent its first year in building up a reputation for getting things done for the neighborhood residents. There were no big victories, but people learned how to work together to carry out the neighborhood improvements decided at the convention. Complaints about municipal services were gathered up and delivered in person by Council leaders to local ward officials and city bureaucrats. The officials snarled and made excuses but soon things began to improve—garbage was collected weekly, streets were repaired, police patrols were increased, vacant houses were boarded up.

The Council launched new programs: a well-baby clinic was opened, neighborhood job fairs brought employers to interview local job-seekers, a credit union was established to cut into the business of neighborhood loan-sharks. The most popular program that first year was a lunch program for school children—1,400 kids were fed hot lunches daily at Davis Square Park's community center.

Behind the scenes Alinsky worked hard to keep the Council moving ahead. Like a shrewd fight manager, he arranged ever tougher bouts for the organization. After every action Alinsky made the leaders take the time to talk about what had happened. They dissected, analyzed, and criticized each event until they understood the reasons why they won or lost. Each victory was celebrated with speeches and impromptu parties. People began to notice that after every successful battle, more residents joined the Back of the Yards Council.

After a couple of months the harassed ward leaders decided to counter-attack. They devised a plan to draw away key neighborhood people from the new organization. That year, instead of sending the traditional Christmas baskets to local poor families, the politicians decided to send the food baskets to neighborhood "influentials." When the Back of the Yards

Council got word of the plot, they delivered bigger and better baskets to the same people, and added a fifth of whiskey to each one for good measure.

The neighborhood youth committee, which had been agreed on at the convention, was set up by the Council. Its members included the district police captain, the high school principal, parish priests, parents and representatives from the unions and local businesses. The youth committee heard all complaints involving local juveniles, discussed the incidents face-to-face with complainants, kids and their parents, and together they worked out a solution. Kids were sent back to school instead of prison; one young thief got a loan to get medical care for his sick mother; neighborhood men and women assisted the probation workers with the supervision of difficult juveniles. Within two years the rate of juvenile crime had dropped significantly in the Back of the Yards.

After a few months of this kind of neighborhood activism, news of the Back of the Yards Council penetrated the "downtown" offices of Chicago's Democratic machine. Mayor Edward J. Kelly decided to teach the upstarts a political lesson. He began his attack by banning all community meetings from Davis Square Park. That meant that the Council lost its meeting hall, and, worse, it was the end of the hot lunch program. But the Back of the Yards people fought back. The organization launched a no-holds-barred publicity campaign against the mayor and forced him to rescind the ban.

Alinsky moved even farther out of the Back of the Yards limelight. One night, after helping Meegan prepare the agenda for a mass community meeting, Alinsky disappeared. As the hall began to fill, Meegan remembers his feeling of panic: "I was scared stiff. . . . It was Saul's way of forcing me to take full responsibility for the organization." After his panic wore off, however, Meegan had no trouble running the meeting without Alinsky. "Halfway through the meeting, Meegan says, "he turned up in the back of the hall, with a huge grin on his face."[6]

By spring, the Back of the Yards Council was the main topic of conversation in the neighborhood. People were proud of what they were doing for themselves. Bishop Sheil said that the organization was being discussed even in Chicago's well-to-do suburbs. "A great respect can be felt everywhere for Back of the Yards, expressed sometimes by 'If the Polacks can do it, why can't we?' "[7]

Technical consultant Alinsky impressed on the Council officers the basic issue of "power." He wanted them to understand that getting the streets cleaned, the garbage collected, the building inspectors inspecting and the politicians paying attention was not enough. The real objective of the Council was to build power—collective power as a community—so that the Back of the Yards residents could really run their neighborhood and make it the kind of community they wanted.

By the spring of 1940, Alinsky had received requests from two other cities for his organizing services. The CIO organizers who had worked with Alinsky in the Back of the Yards had by now moved on to other meat packing centers. They encouraged the stockyard workers in those cities to invite Alinsky to organize their neighborhoods. These local communities had no money to bring in Alinsky, however, and he had no money to make the trip.

Several months earlier when Alinsky knew that he had to leave the Institute for Juvenile Research, he went to see Bishop Sheil. The bishop had the reputation of being the best money raiser in Chicago. Sheil suggested that they set up a non-profit foundation to support Alinsky's organizing efforts in industrial communities. The two men went to New York to talk to Sheil's friend, wealthy financier Marshall Field III.

An upper-class WASP, the Cambridge-educated Field was the grandson of the founder of Chicago's great department store, Marshall Field & Company. In 1936 Marshall Field III had announced his intention to devote his life and fortune to social philanthropy. He became an anomaly among his wealthy friends—a liberal supporter of social change. As his biographer explained, Field "believed in cheering people on; when men wanted to write or make speeches or swear mighty oaths or just think, he believed they ought to go to it, and he spent much of his life defending or advancing the kind of society in which they could."[8]

In August 1940, Field joined with Alinsky and Sheil in

establishing the Industrial Areas Foundation. The Board of Trustees of the foundation was made up of an unlikely group of social reformers. In addition to Sheil and Field, the board included: Britton I. Budd, president of Northern Utilities; Kathryn Lewis, secretary-treasurer of United Mine Workers, District 50 and daughter of John L. Lewis; Stuyvesant Peabody, Illinois coal magnate; G. Howland Shaw, U.S. State Department; and Judge Theodore Rosen of Philadelphia. At that first meeting, the IAF trustees voted to raise $15,000 a year for five years to support Alinsky's organizing efforts in industrial communities. Marshall Field put up the money for the first two years.

Marshall Field and Alinsky became good friends. Until he died in 1956, Field was the chairman of Alinsky's Industrial Areas Foundation. Both men gained from the arrangement: Field gave Alinsky's operation respectability; Alinsky's organizing of working class neighborhoods represented for Field what he wanted the newly established Field Foundation to support—social change projects "in areas of great tension and controversy."[9]

Through the years Alinsky and Field shared many long talks, prime steaks and fine bourbon. For the chesty kid from the Chicago ghetto, rejected by his hard-driving father, it was probably important that Marshall Field understood and supported what Saul was trying to do "to restore the democratic way of life to modern industrial society."[10]

Packinghouse Communities

Unsettled times were a factor in Alinsky's early success as a community organizer. In 1940 democracies everywhere were under attack. The Nazis were overrunning Europe with their terrifying blitzkrieg. Japan's militarists were threatening to conquer all of Asia. At home, America was just beginning to pull itself out of the Great Depression. The rising power of the Congress of Industrial Organizations showed a new strength and solidarity among American workers. The United States was preparing to fight, if necessary, to make the world "safe for democracy."

Alinsky came along, just at this time, with a down-to-earth plan for organizing the masses of city dwellers into local community councils that would make democracy come to life in the neighborhoods as it had begun to do in the factories and foundries.

Some of the tactics Alinsky used were controversial—some said "radical"—but what people saw actually happening in Chicago's Back of the Yards seemed to them as American as apple pie. Churches and labor unions supported Alinsky's organization. A tough generation of Americans who had survived immigration and depression liked the militant tone of the Back of the Yards manifesto: "For fifty years we have waited for someone to offer a solution—but nothing happened. Today we know that we ourselves must face and solve these problems. We know what poor housing, disease, unemployment and juvenile delinquency mean, and we are sure that if a way out is to be found, we can and must find it."[11]

In the spring Alinsky took the train from Chicago to Kansas City, Kansas to meet with members of a residential neighborhood near the stockyards. The district was called Armourdale, after the meat packing company. It was a district of 15,000 people, built on a flood plain of the Kaw River, across from the stockyards.

Armourdale had all the problems of the Back of the Yards and none of the advantages. The residents were mostly ex-sharecroppers from the South. The local churches were Protestant and poor. Everybody worked for the meat packing companies. Worst of all, they all lived with the knowledge that a serious flood would sweep the whole district down the river.

When Marshall Field heard Alinsky's description of Armourdale, he said that it sounded like a disaster waiting to happen. He tried to talk Alinsky out of taking on the project. But Saul was riding high after his success in the Back of the Yards. To him it was a challenge: Could he organize a community of poor, Protestant, white Southern migrants?

Actually, the Armourdale Community Council came together like a dream. The residents were angry about a lot of local issues. They flocked to the meetings. The meat company executives and the local politicians were a lot less sophisticated than their Chicago counterparts. The new council held its first convention months ahead of schedule. Marshall Field's warnings appeared to have been overly pessimistic.

Later in that year Alinsky started a third organization in South St. Paul, Minnesota—a small city of about 10,000 residents, situated thirteen miles from St. Paul. The city's residents were totally dependent on the meat packing industry. Alinsky saw South St. Paul as an opportunity to organize not just a neighborhood but a whole city.

For nearly two years Alinsky plied his trade as an itinerant organizer. Once a month he rode the train from Chicago to Kansas City and South St. Paul. Many years later, Alinsky enjoyed telling young organizers the story of how he was jailed in Kansas City when he first came to organize Armourdale. Although the imprisonment story had gained some luster in the intervening years, he was telling the truth. The local police chief had been warned by the meat packing companies that Alinsky was a dangerous labor agitator. The chief had Alinsky picked up and held in "protective custody" as soon as he got off the train.

The police harassment continued until the chief and Alinsky were able to sit down for a long talk about the city and its problems. The story had a happy ending: the police chief joined the Armourdale Community Council and handled security for its convention. Alinsky said he used these quiet weekends in jail to begin writing a book about community organizing.

During the war Alinsky made only occasional visits to the three community councils. He tried to find a local person in both Kansas City and South St. Paul who would take over the day-to-day affairs of these councils, the way Meegan did in the Back of the Yards. The councils hired a succession of executive secretaries, and Alinsky contributed to their salaries. But none of them came close to being another Joe Meegan.

The community councils Alinsky organized in Kansas City and South St. Paul turned out to be among Alinsky's more modest successes. He did not talk much about them in later years. Neither community had the strong resources of people and local organizations that the Back of the Yards had. The residents worked hard to organize themselves with Alinsky's help. They did it, and they won some signal victories. Perhaps, if Alinsky had spent more time with them, more could have been accomplished. But he didn't.

In 1951, the long-awaited flood swept away Armourdale and, with it, the Armourdale Community Council.

The South St. Paul Community Council continued until the mid-1950's and then went quietly out of business. A couple of years ago a former president of the South St. Paul Council summed up the experience. "After a few years the interest in the council fell off," he wrote. "Saul Alinsky left us to our own devices. . . . I think he developed a number of people in our community into positions of influence and leadership. . . ."[12]

Toward the end of 1941, Alinsky realized that he had several problems with his plan to organize a network of urban neighborhood councils. The knight-errant approach he had adopted did not allow sufficient time in each city to do all the organizing tasks that had to be done with a fledgling council. It took time to survey a city and set up the meetings to dig out with the residents the key issues in a community. It took more time to train the local leaders and to work with them to develop strategy and tactics for their community battles. Alinsky had no doubt that after two or three years of his assistance, the local leaders would be able to handle the day-to-day operation without him. But what would happen in the meantime? He didn't want to get bogged down in Kansas City, Kansas. If only he had a few experienced organizers to assist him. But where do you find them?

At the same time Alinsky was ambivalent about setting up a large network that would require a lot of management. His original idea involved his operating as an organizing "Johnny Appleseed" on the move—the way the CIO organizers operated—planting new organizations in city after city and, each time, moving on to another place.

The rub was that he had no national organization as did the CIO organizers. Alinsky was facing a dilemma. His organizations would have to be firmly established at the local level before they could reach out to form the citywide and multi-city coalitions of organizations needed to deal with issues larger than a single community. He was already discussing national issues with his organizations: "a national housing program, the national health program, the policies being practiced by their political representatives, the development of a common curiosity regarding the reasons pro and con of national programs. . . ."[13]

How was he going to build that kind of local stability and help the local organizations develop a national coalition without losing his independence and, what he feared even more, being forced into a leadership role? Alinsky had no answer to his dilemma. Fortunately for him, the United States entered World War II in December 1941, and he was given a respite. The war effort became the first priority. Alinsky put aside his organizations and their problems for the duration.[14]

Alinsky wanted to be an American spy. He was actually one of those people invited by General William J. "Wild Bill" Donovan to join what was to become later the Office of Strategic Services (OSS). Alinsky had visions of himself parachuting into France in trench coat and beret to work with the Resistance in its fight against the Nazi occupation forces. His actual wartime service turned out, however, to be somewhat less heroic.

What conspired to keep him on the home front was a combination of health problems—his bad back and a thyroid condition—and the machinations of IAF trustee G. Howland Shaw. A veteran foreign service officer, Shaw was, in 1941, an undersecretary in the U.S. Department of State under Cordell Hull. Dean Acheson, also an undersecretary, called Shaw a good administrator, endowed with "saintly qualities as well as some hard common sense."[15] Shaw decided that Alinsky's good reputation in working class communities and his close friendship with the CIO leaders would make him an excellent roving ambassador to the war industry. In his spare time he could help the Treasury Department organize War Bond drives.

On his first coast-to-coast tour of war plants, Alinsky was accompanied by Henry Johnson, a CIO organizer who had

worked in the Back of the Yards. In many of the towns the two
men visited on their morale-building trip, Johnson, who was
black, was not allowed to stay in the hotels. Alinsky solved the
problem for the moment by purchasing the most luxurious
camping outfit available at Abercrombie and Fitch—at government expense. At every factory they visited from Maine to
Oregon, Johnson and Alinsky told of their many nights spent
out under the stars.[16]

At War Bond rallies Alinsky met a number of Hollywood
celebrities who subsequently became supporters of his organizing work. Among them were Melvyn and Helen Gahagan
Douglas and producer Walter Wanger and his wife, actress
Joan Bennett.

Alinsky's favorite Hollywood star was Humphrey Bogart.
The two men enjoyed a few drinks together and found that
they agreed on many things, especially politics. Bogart's main
influence on the younger man may have been his "tough guy"
pose, with his cigarette dangling at a contemptuous angle from
the corner of his mouth. Alinsky used Bogart's cigarette pose
often when facing hostile audiences. Saul liked "Bogie," probably because they were a lot alike. Alistair Cooke has described
Bogart as a "man with a tough shell hiding a fine core."[17]

Alinsky's wartime travels took him all over the United
States. What impressed him most was the incredible richness
and diversity of the nation as it mobilized to fight the war. He
noted fresh stirrings among blacks in Southern cities, brought
on by wartime jobs and the efforts of the CIO organizers. The
rapid growth of Southern California and Texas fascinated him.
Montana's potential for development made him want to organize there too.

As the end of the war approached, Alinsky began thinking
more about a postwar organizing campaign. By now he had a
suitcase full of notes for a book about organizing. In late 1944,
he began writing it in earnest.

Reveille for Radicals

Saul Alinsky published his first book, *Reveille for Radicals*,
in 1945.[18] It became a best seller. In the book department at

Marshall Field and Company, *Reveille for Radicals* was displayed alongside two other current favorites, *Brideshead Revisited* by Evelyn Waugh and *The King's General* by Daphne du Maurier.

The reviews were favorable, even laudatory. Only a couple of reviewers asked where Alinsky was really headed with his People's Organizations. *The Nation* worried about fascism: "Doubtless he (Alinksy) means to regenerate democracy, but the result *might* be something very different. To be candid, in some parts of the world fascism has made use of exactly this sort of 'radical' talk."[19]

As soon as he read the book, Jacques Maritain, the newly appointed French Ambassador to the Vatican, sent a cable from Paris congratulating Alinsky: "Book is epochmaking. Eager to have it published in Paris. . . ."[20]

Actually, Maritain deserves much of the credit for getting Alinsky to finish the book. During the years of the Nazi occupation of France, Maritain lived in the United States. He was a frequent lecturer at the University of Chicago. The philosopher had written extensively about social and political questions. Maritain met Alinsky in Chicago and became interested in the organization Saul was building in the Back of the Yards.

As the war in Europe wound down, Maritain prepared to return to France. He pressed Alinsky to complete his book on the art of neighborhood organizing. Maritain hoped to interest Charles de Gaulle in Alinsky's approach to organizing democratically-run urban organizations. Maritain thought that Alinsky's mass organizations would help offset the Communist cadres who were waiting for the war's end to take over French society.

Part of the reason for the popularity of Alinsky's book was the author's straightforward style and language. It has none of the usual scholarly detachment of political science texts. *Reveille* was a fiery manifesto, written on the run by a young American activist. It was Alinsky's summons to America's citizens to beat their swords into political plowshares and apply them to the reorganization of the nation's troubled cities. Alinsky wanted to catch the attention of the victorious coalition of Americans—the homeward-bound GI's, industry's workers and managers, union and political leaders. He spoke also to the nation's minorities—Negroes, Mexicans- and Japanese-Americans who had fought side-by-side with their fellow Americans and now were demanding their fair share of respect, jobs, housing and education for their children.

Reveille for Radicals caught the nation's citizens during the brief period of rest and relaxation before they took up again their many peacetime interests. Before the great wartime mobilization dissolved, Alinsky spoke to them about America's potential, its many problems and the need to reorganize the nation—beginning in city neighborhoods and in small town communities.

During the war Alinsky had talked to ordinary Americans "on New York's Times Square, Chicago's State and Madison Streets, Kansas City's Twelfth and Grand, small South St. Paul's Concord Street, Atlanta's Peachtree Street, San Francisco's Market and Powell, Los Angeles' Hollywood and Vine ... Butte's Park and Main Streets."[21] He asked them what they wanted out of life and what was bothering them.

More than ever Alinsky felt that most problems in the United States were caused by too little exercise of the democratic process. The American system had not failed, Alinsky argued; it hadn't really been tried in urban neighborhoods or small town America.

In *Reveille for Radicals* Alinsky offered people who felt lost in big cities, workers who hated the boredom of their jobs and minorities who were angry about discrimination a way to organize themselves into tough, independent organizations with the power to make the system work for their interests.

Despite his often overheated rhetoric, however, Alinsky's book was not an invitation to revolt. He wanted no popular uprising that would sweep away the structures of society. He was selling the postwar generation organized participation in the power of a revolution already won—by America's Founding Fathers.

Saul Alinsky was never a revolutionary. He called himself an American "radical." By that he meant he was a political descendant of a long line of American activists that included

Patrick Henry, Sam Adams, Thomas Paine, Thomas Jefferson, James Madison, John Brown, the Abolitionists, the Populists, Horace Mann, and Lincoln Steffens, as well as his contemporaries—John L. Lewis, Marshall Field III and battling Bishop Sheil.[22] The author of *Reveille for Radicals* was an immigrant son, only a generation away from the Russian "shtetl"; Alinsky loved the United States and saw nothing wrong with it that couldn't be fixed by well-organized, hard-working American citizens. With Alfred E. Smith, Alinsky believed that the remedy for democracy's shortcomings was more democracy.

Alinsky wrote with youthful passion in *Reveille for Radicals* (he was thirty-six) about his personal values and democratic vision. He modeled his "radical" after Jefferson's "democrat"— a free citizen, endowed with ideals, dreams, fire and faith in the people. A radical, in Alinsky's description, "is that unique person who actually believes what he says. . . . He personally shares the pain, the injustices and the sufferings of his fellow men. . . . For the radical the bell tolls unceasingly and every man's struggle is his fight."[23]

His ideological mentors were not Marx and Lenin, but Thomas Jefferson and James Madison. The radical principles he put forward for reorganizing America were those he learned in Robert Ezra Park's sociology lectures and in the heady "Great Books" atmosphere of the University of Chicago in the days of university president Robert Maynard Hutchins.

The "People's Organizations" Alinsky proposed in *Reveille for Radicals* were based on a Jeffersonian faith in a sovereign people. "In the last analysis of our democratic faith," wrote Alinsky, "the answer to all the issues facing us will be found in the masses of the people themselves, and nowhere else."[24]

From Jefferson and Madison, Alinsky borrowed his inviolable principle that citizens have a right to form their own voluntary organizations and use them to speak out on public issues, and protest, when necessary, decisions of the government they considered wrong. He treasured Jefferson's response to Shay's Rebellion (1786): "I hold it," said Jefferson, "that a little rebellion now and then is a good thing and as necessary in the political world as storms in the physical."[25]

Alinsky's Back of the Yards Council was an adaptation of

Jefferson's concept of "wards"—neighborhood-sized units of citizens, small enough to allow local people to meet regularly and work out together everyday community decisions. These local units of government were intended by Jefferson and Alinsky to be run by the citizens, not by professional politicians appointed by the "downtown machine."

At the same time Alinsky was aware of the danger in a democracy that a majority could easily crush the rights of minorities in large or small organized communities. James Madison gave Alinsky the answer to the problem of majority rule. Madison had praised the benefit to the democratic process of a pluralistic society: "The society itself will be broken into so many parts, interests and classes of citizens that the rights of the minority will be in little danger from interested combinations of the majority."[26]

Alexis de Tocqueville was another of Alinsky's political tutors. After a lengthy visit to the United States the young Frenchman wrote a book, *Democracy in America* (1835), in which he gave his favorable impressions of the nation. De Tocqueville warned his American hosts, however, how easily they could lose their unique democratic government through political inaction. Americans took their freedom for granted, he said, and spent their time solely in the pursuit of individual and private goods. As a result they were becoming dependent on the government to handle public affairs. In so doing the citizens were gradually giving up their freedom to act, what de Tocqueville called the "habit of self-government," and were quietly slipping into a permanent state of political apathy and powerlessness. Eventually they would lose their liberty. "It is, indeed, difficult to conceive," the political philosopher wrote, "how men who have entirely given up the habit of self-government should succeed in making a proper choice of those by whom they are to be governed; and no one will ever believe that a liberal, wise and energetic government can spring from the suffrages of a subservient people."[27]

Reveille for Radicals was divided into two main sections. In the first part Alinsky explained his political philosophy. In the second part he gave an explanation of how he went about building a "People's Organization." He gave several chapters to the "nuts and bolts" of developing with the people a community program, how to find and train local leaders, how to plan a strategy and use tactics, the place of conflict in community battles and how to direct an on-going program of community political education. The book ended with a plea for an active, organized citizenry directed toward making democracy safe in the United States.

Reveille for Radicals explained Alinsky's entire operation. He held back no secrets. His basic method of operation changed hardly at all in subsequent years.

The only thing the readers could not get in the $2.50 book was the Alinsky "magic" that made his method work. The absolutely essential element was the "organizer"—the outside expert, the catalytic agent who moved into the neighborhood, caught the residents' attention, and showed them how to organize and build themselves into an organized community.

In 1945, when the book was completed, the problem for Alinsky was that he was the only organizer he knew that did this kind of work. He had by now returned to shuttling between Chicago, Kansas City and South St. Paul. He was consulting with a group in Cleveland and laying the groundwork for a new council in Omaha.

Despite the success of the book, trouble was brewing for Alinsky and his Industrial Areas Foundation. His initial five-year budget was almost used up, and the IAF trustees had not raised any additional funds. Alinsky was hoping that his book might bring in some paying customers for his services. He was waiting also for an invitation from Jacques Maritain to come to France. In the meantime he began looking around for some organizers.

Fred Ross

During the war Alinsky made a number of trips to Los Angeles. He decided that the city and all of Southern California would be a perfect setting for a metropolitan network of citizen's organizations.

In 1945, Los Angeles was an exploding metropolis, the

third largest city in the United States. The war production boom in the aircraft and shipbuilding industries had brought a flood of new companies and new workers into Southern California. Alinsky figured that the airplane would do for Los Angeles what the railroads had once done for Chicago. In the sunny Southern California climate new technologies were being assembled: airplanes, petroleum refining, motion pictures and the national distribution center for the nation's fruits and vegetables. All of this meant continued growth for Los Angeles and the whole of California.[28]

In addition to his government service visits to Los Angeles. Alinsky was called in by L.A. Mayor Fletcher Bowron in the wake of the "Zoot Suit"; riots in the summer of 1943. The city fathers wanted Alinsky to advise them as to what could be done to occupy the energies of local Mexican-American street gangs. After he spent a week moving around town and talking to people about the problems of the Mexican-Americans, Alinsky delivered his report to the mayor. The problem, according to Alinsky, was much larger than street gangs; he urged city and county officials to make an effort to alleviate the shocking discrimination directed at Los Angeles' Mexican-American residents. The nervous politicians did not want to hear anything about racial troubles in their city.[29]

One of the people Alinsky met on this visit was the writer Carey McWilliams. He introduced Saul to a number of business and church leaders who were worried about the city's smoldering racial tensions and what might happen when postwar production cuts began affecting the local job situation.

A year later Alinsky returned to Los Angeles to raise money from his Hollywood contacts. He attended a star-studded party at Lady Mendl's (Elsie de Wolfe) fashionable mansion. He did not say whether he got any contributions at the party, but he was struck by the braless starlets and the great number of under-utilized swimming pools in the neighborhood. "Every home I saw could be turned into a community center."[30]

Back in Chicago he made plans for organizing Los Angeles. He decided on a threefold organization. At first there would be a separate council for whites, Negroes and Mexican-

Americans. After six months, or a year at the most, he would bring the three organizations together in the beginnings of a citywide coalition powerful enough to deal with metropolitan-sized issues. If successful, the Los Angeles organization would become the base for a network of citizen's organizations all over Southern California.

The Los Angeles organizing plan was a large step beyond what he had been doing in Chicago, Kansas City and South St. Paul. He figured that if feuding Poles, Lithuanians, Ukrainians, Czechs and Irish immigrants could learn to work together in the Back of the Yards, why couldn't the same happen among the new migrants in sunny California? His friends in Los Angeles agreed to set up a sponsoring committee and help raise the money to pay an organizer. B'nai B'rith gave Alinsky a check for $2,500. He said that he had also received a pledge from the aircraft industry to underwrite twenty-five percent of the organizing costs of the first stage. The Catholic Archdiocese of Los Angeles and the CIO also offered to help.

But by the spring of 1945 the California project had not moved an inch. Alinsky had been working hard to complete *Reveille for Radicals,* and he was trying to get the long-promised Omaha Community Council off the ground. The main reason why he was not pursuing the Los Angeles project, however, was that he didn't have a single organizer to send there, and no idea of where he could get one.

Nearly two years passed before anything happened. Then, one night, Alinsky was playing pinochle with some of his cronies from the University of Chicago. Among the card players was Louis Wirth, professor of sociology and executive director of the American Council on Race Relations. He was complaining about some guy on the West Coast staff of the Council on Race Relations who was organizing Mexican-Americans instead of doing the community research he was being paid for. Alinsky's ears perked up at the word "organize." He asked Wirth to send him more information on his incorrigible organizer. The next day he received a report written by Fred Ross describing his organizing efforts in Southern California.[31]

The report sounded too good to be true, so Alinsky wrote and asked Ross to meet with him in Los Angeles. When he received Saul's letter, Ross and his wife were living in a federal housing project in Long Beach. He was nearly broke, and his job with the Council on Race Relations was over as soon as he finished his final report for Louis Wirth. Ross still remembers how excited he was as he waited for Alinsky two weeks later in the lobby of the Biltmore Hotel: "I had read *Reveille for Radicals,* and I was going to talk to somebody who was an authority on organizing."[32]

The two men got along famously. Before lunch was over, Alinsky offered Ross a job organizing a project in Butte, Montana. Ross said he would like to work for Alinsky, but not in Butte; he wanted to organize Mexican-Americans in California.

For the next three days Ross treated Alinsky to a "sewer-top" tour through the worst areas of the Mexican-American barrios in East Los Angeles, and outside, in Orange and San Bernardino counties. Ross' tour and his rapport with the Mexican-Americans made Alinsky think again about his long-delayed plan to organize Southern California. There was no money in the IAF treasury, of course, but Alinsky hired Ross for the princely sum of $3,000 a year.

Ross wanted to begin immediately, but Alinsky told him to finish his work for Wirth and be ready to start on the IAF payroll in the fall. Ross says that he understood Alinsky's position: "My salary depended on whether or not he could get enough money from the Douglases, Wanger and the rest of them. By that time I wasn't paying attention to the salary. . . . I was finally going to work with someone who would turn me loose to see what I could do organizing the Mexican-American communities."[33] After his busy week, Alinsky returned happily to Chicago. He had just doubled the IAF organizing staff.

Fred Ross, at thirty-seven, was a year younger than Alinsky. Like his new boss, Ross was an organizing soldier of fortune. After he graduated from the University of Southern California in 1936, he couldn't find a teaching position and had to take a job with the federal government's Farm Security Administration. It was the period of the "Dust Bowl" migrations of the homeless Oakies, the American tragedy immortalized by John Steinbeck in his novel *The Grapes of Wrath.* The Roosevelt administration had set up the Farm Security Administration to oversee a network of camps where the migrants were housed and received help in finding jobs on California's farms.

For a time Ross ran the FSA camp at Arvin, where Steinbeck had stayed while he was writing his novel. Among the visitors were itinerant organizers from the radical United Cannery, Agricultural Packing and Allied Workers of America (UCAPAWA). As he talked to these organizers, Ross says he became convinced that migrant farm workers needed a union if they were ever to be treated as human beings. It would be many years, however, before Ross concerned himself with a union for farm workers.

Folk singer Woody Guthrie was another visitor to the Arvin camp. "He used to come through," Ross recalls, "bring his sleeping bag and sleep outside on the lawn and sing those wonderful songs."[34] Like many Americans in the late 1930's, Ross got his radical education at the expense of the U.S. government.

Ross later was named the head of community services for FSA's western region. He supervised seventeen government camps in California and Arizona. After the United States entered the war, most of the migrants left the farms to take jobs in the war plants. The camps were closed or turned over to county governments controlled by the growers. Ross was happy to leave.

In 1942 the federal government began its "relocation" of Japanese-American families from their West Coast homes to government detention centers far inland. Ross went to work for the War Relocation Authority and was put in charge of the relocation camp at Minidoka, Idaho. He thought he would be in a position to be an advocate for the detainees. "The job was a farce," says Ross. "The Japanese could do whatever I was doing, and do it much better."[35]

At his own request he was reassigned to Cleveland. For the next two years he arranged jobs and housing for the imprisoned Japanese-Americans so they could leave the internment camps. When the war was over, Ross returned to California and helped resettle the Japanese-Americans.

Ross' old boss at FSA, Lawrence I. Hewes, asked him in

1946 to join the staff of the western office of the American Council on Race Relations. The Council had been formed in the wake of the wartime racial riots in Los Angeles, Detroit and Harlem, with money donated by the American Friends Service Committee and the Rosenwald Fund. The Council's objective was to set up research and educational programs in troubled communities as a way to offset racial tensions. The West Coast office, according to Ross, "was run on a shoe-string—just Hewes and me and a couple of part-time secretaries."[36]

Ross began organizing local Civic Unity councils, made up of NAACP chapters, Japanese- and Chinese-American leagues and Mexican-American organizations. What he found in Southern California, however, was that Mexican-Americans, the largest minority group, had no local organizations. "They had no one to speak for them; they weren't even registered to vote."[37]

That's where Ross began organizing, in the "colonias" and "barrios" where the Mexican-Americans lived throughout Southern California. "I started out in Riverside," says Ross, "to organize them all together, blacks, and Chicanos, and I did, after a fashion. Next, I went into Orange County and tried to organize three Mexican-American communities all at the same time—if you can imagine trying to do a stupid thing like that. But I was riding a white horse in those days; I wanted a regional council and a statewide and a national federation. Well, you know we all have great dreams."[38]

Then in early 1947, a letter came from Louis Wirth. He told Ross that the racial crisis was over, and that the West Coast office of the Council on Race Relations was to be closed. A month later, a second letter came for Ross from Chicago. This one was from Saul Alinsky.

East Los Angeles

When Ross started organizing the Mexican-American neighborhood of Boyle Heights in East Los Angeles, he was moving into the same neighborhood where Saul Alinsky lived the lonely summers of his adolescence. Brooklyn Street in

Boyle Heights marked the center of the Jewish neighborhood that had been transplanted from New York in the 1920's and 1930's. Saul's father moved into Boyle Heights when he left Chicago in 1922. By 1947, however, the Jews had moved away; East Lost Angeles was now a Mexican-American city.

Months before his first paycheck arrived from the IAF, Ross was spending all his time in Boyle Heights. He found a small group of young veterans who had formed a neighborhood political caucus to elect one of their number, Eduardo Roybal, to a seat on the Los Angeles City Council. Roybal finished "fourth in a field of five," says Ross, "mainly because the Chicanos were not registered to vote."[39]

Even after their loss, however, it took a lot of convincing on Ross' part to convince the youthful Mexican-Americans that they should build an organization with a broader base in the Mexican-American community. What the people in East Los Angeles needed, Ross argued, far more than one seat on the City Council, was a strong local organization with power to deal with community problems, civil rights, and discrimination. They should begin, said Ross, by registering as voters the thousands of Mexican-American citizens in Los Angeles County. By the time they had done that, they would have found dozens of issues around which to organize the local community.

The veterans didn't dispute Ross' analysis, but they were suspicious of him. "He's an 'Anglo.' What are his motives in helping us organize? Is he a Communist?" Before they would work with Ross they insisted he prove to them that he was not a Communist.

That night Ross called Alinsky in Chicago. He told Ross to sit tight for a couple of days. The next day Saul called Bishop Sheil about Ross' problem. Sheil called Auxiliary Bishop Joseph T. McGucken of the Archdiocese of Los Angeles. Ross was given an interview with Bishop McGucken, and he got more than he asked for. The Bishop sent a letter endorsing Ross to all the pastors in East Los Angeles and offered help from the archdiocese for the project. The bishop's letter settled the question of Ross' orthodoxy. By summer, Ross and the veterans were busy organizing Boyle Heights. Ross and his wife survived for months on a few savings bonds they had purchased during the war.

The new organization took the name of the Community Service Organization (CSO). Within two weeks the leaders had added two hundred new members. Ross' first move was to give them a valuable lesson in urban politics. He went with a delegation of CSO leaders and members when they hand-delivered a long list of community complaints to Los Angeles County officials. "They just laughed at us," Ross says. "They knew that no one in the barrio was even a registered voter."[40] The Boyle Heights residents were angry at this rough treatment and decided to make a change in the county's voting patterns.

They continued their recruiting drive for new members and made plans for a giant voter registration drive. When the membership rolls reached a thousand, the CSO leaders asked the Los Angeles election commission to appoint sixty deputy registrars for East Los Angeles. "For the next three and a half months the registrars went door-to-door every evening," says Ross. "They signed up 15,000 new voters and tripled the voting strength of the Mexican-Americans in Los Angeles."[41]

No one who came to the CSO's tiny office with a problem was turned away. The CSO signed up everyone it helped. The local politicians began to pay attention to the neighborhood's complaints. Boyle Heights, in turn, began to take an interest in the Community Service Organization.

Every month Ross had to send Alinsky a detailed report of his activities and the day-to-day progress of the organization. Alinsky came out for the first of his promised twice-yearly meetings with Ross and the CSO leaders. Before long, word of the new Mexican-American organization got around Los Angeles. As a result of the CSO's growing reputation, Alinsky found some new financial "angels." Carey McWilliams introduced Saul to Harry Braverman, an L.A. businessman, who had served on the grand jury that overturned the conviction of seventeen Mexican-American youths in the 1942 "Sleepy Lagoon" murder case in Los Angeles. (The "Sleepy Lagoon" murder trial was the inspiration for Luis Valdez's 1978 Broadway play, "Zoot Suit," since made into a motion picture.)

Braverman raised $9,000 within a couple of weeks to support Ross' work with the CSO.[42]

A few months later Braverman invited a large number of Los Angeles' Jewish businessmen to a dinner in honor of Alinsky, held at the swank Beverly Hills Hotel. Alinsky regaled them with stories of his organizing experiences. He then explained that Ross' objective was to organize branches of the CSO in Mexican-American communities all over California. Before Alinsky left, the businessmen formed themselves into the IAF Los Angeles Committee to provide continuing financial support for Ross and the Community Service Organization.

Ross remembers how much these well-to-do businessmen admired Alinsky. They enjoyed his wit and respected his organization savvy. "They'd get him in the car," says Ross, "and the chauffeur would drive them out to their factories. They'd ask his advice. . . . And you know Saul, when he wanted to be charming, he could charm the pants off a brass monkey."[43]

One of these Jewish businessmen was Seniel Ostrow, head of the Sealy Mattress Company. Shortly after he met Alinsky, Ostrow became a trustee of the IAF. Ross says that Ostrow would take Alinsky with him to the exclusive Hillcrest Country Club, among whose members were Hollywood's George Burns and Groucho Marx. Ostrow and Alinsky would sit in the bar, near the door. "When Ostrow's buddies would walk by," Ross says, "he would reach out and grab him. . . . They would go to work on him for a donation to the IAF. Alinsky loved it."[44]

Usually Alinsky got along well with the so-called self-made business types, those who had not forgotten whence they came. They liked the "realistic" aspects of Alinsky's populist approach. He was compassionate, yet opposed to "hand-outs" from government or social agencies that kept people dependent. Alinsky preferred to organize all the unorganized—sharecroppers, housewives, immigrants, retired workers—so they would have a chance to work effectively for their interests. He was a radical precisely because he believed that the regular application of citizen power would make the democratic system work for all its members.

Ross received his first IAF paycheck on September 1, 1947. By now Alinsky was convinced that Ross would be a first class organizer. His only problem was what Saul called Ross' "express-train-style" of organizing—he wanted to move on to a community every three months. "I was trying to break a record, I guess," Ross now admits. "I was trying to be the Barney Oldfield of organizers."[45] Saul knew from his own experience how long it takes to build a stable community organization.

The hiring of Ross and the establishment of the CSO was a big step in Alinsky's lagging postwar plans. The donations from the L.A. businessmen provided a needed transfusion for the IAF's fragile financial situation. *Reveille for Radicals* was bringing in modest royalty checks. And while invitations to organize were not exactly pouring in to his tiny Chicago office, they were increasing. Alinsky felt sure that 1948 would be a better year for the Industrial Areas Foundation.

Then, suddenly, over the Labor Day weekend, tragedy struck. His wife Helene drowned while attempting to rescue their seven-year-old daughter and her playmate. Helene managed to get the children to shallow water before she collapsed and died. Saul rushed down from Chicago to the cottage they had rented for the summer at the Indiana Dunes—a popular vacation area at the foot of Lake Michigan.

Saul was heartbroken. For all his knight-errant ways, he loved Helene deeply. From the beginning of their marriage, he tried never to be away more than a week at a time. Although Helene was the picture of health, they knew that she had a serious heart murmur, bad enough that her doctor had advised her not to bear children. She and Saul did not let that bother them and adopted two children, Kathryn and David. It may have been her weak heart that caused her death in Lake Michigan that sad day.[46]

For a couple of months Saul was tied up trying to take care of the children. His Chicago friends, Ralph and Rachel Helstein (he was president of the United Packinghouse Workers union), came to his rescue and found him a live-in housekeeper. Instead of returning to work, however, once the children were taken care of, Alinsky withdrew into a long period of mourning for Helene.

Meanwhile, Fred Ross was left entirely to his own resources in California. For months he heard nothing from Alinsky—no paychecks, no instructions, no visits, no answers to his letters. Saul wasn't even going through the motions of working.

In the spring of 1948 he rallied a bit. He met with Ross in Los Angeles for Braverman's fund-raising dinner. Alinsky was surprised at the progress Ross had made in Boyle Heights, but he counseled patience when the CSO leaders talked to him about branching out into the neighboring Lincoln Heights neighborhood.

For many months Alinsky wandered around in a daze; he was discouraged and depressed. His friends, the Helsteins and the Marshall Fields, did what they could to comfort him. He spent a week with Val and "Happy" Macy in New York (she was the newest member of the IAF's board of trustees). *Washington Post* co-owner and columnist Agnes Meyer wrote him long motherly letters and sent Christmas presents for the kids. Bishop Sheil fussed over him. In November Jacques Maritain came to visit his old friend before he returned to France from the second general UNESCO conference in Mexico City. John L. Lewis turned out to be a great comfort to Alinsky during this period.[47]

Ever since the publication of *Reveille for Radicals*, Alinsky had talked about writing another book. Now, at the urging of his friends, Alinsky began work on a biography of John L. Lewis. At first the only thing he said he enjoyed about doing the book were the trips to Washington he made to interview Lewis. The labor leader was not really interested in the biography, but he gave freely of his time to Alinsky out of sympathy for his friend's sorrow.

Every day he was in Chicago, Saul continued to visit the cemetery where Helene was buried. He brought fresh flowers and spent long hours at her grave. One afternoon, nearly a year after her death, a cemetery official approached Saul and apologized for the mixup in the installation of his wife's headstone. He told Saul that Helene's marker had been placed on the wrong grave. Alinsky was shocked. He realized that all these months he had been mourning at someone else's grave. "My

God, what am I doing here?" he said to himself. His mourning was at an end. The next day he started in earnest on the Lewis book.

Alinsky's Mentors

Saul Alinsky completed *John L. Lewis: An Unauthorized Biography* at the midpoint of his career. To the relief of his friends, the book project turned out to be for Alinsky the way out of his personal tragedy.

When the book was published in 1949, Alinsky was forty years old and Lewis was sixty. Saul had started out to write a tribute to the aging labor leader, but as he warmed to the task, he decided to make the life of Lewis an advanced text for organizers, a sort of sequel to *Reveille for Radicals.* He wanted to present Lewis as an authentic American social radical. Since the labor leader was no longer in the limelight of organized labor, Alinsky wanted to convey to a younger generation Lewis' unique blend of personality and power—the goals, dreams, even the blind spots of the man whom Alinsky considered the best the American labor movement had ever produced.

For more than ten years Lewis and Alinsky had been good friends. They had met for the first time in the Back of the Yards, in the days when Alinsky was learning to organize and Lewis' CIO operatives were building the Packinghouse Workers' union. The youthful Alinsky adopted the labor chief as his political model: "I loved him," he said, "not only as my teacher, my close friend, but literally my political father."[48]

After the successful launching of the Back of the Yards Council, Lewis offered Alinsky a job. He asked Saul to organize the industrial neighborhoods in all the cities where the CIO was organizing the industries. But Alinsky turned down Lewis' offer. He explained that he wanted to remain independent, but agreed to work closely with the CIO locals. The two men remained friends. Lewis contributed to the IAF, and his daughter Kathryn served for many years as an IAF trustee.

A scant two months before the presidential elections of 1940, Bishop Sheil and Alinsky were given a chance to serve as go-betweens in a dramatic series of last-hour, secret meetings between CIO chief Lewis and President Roosevelt. Lewis, an early and generous supporter of the New Deal, had gradually cooled toward the President because of what he charged were Roosevelt's "unfilled promises" to organized labor. It now appeared as though Lewis would try to turn the "rank and file" union faithful against Roosevelt in the upcoming election.

Alinsky and Sheil tried to convince Lewis not to break with the President. They got Lewis to agree to meet privately with Roosevelt. The meetings were held but did not go well. Neither man would give an inch. The last session took place early in the morning of October 17, in the President's White House bedroom. The two strong men argued harshly, the session was a stormy one, and finally the labor chief walked out on the angry President. Twelve days later Lewis made a national radio broadcast in which he attacked the President and threw his support to Wendell Wilkie, the Republican challenger.

Needless to say, the thirty year old Alinsky was crushed over his failure to heal the break between his two political heroes. Later, in the Lewis book, Alinsky described the 1940 breakup as a great political tragedy—the beginning of the "long twilight" of John L. Lewis' career.[49] Saul learned one lesson from the incident. Never again did he attempt to play the dangerous role of a political broker.

The book turned out to be an undisguised tribute to the complex and controversial labor leader. It was not that Alinsky refused to deal with Lewis' faults, not the least of which was his autocratic leadership of both the United Mine Workers and the CIO. But the book made it clear that Alinsky considered Lewis far superior to his contemporaries in the American labor movement.

Alinsky's book pictured John L. Lewis at the peak of his long career:

> Into all this (the Great Depression) came a man, John Lewellyn Lewis, to organize an economic revolution: to fight the entire corporate structure of the nation; occasionally with his own government, with the organized labor

union establishment, with large sectors of organized religion. . . . To the establishment he was Satan reincarnate. To
the people he was Jefferson, Jackson, Lincoln, Lenin, Gari-
baldi and Napoleon rolled into one. Every radical of every
suasion flocked to the banner of John L. Lewis. "A man's
right to his job transcends the right of private property."
"We are the workers—they are the enemy."[50]

As might be expected the book received mixed reviews.
Alinsky was praised by some reviewers for "his first-hand
information and such a fair picture of Lewis' actual accomplish-
ments. . . ."[51] At the same time he was roundly criticized for
the reverent, hagiographical tone of the book: "His mild gestures in the direction of negative criticism are soon swallowed
up by page after page of admiration for the man."[52]

Thirty years after the publication of *John L. Lewis*, Nicholas von Hoffman agrees that Alinsky gave Lewis adulatory
treatment. Alinsky did not purport to write as a scholar or an
historian, says von Hoffman. He wrote each of his books,
including the biography of Lewis, as texts for the instruction
and inspiration of future organizers: "He wanted people to
understand the underlying things in Lewis. . . ."[53]

The main elements of his own approach to organizing,
Alinsky said, came from John L. Lewis.[54] The great labor
leader was a master at mobilizing mass popular power. He
knew how to harness controversy so that it helped people rise
up from their lethargy, ready to fight for what was theirs.
Lewis practiced the art of "political ju-jitsu"—the ability to
turn the enemy's blundering strength back upon his own head.
Probably the best lesson he taught Alinsky, however, was how
to manipulate the news media so that society's "little guys" got
their side of the story told.

Lewis was Alinsky's hero; it was as simple as that. He saw
the labor leader as the "George Washington of American labor."[55] It was Alinsky's thesis that Lewis' organizing genius
and tough leadership made it possible to build, in the midst of
the Great Depression, a new kind of American workers' movement. Lewis' CIO was an American, democratic, mass labor
movement which aimed at nothing less than extending the

benefits of the democratic process to all American workers and their families.

Alinsky's book pictured Lewis the way historian Arthur Schlesinger, Jr. said Lewis thought of himself—as the heroic preserver of the American system in the midst of a great national crisis, "standing between the rapacity of the robber barons of industry of America and the lustful rage of the Communists who would lay waste to our traditions and our institutions with fire and sword."[56]

When Alinsky praised Lewis' intransigence in the face of duly constituted authority, one can feel Alinsky's long-neglected radical juices beginning to flow again:

> It is very evident that Lewis still believes in a principle that has been abandoned by the vast majority of American citizens, that publicly elected American officials are "servants of the people." Therefore to Lewis, the flaying of a senator or of a President is not insolence or disrespect, but rather an American citizen telling his "servant" what to do. In a very significant sense, that is a fundamental contribution to the American scene.[57]

After Alinsky finished the Lewis book, he appeared to his friends to be ready to return to his organizing career. Even better news was that he had found a new love. Her name was Babette Stiefel; like Helene, she was tall and shapely and she hailed from Philadelphia. When he was bogged down in the book, Alinsky said that Babette was there to help with research, to edit, scold, cajole.[58] They were talking about getting married, but she understood why Saul was still hesitant about taking that step.

Then, suddenly, before Saul could make up his mind, Babette was dead. She contracted polio in the summer of 1950— one of the last epidemics before the advent of the Salk vaccine. Saul was up north somewhere, on a fishing trip with his son David. Ralph Helstein says that it took him two days to track Alinsky down in the wilds of Wisconsin. Saul raced back to Chicago to Babette's bedside, but it was too late. "She didn't even recognize him," Helstein said. "Within a few hours she died. It all happened in less than a week."[59]

The second personal tragedy in less than three years sent Saul into a new bout of depression. He began drinking heavily. Helstein says that he neglected the kids and became extremely cynical about life and his long-neglected work. A couple of days after Babette's funeral, Alinsky called Fred Ross in California and told him he was through raising money for the Community Service Organization. "He just sort of washed his hands of it," recalls Ross. "He said that he was tired of coming out every few months to raise money. . . . The CSO had to become self-sufficient . . . raise its own money, or to hell with it."[60]

Ross was sympathetic to Alinsky's troubles, but, as usual, he was broke. He left Los Angeles after a couple of weeks and took a job with his old friends from the Friends Service Committee. They sent him to San Jose to organize for the California Federation of Civic Unity.[61]

Alinsky went back to wandering aimlessly, sometimes staying with his friends in New York and Washington, sometimes staying at home with the kids in Chicago. He was a lost soul.

It was during this second period of mourning that Alinsky spent many hours with Jacques Maritain. The French philosopher had returned to the United States in 1948 to teach at Princeton University.

The two old friends walked the tree-lined streets of Princeton and talked about changing the world, and about death and immortality. Maritain understood better than anyone Saul's preoccupation with the thought of death. Years later Maritain gave a glimpse into the soul of Saul Alinsky: "I have known and loved him for more than twenty years. . . . There is in him, I think, much more than he himself is aware of. . . . He says that he knows nothing of God, or the immortality of the soul. Well, God does know him, and the beloved souls whose graves he visits in cemeteries do know him also. And a man whose whole life and work are inspired by dedicated love for the humiliated and oppressed one is surely loved by God."[62]

After his long struggle with death, Alinsky emerged a freer man. "I have learned one lesson," he said. "I learned it in my belly, the astonishing lesson that I wasn't going to live forever. . . . After the full realization, on a gut basis, that I was going to die, my whole life changed."[63] About the same time he wrote to Maritain: "Through the years I have finally realized what has happened . . . and I understand."[64]

By the time Alinsky was ready to go back to his task of reorganizing America, it was the summer of 1951. He found the nation moving in new directions. But he was eager again for the fray—his depression and fears were gone.

3.

Surviving the Fifties

Friends and Finances

In April 1951 the American people were in no mood for Alinsky's reveille for radicals. American troops were bogged down in what was supposed to be a "police action" of the United Nations in South Korea. President Harry S. Truman had just dismissed General Douglas MacArthur as the commander of U.S. forces in Korea. At home, paranoia over the Cold War and the threat of international Communism was touching all facets of national life. At first Alinsky paid no attention to the national mood; he had just recovered from his personal troubles and was eager to get back to work. His friends were cheered by the word they heard that Saul had fallen in love with a lovely New Yorker.

A few weeks before, Alinsky met Terry Lewis at a Manhattan reception for Adlai Stevenson. Lewis, a young writer, spent the whole evening talking with Alinsky. Later that evening, Lewis woke up her roommate, Jean Graham, to tell her about the terrific guy she met at the reception. Lewis was fascinated by Saul's rapid-fire, perceptive critique of American culture and politics. The next day the two women telephoned Alinsky and invited him to dinner at their apartment. They told him they were writing a script for an upbeat television special for Thanksgiving and wanted to pick his brains for some new angles.

The dinner party was a success as far as Alinsky was concerned. He was knocked off his feet by the attractive,

51

intelligent Jean Graham. The next day he asked her for a date. From then on he called Jean every day. Saul was hopelessly in love.

Jean Graham was a sophisticated, thirtyish Manhattanite who was just recovering from a divorce. A native of comfortable Montclair, New Jersey, her pedigree was pure Eastern Establishment WASP: "Scotch-Presbyterian, Republican, Park Avenue," a world apart from Saul's immigrant Jewish background.

After her graduation from Vassar College, Jean had married a young Bethlehem Steel Company executive. When the marriage ended, she went to New York to become a writer. With the help of Terry Lewis and her husband, ABC vice-president Hubbell Robinson, Jean began breaking into the burgeoning television industry.

Everything about Jean fascinated Saul—her "Seven Sisters" sheen, her independent spirit and her New York friends. He went with her to all the parties. One evening, at a party at the home of Val and Happy Macy, Jean introduced him to the painter Jackson Pollock, one of her heroes. In the course of a long party, Alinsky told Pollock that he had no use for any of his incomprehensible paintings. More than that, Saul told the painter that he could not understand paying so much for paintings when so many people were poor. The next morning Pollock tried to continue the discussion at the train station. He brought along several of his canvases and offered to loan them to Saul to study at his leisure. He was sure that Alinsky would feel better about his work if he lived with the paintings for a while. But Alinsky refused to accept the pictures. Jean describes the funny, touching scene of Pollock running along the platform, with the rolled-up paintings under his arm, trying to press them on the reluctant Saul.[1]

Saul described Jean to his friends as the "pink sheep" of her family. He described her mother as having a "puss that makes the dame in Grant Wood's 'American Gothic' look like a happy-go-lucky babe."[2]

Mrs. Graham, as it turned out, was even less impressed with Alinsky. "Jean's mother hates three things," Alinsky wrote later to his friend Milton Mayer, "the Catholic Church, Jews and John L. Lewis. She says that Jean deliberately scoured the nation to find the one person who embodies all three."[3]

The new romance brushed away the last clouds of Saul's long mourning period. His energy had returned. He was writing good stuff—an article on Bishop Sheil's battles for social justice[4] and a first draft of a book on Catholic social activist Monsignor John O'Grady, executive secretary of the National Conference of Catholic Charities. G.P. Putnam's Sons, the publishers of *John L. Lewis,* gave him a modest advance for the O'Grady biography.

The top priority for Alinsky in 1951, however, was a new IAF operation. Six years behind his original schedule, he returned to his postwar scheme to organize a national network of big-city organizations. He was confident that he could get the funds he needed from foundations interested in social reform. His proposal called for hiring and training organizers to work in a dozen cities around the country. Alinsky decided that the time had come to get away from the hand-to-mouth money-raising of his early projects.

At best, Saul was a reluctant fund-raiser. He hated to ask for money. In later years, he said that the main reason for rejecting his mother's plan for him to enter the rabbinate was because rabbis had to ask continually for money.

He treasured his few faithful financial supporters, like the group of Jewish businessmen on the West Coast. He visited them twice a year, went out to dinner with them and told them great stories. He neglected them, however, along with Ross and the CSO leaders during the long period after Helene's death. Never again did Alinsky receive much support from Jewish groups. After the foundation of the State of Israel in 1948, Alinsky's Jewish supporters sent their money to that young, beleaguered nation.

Harriet "Happy" Macy was elected an IAF trustee in 1945. She was shocked when she learned of the precarious state of Alinsky's finances. She volunteered to set up an annual fund-raising drive for the IAF. Saul gave her permission to prepare a brochure about IAF's project, to be sent with a letter asking for donations to a select list of likely benefactors on the East Coast. Macy was also busy lining up speaking dates for Alinsky before groups of well-heeled New Yorkers.

"Happy" Macy became a faithful member of the elite group of Alinsky's socialite supporters. Marshall Field had introduced Saul to Harriet and Valentine Macy. They were the owners of a string of Westchester (New York) newspapers. Solid Republicans, the Macys were nevertheless worried about racial discrimination and the increasing ideological threats to the American democratic system. They were also genuinely fascinated by Saul and his efforts to build democratic community organizations.

As long as Alinsky was organizing one community at a time all by himself, he was able to get along on annual donations from the IAF trustees and a handful of other benefactors. When it came to spending money, his own or the IAF's, Saul operated with the caution of an accountant from Scotland. Every year IAF board members Marshall Field, Harriet Macy, and Sears, Roebuck heiress Adele Rosenwald Levy gave $5,000 each. Other trustees gave smaller amounts. But, with the exception of Sheil and Shaw, none of the trustees brought in any outside money. Saul told Harriet Macy: "The IAF board members are nice people, but they don't spend much time going out and raising dough."[5]

The other key benefactor on the East Coast was Agnes E. Meyer, co-owner with her husband Eugene of the *Washington Post* (the Meyers' daughter Katherine is today chairman of the board of the Washington Post Company; their grandson Donald Graham is the publisher of the *Washington Post*).

Agnes Meyer first met Alinsky in 1945, in the course of writing a series of articles for the *Washington Post* on social conditions in the United States after the war. She spent three days with Alinsky, roaming around the Back of the Yards, which she described as this unique "community project that pulsated with the will of our masses to manage their own affairs." She called the Back of the Yards Council an "orderly revolution. . . . 'We, the people, will work out our own destiny'—that I found was the slogan of 120,000 people in Chicago's Packingtown who had formed themselves into the Back of the Yards Neighborhood Council under the able leadership of Saul Alinsky, a young criminologist who prefers to do the kind of work that keeps people out of jail." In the articles Meyer captured the feeling of pride experienced by the Back of the Yards' residents in their six-year-old organization.[6]

Like the Macys, newspaper owners Agnes and Eugene Meyer were long-time Republicans. Eugene was named a governor of the Federal Reserve Board during the Hoover administration. He was condemned, along with other contemporary financiers (J. P. Morgan, Andrew Mellon, and Ogden Mills), by Father Charles E. Coughlin, who called them the "Four Horsemen of the Apocalypse."

Agnes Meyer joined the small group of Alinsky's supporters because she approved of the democratic spirit of his citizen organizations and the self-help attitude they brought to troubled neighborhoods. For many years Meyer continued to be one of Saul's strongest supporters; she sent him money for his projects, worried about him when he was troubled, and warned him repeatedly to steer clear of Walter Reuther, Henry Wallace and other union leaders she considered too radical. She was a woman ahead of her time. Chalmers Roberts describes her as "strong-willed, tough-minded on civic issues, bursting with opinion, and always ready to express them verbally or in writing. . . ." Often she had to insist that the *Washington Post*'s editors carry the articles she wrote on America's social problems. "When she sent in stories from New Mexico on the impoverished Chicanos," says Roberts, "Casey Jones (managing editor) would have none of them: 'Who in the hell in Washington cares about a lot of Mexicans?' But she persisted. . . ."[7]

Casey Jones was not the only Washingtonian who heard from the irrepressible Meyer. She urged President Harry S. Truman to create a federal department of health, education and welfare. Truman complained about her lobbying: "There's hardly a day I don't get a letter from that woman or from Eleanor Roosevelt telling me how to run this job."[8]

In the mid-1950's, though, Meyer broke off her support to Alinsky, evidently as the result of a difference of opinion over their mutual friend Bishop Sheil. Non-Catholic Meyer was the battling bishop's greatest fan ("a great treat to find a clergyman who is religious," she wrote). The trouble started when she wrote to Cardinal Francis Spellman of New York, asking him to see to it that the Pope appoint Sheil the Archbishop of Omaha. Soon after, Meyer complained to Alinsky that the article about Sheil was "too belligerent." She was worried that the tone of Alinsky's piece might hurt the bishop's chances for the Omaha post. A year later, when Sheil fell out with Saul over the IAF's agreement to work for Cardinal Stritch, Meyer sided with Sheil and removed herself from the list of Alinsky's supporters.

Looking back, it seems unfortunate that Alinsky did not make better use of the talents of Agnes Meyer and Harriet Macy. With a little encouragement on his part, these two remarkable women could have developed an effective fund-raising operation for the impoverished IAF. When it came to working with women, however, Saul was not ahead of his time. He saw these two women as friends and well-to-do supporters of his work, not as potential organizers.

When Harriet Macy's genteel effort to shake down her socialite friends did not have immediate results, he comforted her instead of helping her to organize it better. When Meyer offered to ask the Wilsons and Swifts for money to help the Back of the Yards Council set up a Veterans' Center after the war, Saul did nothing to encourage her.

Part of the reason was that he did not think that rich people would fund social change for long—chicken farmers rarely befriend the wily fox. But there was more to it than that. As shrewd a judge of people as he was then and later, Saul did not believe that women were as capable as men of doing the job of the professional organizer.

In the fall of 1951 Alinsky drew up a list of a dozen foundations that would likely support his national organizing campaign. He opened the campaign with a letter to Jacques Maritain, asking the philosopher to set up a meeting for him with Robert M. Hutchins, the newly appointed associate director of the Ford Foundation.[9] Next he paid a call on Professor Louis Wirth, the executive director of the Emil Schwartzhaupt Foundation. He sent copies of the IAF proposal to ten other foundations and followed up with visits by himself, Bishop Sheil and G.H. Shaw.

The proposal was certainly ambitious. Alinsky's objective was to hire and train a dozen organizers and send them to work in as many cities. His list included the organizations already functioning in Chicago, Kansas City, South St. Paul, Omaha and Los Angeles. The other cities named in the first draft were New Orleans, Atlanta, Birmingham, El Paso, San Antonio, San Diego, Pittsburgh, Philadelphia, Newark and two sites in Montana. All of them were cities he had visited during the war.[10]

According to the proposal, the IAF would "develop voluntary community organizational procedures designed to provide the opportunities and stimulus for citizen participation and education into the character of the democratic process." Local groups would provide the invitation, the people and the issues; the IAF would provide the start-up funds and a trained organizer for each community. Alinsky wanted to show the nation that American-style democracy, fully utilized, can provide a most effective system for realizing people's dreams, hopes and aspirations. Saul underlined the fact that the proposal was backed up by twelve years of successful operation of Chicago's famous Back of the Yards Neighborhood Council.

The total amount of the budget Alinsky requested was in the vicinity of $900,000, over a three-year period. Each foundation was asked for a grant ranging from $75,000 to $100,000. It was a realistic request. In preparing the budget, Saul had the help of Leonard M. Rieser, an attorney with a large Chicago firm. Rieser was an expert on foundations. He had been a trustee of the Rosenwald Fund and was one of the architects of the Schwartzhaupt Foundation, and he was also a trustee of the Industrial Areas Foundation.

Alinsky's proposal went out to the foundations in the fall of 1951. He planned to launch the new program in early 1952, but when he received little response to his proposals from the foundations, he began to worry about his timing. Actually, only one foundation showed any interest at all in IAF's grassroots reorganization of America's cities.

The early 1950's were a bad time for radical programs of any kind. Senator Joseph McCarthy and the House Un-American Activities Committee (HUAC) ranged the land, chasing suspected spies, Communists and fellow travelers. As the national witch hunt grew in scope, anyone suspected of thinking radical thoughts or heard expressing dissenting opinions was considered by some to be guilty of treason. In a time of national fear and conservatism, Alinsky's radical populist Americanism was anathema to nervous foundation trustees.

Sometime during this period Alinsky received a visit from staff members of McCarthy's Government Operations Committee.[11] But Alinsky was never a Communist. In the 1930's he worked with American Communists, and a number of them were his friends. Alinsky was a pragmatist. American Communists were on the right side of most of the social struggles of the 1930's—the labor movement, desegregation, anti-fascism, the New Deal programs. Saul shared with these men and women many of the same fears and hopes for a better society. The main reason he said he never joined the Party had to do with its ideology. He was suspicious of dogma, anyone's dogma, distrustful of utopian schemes and ever ready to fight any attempt to curtail his, or anyone's, freedom.[12]

For years, however, Alinsky's meaner enemies continued to bring up the charge that he was a Communist every time the IAF started a new project. Most of the time he ignored these attacks and let the organizations speak for themselves. But the general malaise of the 1950's surely hurt his organizing and made it more difficult to raise money. His dream of a national network of community organizations never materialized. For a long time he could find no one who wanted to be an organizer. Would-be radicals vanished. Alinsky worried about who would hand on the battered torch of American radicalism to the next generation.

One by one the foundations turned down Alinsky's proposal. Even the somewhat liberal Ford Foundation greeted his request with monumental silence. Maritain said that he had written twice to Robert Hutchins on Alinsky's behalf, but found him absorbed in educational projects and totally uninterested in community organizations. Maritain had tried earlier to warn Alinsky that the Ford Foundation was the wrong place to go for money: "Too big—too big," he said, to pay attention to

Saul's brand of energetic citizenship.[13] Alinsky backed off. Maritain's warning recalled for Alinsky an earlier incident with the Rockefeller Foundation. When G.H. Shaw went to John D. Rockefeller III on behalf of the IAF, he was told by the philanthropist that Alinsky's program was a bit too "rugged" for Rockefeller tastes. The Rockefellers preferred to fund "benevolent" or "welfare" organizations.[14]

The one positive response came from the Schwartzhaupt Foundation. Established a year earlier by the will of Emil Schwartzhaupt, a German-Jewish immigrant who had made a fortune in the liquor business, the new foundation was intended by its founder to promote the "upbuilding and betterment of American citizenship."[15]

Because millionaire Schwartzhaupt believed, like his friend Julius Rosenwald of Sears, Roebuck, and Company, that each generation should solve its own problems and raise its own money to do it, he insisted that the foundation should dispose of all its assets within twenty-five years of his death. When Alinsky heard about this requirement, he offered to help the Schwartzhaupt trustees spend the endowment as soon as possible.

Because they were unsure of how to carry out Schwartzhaupt's will, however, the trustees gave the first grant to Louis Wirth to establish an interdisciplinary committee of University of Chicago faculty members to draw up guidelines for the foundation. When Wirth died suddenly in May 1952, the Committee on Education for American Citizenship, as it was now called, moved beyond Wirth's interest in long range research to a more immediate task of providing the trustees with guidelines for funding projects. The trustees appointed Carl Tjerandsen, a graduate student, to serve as a part-time executive secretary of the foundation. Tjerandsen began by cataloguing the flood of proposals already received by the foundation.

In early 1952, therefore, the Schwartzhaupt Foundation trustees were not ready to respond to Alinsky's proposal for a national network of community organizations. They told him, however, that they liked his concept of organized citizen participation in local urban communities. The foundation gave him $15,000 as earnest money until the trustees were better

prepared to consider his proposal. After many disappoint-
ments, Alinsky was convinced that IAF's stock was, at last, on
the rise.

With the Schwartzhaupt Foundation's promise of money
as bait, Alinsky was able to get Fred Ross to come East to give a
couple of workshops on organizing. Ross had not seen Alinsky
since he had been abandoned by Saul five years before. On his
own now, Ross was organizing a CSO in San Jose, but he had
no money.

Ross met Alinsky at Rutgers University, and together they
conducted a workshop. Ross could hardly wait to discuss the
Schwartzhaupt Foundation and his plans to organize chapters
of the Community Service Organization in the Mexican-American barrios throughout California. But Alinsky put him off
and told him they would have time to talk after the second
workshop they were giving in Cleveland. Finally, it was the
last day before Ross was scheduled to return to San Jose. Ross
went back to the hotel for the long-delayed discussion. Alinsky,
however, was on a high and wanted to go to the ballgame. An
incorrigible White Sox fan (South Side Chicago), Saul wanted
to see the White Sox play the Cleveland Indians that afternoon.
He told Ross that they could discuss the CSO during the
ballgame. Ross was furious: "I was upset because I wanted to
spend the afternoon talking to him and not be interrupted by
any Goddamn baseball game." On his way out the door,
Alinsky told Ross not to worry because the Schwartzhaupt
Foundation was going to fund a giant IAF proposal in which
the CSO was included, adding: "We will never have to worry
about money again."[16] On the train back to California
Alinsky's vague promise of money provided scant comfort to
the impoverished Ross.

About this same time, Alinsky was meeting regularly with
Monsignor John O'Grady, the head of the National Conference
of Catholic Charities. Saul was supposed to be interviewing
O'Grady for the book he had promised G.P. Putnam's Sons.
The book was not going well, however, his advance was gone,
and each time the two men got together, they ended up talking
about how they could get the Catholic Church to back
Alinsky's organizing campaign.

Community Service Organization

Probably the most effective and interesting IAF organizations in the 1950's were not organized by Alinsky, but by his West Coast operative, Fred Ross. As mentioned earlier, Ross was left without funds or direction after the death of Alinsky's wife in 1947. For three months he continued to work on his own with the CSO in East Los Angeles; then he went to work for the Friends Service Committee in San Jose. At that time San Jose had the largest concentration of Mexican-Americans in the United States. In that city Ross organized a Community Service Organization modeled after the one in Boyle Heights. The barrio in which he began the organizing was called by its residents "Sal Si Puedes" ("Get out if you can"). The overriding issue in the barrio was flooding. Every time it rained, the neighborhood was awash with filthy water. The kids were sick with amoebic dysentery from the polluted water supply.

At one of the first meetings Ross met a quiet-spoken twenty-five year old ex-migrant, now working as a lumber-handler in San Jose. Ross says that he knew that night that the young man would make a good organizer. He wrote in his diary after the meeting, "I think I've found the guy I'm looking for."[17] The young man's name was Cesar Chavez.

Later, when Alinsky called Ross back to his old job as IAF's West Coast director, Ross asked the Friends' Josephine Duveneck to hire Chavez to take his place in San Jose. In her autobiography Duveneck wrote: "I remember his (Ross') saying about Chavez, 'He's pretty young and inexperienced, but he has great potential. I'd like him to take on the job.' " Some of Duveneck's co-workers thought Chavez too shy and unsophisticated to be an organizer. They worried that he might be "lacking in drive." But there was no one else around, so they hired him.[18] Ross was happy; he was going to hire Chavez for the IAF just as soon as he could convince Alinsky that he needed another organizer in California.

A year or so later, when Alinsky received the long-awaited grant from the Schwartzhaupt Foundation for the CSO project, Ross asked Saul to hire Chavez. Alinsky wanted to interview him first. Chavez remembers that first meeting: "I really didn't like Alinsky the first time I met him. He sat in on the CSO executive meeting. I was very uncomfortable all evening. After the meeting . . . we went to dinner. He was very smart, very quick and very rough in his approach. Later, though, after I got to know him, I realized that underneath all that, he was compassionate and warm—a real great man."[19]

Starting from the two CSO's already operating in East Los Angeles and San Jose, Ross and his young assistant took to the roads to organize the Mexican-Americans in the rest of California's cities and towns. They operated on a shoestring, but they were happy. Chavez says: "I was getting thirty dollars a week plus gas. . . . I loved it. It gave me an opportunity to organize and get a little money at the same time."[20] The only other staff member was a part-time secretary who was an expert on U.S. immigration regulations. Immigration problems were a major issue in every barrio in California.

First they moved southward from San Jose. Chavez organized Madera, Bakersfield and Hanford in the San Joaquin Valley. Ross started in Salinas and moved on to San Bernardino and the agricultural towns in the Imperial Valley near the Mexican border. Later they moved northward to organize CSO chapters in Stockton and Sacramento. Less than two years after Ross returned to Alinsky's payroll, there were enough local CSO chapters to hold a statewide convention at Asilomar, near Monterey. At that meeting the delegates formed the National CSO, Inc. The "National" in the title may have been a bit premature, but Ross and Chavez were well on their way. Alinsky's old dream of organizing California appeared to be coming true—if not quite the way he planned it.

Like the early Franciscan missionaries, led by Junipero Serra, who roamed California in the years when the territory was a colony of Spain, Ross and Chavez traveled from town to town, planting CSO's as they went. The only difference was that the organizers rode beat-up jalopies instead of mules.

The key organizational tool they used in the CSO's was the house meeting. Unlike the Back of the Yards Council and the other industrial neighborhood organizations Alinsky built, the barrios had few local organizations and no political power base in any of California's cities. Organized labor was no help because the Mexican-Americans represented only a tiny minority of the membership of any union. Although most Mexican-Americans were Catholics, they had little influence in the Church. The family group was, for them, the basic community institution. So Ross made the family the building block of the CSO.

Ross or Chavez would move into a new town, armed only with names of local persons supplied by CSO members elsewhere. In classic Alinsky style the organizer hung around for a couple of days to get the lay of the land. He wandered around the barrio, listening to the residents; at night he visited the taverns and cantinas; he interviewed the local parish priest. When he had made a couple of good contacts, the organizer asked those individuals to invite a group of friends and relatives to a meeting in their homes. The organizer introduced himself to the group and described what the CSO's were doing in other places. With a few questions he had them talking about the issues that needed attention in the local community. The list in the barrios was always long: substandard schools, discrimination against Mexican-American kids using public swimming pools and skating rinks, no school buses, police brutality, and the usual lack of city services—not enough sewers, sidewalks, stop signs or street lights. With only a nudge now and then from the organizer, the group discussed, with growing anger, their lack of political clout and the dearth of registered voters in the barrio. Before the meeting broke up, the organizer got promises from members of the group to invite him to meet with others of their friends and neighbors.

After a few weeks, a temporary committee was formed to address the key issues. By now the organizer was sorting out the natural leaders he had discovered in the community. A couple of months later, the group held an organizing convention. Officers were elected, committees were appointed and a plan of action was accepted by the members. As soon as the new CSO was operating on its own, Ross and Chavez moved on to another town.

In the summer of 1955, when Alinsky's friend Monsignor John O'Grady wanted to see some IAF organizations in action, Saul sent him to tour the hot, dusty California valleys with

Fred Ross. In whirlwind fashion O'Grady visited fourteen CSO chapters in as many towns. He was overwhelmed with what Ross and Chavez had been able to accomplish in such a short time with very little money.

Alinsky came from Chicago twice a year to confer with Ross and Chavez and meet with the CSO leaders. Ross says that Saul did his best to avoid the formal CSO meetings whenever possible—"He found them boring." In his usual style, Alinsky preferred informal sessions with the organizers and CSO leaders late at night, when the phones were quiet and neighborhood crises had to wait until morning. "What he liked to do," Ross recalls, "was talk about what he was doing in other places and new plans that he wanted for the CSO network. He wanted reaction to his ideas."[21]

Throughout the 1950's the crucial problem for Mexican-American communities remained that of discrimination. Involved in this discrimination were interrelated problems of language, U.S. citizenship requirements and voting rights. Ross and Chavez were able to convince the CSO leaders that they had to concentrate their efforts on helping their members become American citizens and on building up Mexican-American voting strength throughout the state. In California most school districts showed little interest in providing basic education for Hispanic-speaking adults, so the CSO's developed their own adult curriculum, with a focus on English language and citizenship classes.

In San Bernardino, the CSO Citizenship Committee recruited volunteer teachers, developed materials, recruited students and ran classes in the neighborhood churches. "In spite of difficulties and the lack of adult school help," Schwartz-haupt Foundation's Tjerandsen reported, "the San Bernardino CSO organized, in 1954 alone, thirty citizenship and English classes with a total enrollment of between 700 and 750 students." At the peak of the CSO citizenship drive there were more than one hundred classes meeting in the cities of California. "Over a ten year period," according to Tjerandsen, "perhaps 30,000 completed CSO-sponsored classes in English and citizenship."[22]

Citizenship classes were not enough, however, to end discrimination against the Mexican-Americans. Hand in hand with the citizenship drive the CSO chapters organized an unending series of voter registration campaigns. The CSO's trained hundreds of their members to serve as deputy registrars. Others were sent out as "bird dogs" to search door-to-door for unregistered voters. According to the Schwartzhaupt Foundation, the CSO registered a grand total of 435,000 new voters in the 1950's and early 1960's.[23]

With increased voting strength among Mexican-Americans in the cities and towns came community recognition and a more equitable share of political power and municipal services. One CSO president told Alinsky: "In the pre-Community Service Organization days, whenever a Mexican-American had a problem, regardless of whether that problem was related to the police department or to various services concerned with streets, lights, health, education or no matter what, that Mexican-American was always referred to the dog catcher. . . . The post was always filled by either political party with a Spanish-speaking person. . . . Imagine, everytime something came up which had anything to do with the city, we would have to go to the dog catcher. But not anymore. . . . You saw yourself, Mr. Alinsky, at the meeting tonight. There is the mayor, the chief of police. . . . Ever since we registered people and did all those other things, lots of changes have come about."[24]

In 1955, Ross and Chavez received a second three-year grant from the Schwartzhaupt Foundation. This time the total was $186,000. The two organizers used the money to retrace their steps through California's valleys, returning to each of the CSO chapters they had organized for a period of "consolidation." After three years the initial enthusiasm of some of the chapters was waning, and they needed new ideas, new leadership and, always, money. The organizers told the CSO leaders that if the chapters did not soon develop independent sources of operating funds, the whole network would soon be out of business.

Ross remembers the fund raising as the hardest part of the consolidation campaign. Most of the money-raising ideas came from Chavez. "In the beginning we were experimenting with various types of fund raisers that the local chapters could run themselves. Cesar started a rummage store—you know, they'd go around town and collect old washing machines, clothing, radios. With the money from the second-hand store's profits, they were able to hire a part-time organizer or staff person. Cesar ran a big carnival in San Jose and raised a lot of money." Only one of Chavez's projects failed completely. Ross says that Cesar and some of the leaders drove up to Oregon to buy a couple of truckloads of Christmas trees. When they began selling the trees, however, the local leaders dropped out, one by one, during the long, cold nights before Christmas. Finally, according to Ross, there was only "poor Cesar out there night after night among those thousands of Christmas trees, freezing his ass off, and nobody buying any trees."[25]

The best idea in the consolidation campaign proved to be the local service center. For three dollars a year (gradually raised to twelve dollars), any member could drop in at the CSO office and get immediate help with a problem. The service center caught on quickly in most communities, and a steady stream of people brought their problems and complaints to the center staff. The most common were problems with the immigration authorities and police and everyday issues of welfare, unemployment, workmen's compensation, insurance, housing and city services.

The CSO service center was not the traditional social agency where professionals from outside the community did things for people. Ross and Chavez trained local people, unemployed women and senior citizens, to run the center and investigate the complaints. The CSO leaders took over problems that turned out to be more than could be handled by the volunteers. To supplement the annual membership dues, most chapters held community fiestas (a combination street dance and barbecue). The consolidation program paid off: new members came and brought increased revenues and new blood into the local chapters and to the National CSO office.

Probably the most interesting innovation contributed by the CSO's to Alinsky's organizing approach was what were called "Educationals." Carl Tjerandsen, the executive director of the Schwartzhaupt Foundation, was, by profession, an adult educator. When he first met Alinsky, Tjerandsen was directing the Institute of Citizenship at Kansas State University. The institute trained leaders for community development in rural areas. One of the guest lecturers at Tjerandsen's institute was Saul Alinsky. During the two-day visit to Kansas State, Alinsky and Tjerandsen spent most of the time talking about mass organization.

A few years later, when Tjerandsen moved to the Schwartzhaupt Foundation, he and Saul resumed their conversations. When the foundation agreed to give Alinsky a three-year grant for the CSO program, Tjerandsen wrote a long letter to Alinsky in which he raised some important questions about the IAF's organizing program.

The greatest danger in Alinsky's approach, according to Tjerandsen, was its tendency to activism—to "operate" on a community's problems without making room for the people to reflect on what they were doing. The organizers did not take time to build into the organizing process an educational component. Tjerandsen did not minimize the good Saul was doing: "There are injustices and inequities," he wrote. "It is possible to identify leaders, work with them to build a power organization, and apply the pressure to correct the injustices. But is not your basic objective to develop certain capacities among the people with whom you work? ... Are you developing (through the CSO's) a set of political bosses, new style, in the pattern of ethnic political bosses as we have known them in Chicago or Boston?"[26]

Tjerandsen's letter bothered Alinsky; it reminded him of something he had written in *Reveille for Radicals* about the necessity of citizen education. He had quoted Thomas Jefferson on popular education: "Enlighten the people generally, and tyranny and oppression of body and mind will vanish like spirits at the dawn of day."[27] Saul understood that organizing was more than power. He agreed with Tjerandsen that the "function of the citizen is to deliberate, to act, and to evaluate the results of the action ... he is responsible for knowing why he does what he does."[28]

Alinsky knew from experience, however, how difficult it was to get an active organization to take time to reflect on what it is doing. In the actual organizing he did, Alinsky had become content with the bits and scraps of education that took place in the course of the everyday operation of his people's organizations. In the early days of an organization there were a lot of learning groups. People turned out in droves to every meeting, and discussion was heated. After every action, whether the organization won or lost, there were plenty of opportunities for the organizer to slip in a little political education. But Alinsky knew it was not enough.

Organizations tended to ossify. After a few years of operation, when the immediate problems of a community were solved and no new crises were looming, an irresistible process of institutionalization began. The organization took on a life of its own, apart from its community, individual members no longer knew what was going on "behind the scenes," and an "old guard" of leaders and insiders now looked upon themselves as the guardians of the new status quo in the community. Things got done, programs were administered, services were rendered, the rent and the staff were paid, but the excitement was gone, the rank-and-file members lost interest, meeting attendance fell off—organizational arteriosclerosis set in. Alinsky had begun to think that there was no way of preventing this institutionalization short of revolution.

Tjerandsen's idea of using specially trained educational leaders to work within the organizations seemed worth a try. Alinsky asked for $60,000 for an educational program in the second CSO grant. He met also with the adult educators suggested by Tjerandsen, but they were not much help. The educators wanted to talk about formal classes and the usual vocational and remedial programs for adults. Only one of the professionals seemed to understand Alinsky's problem: Glen Burch, a former dean at the University of California at Davis, who was now directing a study/research project for the Fund for Adult Education. Burch agreed to help Alinsky develop an educational program for the CSO's.

The "Educationals," as they were called, became a part of the consolidation program in a select few of the CSO chapters. At first, as Alinsky feared, no one among the CSO leaders was the least bit interested in an educational program. "Call them strategy sessions," Saul advised Ross. "The minute we call them education, nobody will come around." Ross, too, was skeptical of the program. He was afraid that it would slow down the organizing. But, at Saul's request, he did his best to find an educational director. He came up with Abilizio "Abe" Chavez, from the Salinas CSO. Chavez, in turn, signed up five young CSO members to be the first educational fellows. They were trained on-the-job by Alinsky, Glen Burch and Abe Chavez to direct a series of educational sessions in the five selected CSO chapters. The fellowships they received provided them with $500 annual stipends for the three-year program.

In an unusual burst of concern Alinsky agreed to spend three months in California in the summer of 1956 to "supervise personally the development of five pilot projects in our Salinas, Monterey County, Soledad, San Jose and ... Oakland projects."[29] He brought Jean with him. She was not feeling well. She had been suffering off and on with spells of dizziness and double vision. Saul thought that a summer on Monterey Bay would do her good. He was right. Not only did the change of climate seem to improve her health, but Jean fell in love with Carmel—its artists and small shops, the magnificent Pacific Coast. On their return to Chicago, she told Saul she wanted to move to California.[30]

The educationals began slowly. The meetings were small, no more than ten or twelve participants, usually held in someone's house. The attendees were mostly the younger and more recent members of the local CSO.

The meetings followed a general pattern. According to Ross, "The fellow would encourage members of the group to choose a topic (something about their community), and then he would build a network of questions around it and bring the discussion out of them. The people already knew the answer; it was just a matter of drawing them out. They loved it. They ate it up. And after the session was over, the group would head for the CSO membership meeting. There they would lock horns with the leaders over some issue that the executive committee had already decided."[31]

It didn't take long to win Ross over. When he saw the results, after only a few educational sessions, in the local CSO chapters—the informed, aggressive participants, the hot and

heavy discussions they started at the CSO meetings—he asked
Saul if he could take over the training of the fellows after the
first year. "I stopped being a two-bit Messiah," Ross admits,
"and became a two-bit Socrates."[32]

The educationals produced marvelous discussions. They
also produced a new breed of loyal insurgents from the rank-
and-file. Ross says: "They would mow down the executive
board. It caused no end of trouble." Soon the CSO leaders were
complaining to Ross about the educationals. Ross told the
leaders to go to the sessions. In the places where they did
attend, the leaders were won over to the program. In other
chapters, however, the leaders boycotted the educationals and
tried to freeze out the participants. They soon found themselves fighting for their lives against the savvy insurgents.[33]

In Stockton, the CSO leaders gave their unquestioning
support to a city redevelopment plan because it included the
barrio area. But after the educational group studied the city
plan, they explained to the CSO members that barrio residents
would lose their homes and be unable to afford the new housing that would be built on the land. The CSO members overturned the hasty decision of the executive board and fought to
change the city's plan.

In Hanford, the CSO, led by the educational caucus,
helped change a state highway program to include replacement
housing for the displaced residents.

In San Jose, a well-publicized case of discrimination was
brought by the NAACP against a Mexican-American tavern
keeper. The CSO educational group investigated the incident
and convinced the CSO leaders to join in the NAACP's suit
against the tavern owner. As the CSO president explained,
"We are trying to integrate our people into the community by
dispelling discrimination. How in the world are we going to do
it if we do the same thing?"[34]

Alinsky was delighted by the new vitality brought to the
CSO's as a result of the educationals. In a letter to Tjerandsen
he admitted his initial doubts that an eucational program could
actually bring about "a situation of constant questioning, chal-
lenging, unrest and controversy all inimical to the hardened,
settled condition so essential to institutionalization. . . . Frank-

ly," he continued, "I wouldn't have . . . given a hundred-to-one bet on it, but it seems to have worked."[35]

Later, the educationals provided another development in IAF's history. When Ross was organizing the CSO in Stockton, he discovered a remarkable young woman named Dolores Huerta. She had a talent for organizing, but told Ross that she had her heart set on being a flamenco dancer. In time, however, Ross convinced the lovely, vivacious woman that she should join with him and Cesar Chavez to build the CSO network. Alinsky agreed to hire her, and Dolores Huerta became the first woman to be an IAF organizer.

Once the educationals were accepted by the CSO leadership, Huerta convinced Alinsky to let her run a series of educationals for women in the CSO. She argued that women needed political education and greater freedom of movement within their communities. Alinsky brought her proposal to the IAF Board and the Schwartzhaupt Foundation. He explained to them: "It must be remembered that since the bulk of membership of the CSO's are of Mexican-American ancestry, the Latin tradition emphasizing a secondary status for the female is still definitely present in these groups. The program will unquestionably result in more and more women rising into positions of leadership in the various activities of the organizations."[36]

The CSO educationals provided an important new component in the organizing approach of Alinsky and the IAF. How it would be made a part of future IAF organizations, however, remained to be seen.

Another important contribution to Alinsky's thinking was made by Dolores Huerta and her sisters in the CSO. They convinced Saul that women had much to contribute to leadership in local communities. He still had doubts about women's ability to organize, but the CSO women had given him a lot more to think about.

The CSO network continued to expand throughout the 1950's. At its high point in membership, there were over thirty chapters affiliated with the National CSO, Inc. The CSO chapters in California extended from Sacramento in the north to Calixico in the south, and there were three chapters in Arizona.

In the late 1950's the National CSO became independent of the IAF. At that time Cesar Chavez moved from Alinsky's payroll to become the director of the CSO's organizing staff. Ross remained IAF's West Coast director and continued as a consultant with the CSO leadership. Until well into the 1960's Alinsky came, as usual, for his twice yearly visits.

All during the years that Ross and Chavez were organizing and consolidating the CSO, Alinsky was back in the East, working to build support for his program to reorganize America's cities. He remained convinced, despite the exponential growth of suburban communities since World War II, that the nation's large, older cities were essential to the health of the sprawling metropolitan communities. Alinsky was convinced also that the Catholic Church, with its system of urban parishes, would remain the backbone of the older cities, with their many-splendored neighborhoods.

The effective organizing done by Ross and Chavez in California helped Saul realize that his main function should now be that of organizing the organizers. It became obvious that someone had to sell interested communities on organizing themselves, and recruit, train and oversee the IAF's organizers and raise the money needed to start the new organizations. By the mid-1950's Alinsky was ready to put together a Chicago-based team of IAF organizers that would match the West Coast staff of Ross, Chavez and Huerta.

Monsignor John O'Grady

During the Eisenhower years, the labor unions moved away from the neighborhoods. That was bad news for Alinsky. It meant that he was losing one of the two fundamental voluntary institutions upon which he had built the Back of the Yards Neighborhood Council and the organizations in Kansas City, South St. Paul and Omaha.

There were many reasons why the unions moved away from what Alinsky called industrial area communities. The postwar population changes, with people moving from cities to suburbs, was a factor; the mobility of industry in an era of inexpensive automobile-truck-superhighway transportation was another. The unions went through political changes as well, not the least of which was increased anti-union regulation by federal and state governments. Unions became more cautious about their activities. The anti-Communist crusade of the early 1950's was a period of painful purges within the labor movement. Alinsky's mentors were gone: John L. Lewis was too old and too isolated to have an influence on the union leadership; the radical organizers who gave life to the lusty CIO locals during the 1930's and 1940's disappeared into less radical pursuits. Besides, the economy was booming and the American workers were busy buying refrigerators and automobiles. There were lots of reasons why the local unions were no longer what Alinsky once described as the "secular equivalent of the parish church ... the medium through which these people (in the Back of the Yards) express their secular hopes and desires for economic security."[37]

Alinsky was sorry to see the unions give up their involvement in local community affairs. The sociologist and the organizer in him thought that organized labor was making a big mistake. Mass-based organizations like labor unions, according to Alinsky's gospel, grow and flourish from the bottom, not from the top.[38] He was convinced that the unions would lose their base among the workers if the action was to take place only at the national level or at the local level only every three years, at contract time. In later years he grumbled about the AFL-CIO becoming a member of the establishment. He continued, however, to hope for a grass-roots revolution in organized labor, a return to "organizing the unorganized." In the meantime he looked elsewhere for his support.

What also bothered him, as the 1950's progressed, was how the business community had the gall to publicize itself as a revolutionary, progressive force in American society. The editors of *Fortune* described the next phase of America's ongoing revolution as a function of the corporations: "U.S. capitalism is *popular* capitalism, not only in the sense that it has popular support, but in the deeper sense that the people as a whole participate in it and use it."[39]

Not for a moment did Alinsky take seriously *Fortune*'s brand of populism, nor did he agree with the dictum of Charles Wilson that "what was good for our country was good for General Motors and vice versa."[40] For Alinsky, the combination of political consensus ("I Like Ike"), middle class prosperity and benevolent corporate management would never be able to preserve the American democratic process. The nation needed, more than ever, an active, multi-cultured citizenry, organized to ensure popular participation and healthy dissent. Instead of staying within the old neighborhood boundaries, as in the past, Alinsky realized that he would have to extend his organizing to citywide and regional "communities of interest." The issues, not geography, would be the binding force of the mass organizations of the future.

So, in the 1950's, Alinsky turned for support to the churches. He found that they too had changed since the war. Many Protestant and Jewish congregations were moving to the suburbs in an attempt to catch up with their migrating members. For the most part, however, the Catholic Church remained committed to the cities; it had too much at stake in the old cities—its unique network of parishes, parochial schools, hospitals and social agencies. For many years Saul had felt right at home with Catholic bishops and pastors.

His chief collaborator in this period was a tall, ruddy-faced Irish-American monsignor, John O'Grady. The two men had been friends for a decade, ever since the day in 1940 when G. Howland Shaw took Fr. O'Grady to meet Saul Alinsky and to observe the Back of the Yards Council in action. In spite of O'Grady's appearance—his silver hair, twinkling blue eyes and soft brogue—the monsignor was, in his clerical way, as radical and persistent a social activist as Alinsky.

Over the years in his post as director of the National Conference of Catholic Charities, O'Grady had built up a network of contacts within the U.S. Catholic Church that even the Pope couldn't match. Twenty years Alinsky's senior, O'Grady had been educated and ordained a priest in his native Ireland. After ordination he was dispatched by his Irish superiors to serve "Holy Mother Church" in Omaha, Nebraska. Until 1908, and even longer in some places, the United States was looked on as a missionary land by Vatican authorities. The Irish bishops, in particular, continued for many years to send, from their abundance of priests, young men like O'Grady to care for the souls of Irish-American Catholics in the cities.

That is how, in 1910, the youthful John O'Grady came to land in New York. He knew nothing about Omaha. "All I knew about it," he said later, "was that at one time it had been Indian territory."[41] He did not stay long in Omaha, however; the bishop sent the bright young priest to do graduate work at the Catholic University of America in Washington, D.C. O'Grady studied economics and sociology and completed his doctorate in 1915. But instead of returning to Omaha, he received permission to join the faculty of Catholic University. For many years he taught the social sciences, and when the university opened its school of social work in 1934, O'Grady was named its first dean.

Even in those early days, O'Grady was more of a social activist than an academic. He helped establish the National Conference of Catholic Charities and became its executive secretary in 1920. In that post he did much to organize the U.S. Catholic Church's program of social welfare and its nationwide network of Catholic Charities. After World War II, O'Grady came to Alinsky for help. He was worried over the growing emphasis on social work professionalization in Catholic Charities and the concentration on middle class social service, especially adoption services and institutional care. He wanted Catholic Charities workers to be moving out into crowded city neighborhoods and isolated rural areas. He told Alinsky that the IAF's community organizing, with its coalition of local parishes and community, could provide the environment in which Catholic Charities could return to the streets. "The time had come," O'Grady argued, "for more welfare organization on the neighborhood basis. . . . The time had come to help people to think and plan for themselves."[42]

For the next couple of years, O'Grady arranged for Alinsky to speak at the annual meetings of the diocesan directors of Catholic Charities. For two summers Saul also taught a course on mass-based organizing at Catholic University. At O'Grady's request, IAF trustee G.H. Shaw became the treasurer of the National Conference of Catholic Charities. Shaw joined the monsignor in urging Catholic social workers to break out of rigid patterns of individual case work and "to stimulate the genuine and democratic organization of the communities in which they are located . . . democracy at the grassroots level."[43]

O'Grady wanted nothing less than for Alinsky to help him reorganize Catholic Charities and make it part of the network of people's organizations across the country. Saul, for his part, was eager to help O'Grady because he saw the churches, more than ever, as the backbone of his community organizations. In the conservative climate of the 1950's Alinsky needed allies, money and staff if the IAF was to get rolling again.

Monsignor O'Grady's first target was the Archdiocese of Chicago, the largest Catholic community in the United States. He went to Cardinal Samuel Stritch, Chicago's archbishop, with his plans for neighborhood conservation and organization in the city. Stritch readily endorsed O'Grady's program. He liked especially the part about conserving the older city neighborhoods because that's where the Catholic Church was in Chicago.

At O'Grady's request, Cardinal Stritch called a meeting of 150 pastors from Chicago's urban parishes. Stritch spoke movingly to the priests about the city's expanding slums, its bad housing, and the terrible effects these living conditions inflict on families. To the surprise of many of the priests, the cardinal was harshly critical of the city administration's slum clearance program. He called the wholesale destruction of old housing a short-sighted solution to the city's neighborhood problems, a solution that would cause more problems than it would solve. In particular, Stritch warned the pastors that they must resist attempts by their parishioners to keep "certain groups" out of their neighborhoods. "Blight and black," he said, are not the same. Alinsky thought Stritch's presentation was down-to-earth, informed and compassionate.

Before he sat down, Cardinal Stritch made an appeal to the pastoral interests of his priests. "As things are going now," he said, "we are building a new Archdiocese on the perimeter of Chicago." To avoid this costly flight of their parishioners to the suburbs to escape from blight and blacks, Stritch urged the priests to work together to "save Chicago, save Chicago from itself, save Chicago from some of its greedy citizens. . . . We cannot only recapture some of the blighted areas . . . but we can prevent other areas from becoming blighted."[44]

After lunch Alinsky talked to the pastors about his plan for a citywide network of neighborhood organizations and urged the priests to join him. He explained the benefits to the churches from being a part of a strong program of neighborhood control. The thirteen year old Back of the Yards Council was a good example, he said, of what can be done if a neighborhood is organized.

As a result of the meeting, the pastors, with Stritch's blessing and O'Grady's prodding, formed the Pastors' Conservation Council (later the name was upgraded to the Cardinal's Conservation Council) to study ways to curb "premature deterioration of parishes, the panic about our people rushing out to the suburbs, and the growing need for new parishes on the fringes of Chicago."[45] O'Grady was named the council's advisor and Alinsky was its unpaid consultant.

At the next meeting in 1953 the pastors heard a success story from Father Adrian Fisher, O.F.M., pastor of St. Augustine's Church in the Back of the Yards. Fisher, a leader of the now-famous neighborhood organization, made his point clear: "We have found that the only way to attack the problem is to have a good neighborhood organization which is democratic and represents all the elements in the neighborhood. With the power you have by virtue of this organization, you can get first-class services from the city, and you can throw your weight around and get what has to be gotten to save your neighborhood."[46]

To the dismay of O'Grady nothing much happened for the next couple of years except more meetings. The pastors complained that whenever they tried discussing neighborhood conservation in their parishes, it led to arguments with their people over keeping Negroes out of the neighborhood. Race was fast becoming the key neighborhood problem in Chicago. The city's black population had doubled from 280,000 at the beginning of World War II to 509,000 in 1950. By the mid-

1950's it was well on its way to 749,000. The city pastors were afraid that any move on the part of Negro families into all-white neighborhoods would drive their parishioners to the suburbs. It was common knowledge among the priests that a couple of the pastors in fringe areas, near all-black neighborhoods, were working behind the scenes to make sure their parishes remained lily-white. At this point John O'Grady became bored with the Chicago discussion and began to look for another diocese in which to launch his community organization plan for the National Conference of Catholic Charities.

In 1953 the NCCC's annual meeting was to be held in St. Louis. Joseph E. Ritter, the Archbishop of St. Louis, had become something of a hero in liberal Church circles for his desegregation of St. Louis' Catholic schools in 1947. When a group of angry Catholic parents took the Archbishop to court to stop his desegregation order, he threatened them with excommunication unless they dropped the suit. The parents backed down. O'Grady decided that St. Louis might be the second-best place in which to launch his community organization program.

At the national meeting of Catholic Charities directors that year the principal address was given by Saul Alinsky. Archbishop Ritter sat in the front row. Saul looked over the impressive audience of bishops, priests, sisters and social workers. His address was a masterful argument for the Church's professionals to develop a new kind of social mission, a city-wide, parish-based program aimed at "unslumming the slums." Alinsky told them that no amount of technical organization (government grants, public housing, professional planners) would solve by itself the multiple problems of blighted urban areas. The basic priority was to enlist the human resources of each diocese, each community, each parish church; in short the Church's own people had to be "organized, informed, participating and pressing for proper action." Only then, said Alinsky, could they make use effectively of federal funds and municipal programs to renew the city.

Toward the end of his talk, Alinsky addressed the underlying issue of the growing migration of black citizens to the large cities. The St. Louis meeting was held one year before the U.S.

Supreme Court's historic ruling in "Brown vs. Board of Education" which ushered in a new era of civil rights efforts on behalf of America's blacks. But initiating changes in racial attitudes was not a high priority for the Catholic Church in 1953. Alinsky warned his audience, however, that the cities where the churches were could not be saved without dealing with the Negro question. He left the NCCC members with these words: "The night of segregation is done. The day is here in which our people must learn to live together in integrated communities. . . . The organized community must direct the politicians—but first, it must make up its mind whether to become part of the migrating group ever fleeing in its obsession of color or of living in stable, healthy community with their fellow Americans."[47]

Before the week was over, Archbishop Ritter invited O'Grady and Alinsky to start a neighborhood organization in the area surrounding the cathedral parish in downtown St. Louis. To assist O'Grady, Ritter appointed two of his priests, one of whom was the administrator of the cathedral.

In 1953 Monsignor O'Grady was in a hurry. He was sixty-seven, and his health was failing. He hoped to make the change in Catholic Charities his last accomplishment before he had to retire. He explained to Alinsky that he wanted to organize two or three councils like the Back of the Yards to serve as models for the National Catholic Charities network. When Alinsky questioned him about money for these ventures, O'Grady assured him that money would be no problem once he had the sites for the NCCC demonstration projects. Alinsky wasn't so sure; he knew O'Grady's greatest failing was to be "more enthusiastic than time, strength or resources warranted."[48]

Alinsky was not convinced, either, that the diocesan directors of Catholic Charities were as interested in supporting community organization as O'Grady was. Most local Catholic Charities agencies had become heavily dependent on the United Fund to support their community programs. Saul's experience in Chicago had taught him that social service agencies tended to be more interested in ministering to society's victims, one-by-one, than in supporting organizations bent on changing that society.

Organizer Alinsky was forty-four the year he spoke in St. Louis. He was becoming less romantic about his itinerant organizing career. Perhaps it was his observing of O'Grady's frantic pace as he raced along, caring for the social development projects he had started in the United States and in Italy and Africa, before his failing health caught up with him. Whatever the reasons, the lone organizer found himself becoming more cautious about hanging out somewhere in the boondocks on a budgetary shoestring. He certainly did not paint a rosy picture of the organizer's life for the St. Louis audience: "Nights, days, meeting in homes, lodge halls, church meetings, persuading, persuading and persuading in a constant fight against apathy and the feeling of anonymity of 'we don't count, nobody cares for us and there isn't much we can do about it.' "[49]

Saul's friendly agreement with O'Grady meant that he would receive his expenses and little more, but at least it meant he would be traveling around, able to look for new organizing jobs and training on the job some young organizers he then could steal for his IAF team. O'Grady would be in full control of these NCCC projects. He would contact the local people, raise the money, set up the sponsoring committee and oversee the project—all from his base in Washington, D.C. Alinsky was O'Grady's consultant, advising him, screening applicants for the local staff and training them on his regular visits to the site. This would leave Alinsky plenty of time to work with his other organizations and to take on any new projects that came along.

The St. Louis organization was a long time aborning. O'Grady complained constantly about the inactivity of the local priests appointed by the archbishop. They took forever to gather the sociological data on the area; they still had not found enough people to make up the steering committee. Finally, after nearly two years and a half-dozen trips to the city, the Central West Neighborhood Organization (at least it had a name) was enough of a reality for O'Grady to request a grant from the Schwartzhaupt Foundation. On the advice of Carl Tjerandsen, O'Grady put the money in a special NCCC account. Out of the grant he would pay his and Saul's expenses and the salary of the organization's staff. Only when the organization was fully operative would the grant be turned over to its officers. Everyone was being extremely cautious about St. Louis.

In fact, only the irrepressible John O'Grady was excited when the St. Louis organization showed signs of being successfully launched. He knew that a successful start in St. Louis, a major Catholic diocese, would inspire others to follow suit. The long delay in getting started meant, however, that O'Grady had several new irons in the fire, and he didn't have the time to visit St. Louis as often as he had planned during the early days of the new organization. In the fall of 1955, he asked Alinsky to go to St. Louis and meet with the steering committee. While Saul was there, he was instructed to screen candidates for the post as the organization's director. Alinsky came away from that visit with a lot of questions about what was really going on in Central West St. Louis.

A couple of months later the St. Louis project suddenly went sour. O'Grady came in for a visit, stayed a few days and saw the steering committee in action. It was evident to him that the committee was steering the organization away from a democratically controlled organization like the Back of the Yards Council. The faction that had taken control of the budding organization was obviously more interested in working with the city's business and political establishment than it was in building a people's organization. At a special meeting called by O'Grady, the monsignor unleashed his Irish temper. There was a towering exchange of opposing viewpoints, but no change of minds. That night, after the meeting, O'Grady called Tjerandsen at the Schwartzhaupt Foundation and told him that NCCC was pulling out of the Central West Organization of St. Louis.

Tjerandsen said later that O'Grady "discovered to his horror and chagrin that what was really going on in St. Louis was a move to keep Negroes out. So he jerked the project out . . . and began casting about frantically to find another location."[50] What angered O'Grady even more was his discovery that the St. Louis director of Catholic Charities was a part of the opposition faction. The priest said he was afraid that an Alinsky-style community organization would hurt his agency's standing with the United Fund of St. Louis. Alinsky had figured that one correctly.

For Saul the whole St. Louis mess was symbolized by the two priests the archbishop had assigned to help O'Grady with the organization. On Alinsky's first visit to the new organization, the two priests stuck Saul with a large restaurant tab. He protested to O'Grady on his expense voucher: "Regardless of its being Lent, they had the best prime rib of beef and the best of everything. . . ."[51] Like the biblical organizers, O'Grady and Alinsky shook the dust of St. Louis from their feet and moved on to another town.

Two Model Organizations

At dinner one night in Chicago, O'Grady asked Alinsky to talk to a couple of young men who were working with a small enclave of Puerto Rican families on the city's South Side. The two men, Nicholas von Hoffman and Lester Hunt, had recently quit jobs at the University of Chicago to organize the Puerto Ricans. O'Grady told Saul that things were not going well with the Puerto Rican project and that the two young men needed Saul's expert advice. Alinsky agreed reluctantly to the meeting.

The next night, O'Grady assembled around his table at the Blackstone Hotel's restaurant von Hoffman, Hunt, Father John J. Egan, a young Chicago priest, and master organizer Saul Alinsky. With a bit of persuasion from O'Grady, von Hoffman told about how he and Hunt got involved with the Puerto Ricans through some friends who were members of a Catholic social action group, called the Young Christian Workers. The YCWers were trying to assist the newly arrived Puerto Ricans with their problems of living in Chicago. They found that the immigrants needed everything—jobs, decent housing, medical care and, above all, English-speaking assistance in dealing with Chicago's police, landlords, city officials and their neighbors in the all-black Woodlawn neighborhood.

Von Hoffman and Hunt convinced the YCWers that it

would be better in the long run to organize the Puerto Ricans to take care of themselves. But there was no money to hire the two hopeful organizers. On the advice of the group's chaplain, the YCWers went to see Father John J. Egan, an up-and-coming young priest who was in charge of family programs in the archdiocese. Egan pulled the proper ecclesiastical strings and got $10,000 from Cardinal Stritch to finance the work of the newly named Woodlawn Latin American Committee.

At that point Alinsky interrupted von Hoffman's narrative. "Okay," he said in a gruff, impatient tone, "so you got the money—now what the hell are you going to do for the Puerto Ricans?" When von Hoffman began explaining his plan, Alinsky interrupted again to tell him that they were going about it all wrong. An angry von Hoffman fought back, charging Alinsky with being "over the hill" as an organizer, afraid to take on anything new. The rest of the meal was a shouting match. Only the venerable Monsignor O'Grady remained silent. He sat back and watched the proceedings with a beatific smile on his face.

O'Grady had been impressed with von Hoffman from the day he met him. After listening to the young organizer's colorful account of the Puerto Rican project, O'Grady, with his rich brogue, told him: "Young man, you've got fire under your feet. I want you to meet my friend Saul Alinsky." The Blackstone Hotel dinner was the result. When the noisy party finally took their leave that night, the Blackstone's maitre d' was visibly relieved.

The next day Alinsky called von Hoffman to his office. When the youthful organizer appeared, apprehensive but unbowed, Alinsky barked at him, "Oh, sit down! I still wouldn't touch that organization of yours with a ten foot pole, but I'll hire you to work for me—on the condition that you'll get a haircut and buy a decent suit of clothes."[52]

Just as he had started on the streets of Chicago twenty years earlier, Alinsky sent von Hoffman out to find out what he could about the neighborhoods on the West Side. "Look around, take notes, give me weekly written reports and don't bother me until further notice"—those were his instructions.

Nine weeks later, when von Hoffman was sure that Alinsky had forgotten him, he was again summoned to the Michigan Avenue office.

"He had all my reports in front of him," recalls von Hoffman. "He had read them all. He said, 'You know, you might eventually turn into an organizer.' "[53]

On February 15, 1954, Alinsky hired von Hoffman as an apprentice organizer with the IAF. A few days later, he hired Nick's friend, Lester Hunt. Since Saul had no money, as usual, he farmed them both out to work for the Archdiocese of Chicago. Hunt, who spoke Spanish fluently, was sent by Catholic Charities to continue organizing the Puerto Ricans on the South Side. Nicholas von Hoffman became Cardinal Stritch's "eyes and ears in the neighborhoods."

As already mentioned, Cardinal Stritch was troubled about the city's older neighborhoods, the worsening racial situation and Chicago's slum clearance plans. Von Hoffman was sent out to find out everything he could about what was going on in those neighborhoods. Once a month von Hoffman reported personally to the cardinal at his episcopal residence. It sounds like something out of the Renaissance, as von Hoffman tells it: "There would be a rustle of red moiré at the door, and there he was, His Eminence Cardinal Samuel Stritch. He would sit at his desk, finger his pectoral cross and say, 'Sonny, tell me about Chicago.' "[54]

During this period von Hoffman and Hunt (Fred Ross called them the "Bobbsey Twins") underwent Alinsky's organizer-training course. It consisted mainly in several-times weekly, late-night sessions at Saul's Hyde Park home. With Ross and Chavez working hard in California, and now with von Hoffman and Hunt in Chicago, Alinsky figured he had the makings of a first-class team of IAF organizers.

A few months after the Blackstone Hotel dinner, O'Grady announced that he had found a new site for the NCCC's model organizing project. The director of Catholic Charities in Buffalo, Monsignor William Wozniak, had agreed to sponsor an organization in his diocese. His enthusiasm for the organizing project, as it turned out, was less enthusiastic than O'Grady made it sound. The Schwartzhaupt Foundation agreed to

O'Grady's request to transfer the unused St. Louis grant to Buffalo. Wozniak promised that the local Catholic Charities would pick up the organization's support after the three-year period covered by the foundation grant.

Once again, as in St. Louis, Alinsky agreed to organize the project and train the new organization's permanent staff. This time, however, instead of Alinsky, O'Grady got Alinsky's assistant, the tough, smart, outspoken and totally inexperienced Nicholas von Hoffman.

The first site chosen by O'Grady was Fruitvale, a run-down section of Buffalo with a large population of senior citizens. The NCCC had been conducting a study in that neighborhood of problems of the elderly. The local Catholic and Protestant churches and the director of the neighborhood house liked O'Grady and welcomed the "citizen participation" project to be funded by Catholic Charities. But as soon as Nick von Hoffman arrived to begin organizing, word spread through the neighborhood that he worked for Saul Alinsky and was probably a "Communist agitator." O'Grady wanted no more delays; he chose a new site for the project.

This time he and Monsignor Wozniak agreed on Lackawanna, an industrial suburb of 30,000 residents, south of the city of Buffalo. On November 25, 1956 Nick von Hoffman started organizing. To prevent a repeat of the Fruitvale allegations, von Hoffman was hired by NCCC for the princely salary of $6,000 per annum.

Lackawanna, New York was a seedy, smoky place whose life was entirely dominated by the giant Bethlehem Steel Corporation. Every family in Lackawanna had at least one member who worked for the steel company. The only other major employer was the Catholic Church, which ran a large orphanage and a home for unwed mothers. The United Steelworkers of America, after years of bloody labor disputes, was finally able to organize Bethlehem Steel in Lackawanna during World War II. By the mid-1950's, however, the union had settled down to "bread and butter" unionism, and its leaders showed little interest in community problems.

Lackawanna's population in 1956 certainly did not fit the "melting pot" theory of immigrant assimilation: O'Grady counted fifty-one nationality groups represented among the city's residents. The largest ethnic group was the Poles—they were Catholic, conservative and cautious about outsiders. The Lackawanna city government was corrupt and inept, the result of many years of paternalistic control by the steel company. A large railroad yard divided the city in half. On the wrong side of the tracks lived the black workers and their families. The city had no building code; city ordinances could be found only by sifting through years of city council minutes. The air was polluted, sewers were inadequate and streets were unpaved. Von Hoffman called Lackawanna "a city with an inferiority complex."

Nevertheless, the optimistic Monsignor O'Grady saw in Lackawanna the potential for a dramatic demonstration of what Alinsky's mass organizing could do for a downtrodden, apathetic community. To O'Grady Lackawanna was a tragedy. He found it difficult to comprehend "how a town of over thirty thousand people who were highly paid and very well organized in churches, unions, fraternal clubs, national group and veterans organizations could be so plaintively helpless."[55] If Lackawanna could be organized and made to work, Alinsky's approach would work anywhere.

Von Hoffman followed Alinsky's organizing blueprint to the letter. He held a series of small group meetings, drew the issues out of the people who attended and found the community's natural leaders. The Lackawanna Neighborhood Cooperative Committee, as the steering group was called, had the enthusiastic support of Monsignor Julius J. Szabo, the pastor of the city's Assumption Church and the associate director of Catholic Charities of Buffalo. When Alinsky met Monsignor Szabo for the first time, he told Saul about the Christopher Movement, a Catholic modern-day tractarian society, a branch of which he had started in Lackawanna to deal with some of the community's problems. He said that the Christophers' motto was: "Better to light one candle than to curse the darkness." From what Saul already knew about the problems of Lackawanna, he responded: "That's okay, Father, but it would be better if you took the candle and held the flame to the rear ends of some of the people who are the cause of the problems."

For the first six months von Hoffman worked hard to build the organization in Lackawanna, O'Grady dashed in and out at irregular intervals, and the closest Alinsky came was New York City, four hundred miles to the east. Once a month he met with von Hoffman to discuss the Lackawanna project at Peter's Backyard, a Greenwich Village steakhouse.

Before the exhausted von Hoffman returned to Chicago in the spring of 1957, he hired two men to continue the organizing, Tom Murphy, a fifty-two year old Lackawannian, and Ed Chambers, a twenty-six year old ex-seminarian from Iowa who had been working at Friendship House, a Catholic lay organization with branches in Harlem and Chicago.

Everything went well at first. There were ready-made issues in every neighborhood in the troubled city. The residents were sophisticated, to some extent, about what organized power could do because of their experience in the steelworkers' union. Von Hoffman started with a modest victory involving 120 families who were slated for relocation to make room for a state highway project. The residents, mainly poor blacks and elderly whites, found out that the state agency had no intention of helping them relocate. For months the issue was kicked around by the local politicians, with no solution in sight. The Lackawanna Neighborhood Cooperative Committee (LNCC) took the side of the residents, organized them and won a promise from the local housing authority to give the displaced residents priority access to public housing.

The incident made an impression on the whole city. O'Grady wrote to the Schwartzhaupt Foundation's trustees: "This small achievement provided the impetus ... to keep the organization in existence. People began to talk about things that had been bothering them but which they had held back because they did not really think anything could be done about them."[56]

In the first year, other issues the LNCC took on turned out successfully. A long-needed flood control project was pushed through; residents of a new suburban housing development were organized to fight for basic services promised but never delivered by the city—sewers, street lights, garbage collection; a tenants' association was formed in a large World War II era public housing project when it was acquired by speculators who began raising rents and reducing maintenance. LNCC meetings soon overflowed Father Szabo's parish hall.

But the new organization had problems too. The highly publicized controversy surrounding the tenants' association alerted Bethlehem Steel officials and their political lackeys that a new force was growing in their front yard. The Catholic parishes, with one exception, adopted a kind of wary neutrality toward the organization. Battles among the organization's leaders postponed the first community convention for sixteen months. Only in March 1958 did the LNCC become a full-fledged organization, the Citizen's Federation of Lackawanna. That convention was the occasion of Alinsky's only visit to Lackawanna.

Two years later, Monsignor O'Grady turned the sponsorship of the healthy organization over to Catholic Charities of Buffalo. With O'Grady out of the picture, Church support dwindled, and the Citizen's Federation faltered, then disappeared shortly after its fourth convention in 1961.

In his later years Alinsky did not talk about the Lackawanna organization except to say that it was never an IAF project. Schwartzhaupt's Carl Tjerandsen calls CFL a failure.[57] The organization was successful, however, to the extent that it brought together a disorganized and discouraged populace and taught the community how to use its power to make necessary changes in the city.

The organizers were burdened with unusually heavy obstacles in building the Federation. Among them were Bethlehem Steel's tight control over the city, the steelworker union's lack of interest in the everyday affairs of the community, and the unwillingness of the local churches to get involved in controversial issues.

Alinsky did not help. He left the oversight of the project entirely to O'Grady, and the monsignor was too old and too busy to handle it alone. Von Hoffman was good, but he stayed less than six months. Afterward, when he was supposed to be guiding the work of the two apprentice organizers he left behind, he was taken up with another project in Chicago. The two organizers, Murphy and Chambers, did not get along, but

O'Grady could not bring himself to appoint one of them as the boss. When the Schwartzhaupt grant ended, the organization's days were numbered.

Recently, Chambers said that despite all the problems the CFL could have been more successful if there had been an adequate organizing staff.[58] If so, then Lackawanna was another example of Alinsky's perennial overcommitment of IAF's resources. Saul had other irons in the fire. As a result he barely fulfilled IAF's agreement with NCCC. O'Grady did not get the clearly successful demonstration project he needed to capture the attention of the Catholic Charities directors. Tjerandsen says that the officials of Buffalo's Catholic Charities never "understood what the whole thing was really supposed to accomplish in the first place."[59]

Nevertheless, Alinsky came away from Lackawanna with some valuable assets. The LCF provided the baptism under fire of two men who would become the IAF's top organizers. Von Hoffman and Chambers came to Lackawanna without any experience. When they returned to Chicago, they were ready to take on major organizing projects.

O'Grady's second attempt to build a model community organization for Catholic Charities turned out better than St. Louis. In his effort to find Church support, O'Grady was forced to go wherever the local bishop and the Catholic Charities director invited him. There were few invitations to choose from.

When the Lackawanna organization seemed safely launched, O'Grady started a third project in the copper-mining city of Butte, Montana. The Schwartzhaupt Foundation provided him with another three-year grant, on the condition that Alinsky provide an IAF organizer to start the project and train two local people to take over after he left.

This time Alinsky loaned von Hoffman's buddy, Lester Hunt. He was to receive $4,000 for salary and expenses from O'Grady for a three-month assignment. Also, this time Alinsky agreed to come personally to consult with Hunt and the local leaders on a regular basis. At the urging of the Schwartzhaupt board (they were not pleased with Alinsky's "no-show" record in Lackawanna) O'Grady and Alinsky wrote a contract outlining the terms of IAF's consulting relationship with the Butte project.

Again everything went well at the start. Hunt, like von Hoffman, was a born organizer; all he lacked was experience. Unlike Lackawanna, however, the director of Catholic Charities in Montana was an enthusiastic supporter of the organization from the beginning. Monsignor D.B. Harrington became chairman of the temporary steering committee. At the convention he was elected the first president of the Butte Citizen's Project.

The city's top union boss was behind the project. Ernie Selvas, the president of the Mine, Mill and Smelters Union, made the new organization a top priority of the union. Selvas was an officer of BCP.

The community issues stood out clearly in the troubled mining city. Butte needed a new bus system to replace the one that had gone bankrupt, leaving the city without public transportation; housing was needed for young couples with moderate incomes if they were to stay in town; the city's schools were in serious financial straits; on-going strikes against Anaconda Copper were crippling what strength remained in the community.

Over a thousand people turned out for Hunt's first organizing meeting. The constitutional convention was held in the fall of 1959. A few months later the Butte Citizens Project held a citywide congress. O'Grady and the leaders were so pleased that they began talking about branching out to the nearby cities of Anaconda, Missoula and Helena within two years. But a couple of months later, when Hunt left, the two local men he had trained to staff the organization proved to be unequal to the task. The project managed to limp along until 1964, when it went quietly out of business.

Butte, like Lackawanna, was a one-company town. Anaconda Copper owned everything in Butte except the union. The city was dying. With the introduction of open pit mining in the early 1950's, Anaconda began laying off miners. A long period of bitter strikes followed. The population of Butte declined from a high of 100,000 to less than 30,000 at the time of the organization.

Parts of the city looked like a ghost town. "God, what an ugly town it is!" was Hunt's opening line in his first report to Alinsky. "My immediate reaction to meeting their economic crisis is that it is a good place for any industry to locate if it wanted to incur substantial losses for tax purposes."[60]

But Hunt said also that the people were wonderful, especially the tough, close-knit union families who understood things like "solidarity" and "power." Technically the Butte organization was exactly what O'Grady hoped for. "What we did," Hunt said, "was to organize sort of a community marriage between the Catholic Church and the Mine, Mill and Smelter Workers Union."[61]

The only problem was that the Butte Citizens Project arrived too late. Tjerandsen says: "There was no way, given the absolutely dreadful economic conditions in Butte, that the organization could ever have become self-sufficient. The town was being destroyed by a no-win battle between Anaconda Copper and the union."[62]

During the crucial second year of the project, Monsignor O'Grady became seriously ill and was forced to retire as director of the National Conference of Catholic Charities. His successor, Monsignor (now Bishop) Raymond Gallagher, showed no interest in community organization projects.

In Butte, as in Lackawanna, Alinsky was not much help. He was involved during most of this period in an organization in New York City that proved to be a debacle. The difficulties with the New York organization explain to some extent why he gave so little attention to O'Grady's project. For the first time in his career, he now had a stable of eager, talented organizers ready to work. But Saul continued to operate as the lone organizer whenever it suited his mood. As a result, in the late 1950's Alinsky and the IAF sustained some painful bruises.

New York City

Every great innovator has at least one disaster to his credit. The radical from Chicago's West Side tried to organize the Lower West Side of New York. He ran up against that city's hostile and well-organized social worker industry. It was a bruising battle and ended in a stalemate. In Gotham, Alinsky's radical reveille made a sound like an uncertain trumpet.

The IAF's New York project began in the early 1950's during the period when Saul was recovering from his personal tragedies. While he was courting Jean, she showed him all kinds of wonderful places in the city. She took Saul on long walks in Central Park, and they enjoyed quiet dinners in neighborhood restaurants away from Midtown.

Most of the friends who cared for him during his sadness lived in the New York area. Marshall and Ruth Field and Val and Harriet Macy lived in the city, Jacques and Raissa Maritain were in nearby Princeton, N.J., and Agnes Meyer's summer home was in Mount Kisco, N.Y. The ubiquitous John O'Grady introduced Alinsky to Herbert H. Lehman, U.S. Senator from New York, and his circle of liberal friends. One of the nice things about Saul's radicalism was that he never let it interfere with his love of good friends, fine food, comfortable surroundings and long, late-night conversations. He was a multi-cultural man—at home in Park Avenue apartments or in Southwest barrios. Alinsky had dedicated his life to social change, but his was an orderly sort of social revolution.

New York City had begun to grow on him. At the time of their marriage Jean and Saul discussed his moving the IAF to New York, but then decided against it as too drastic a move for his kids. But Saul continued to use any excuse to visit his New York friends.

One of his earliest supporters was Adele Rosenwald Levy, an IAF trustee and a faithful contributor. In the early 1950's Adele Levy suddenly stopped attending IAF's annual meeting. In 1953 she refused to send her annual contribution. She complained to IAF treasurer Bishop Sheil that Alinsky's East Coast trustees were nothing but figureheads and that her New York friends kept asking her why Alinsky had never organized any neighborhoods in the city. Unwilling to lose her yearly $5,000 check, Alinsky dispatched Harriet Macy to talk Levy back into the fold. Fortunately, by the time he heard about Adele Levy's boycott of the IAF treasury, Saul was already negotiating with the New York Foundation for a small project in the city.

In the fall Alinsky had been approached by Senator Leh-

man and Leona Baumgartner (Lehman was a trustee and
Baumgartner was the executive director of the New York
Foundation) about ways to involve the foundation in the many
problems of the city's rapidly growing Puerto Rican popula-
tion. The two New Yorkers had been impressed with Monsi-
gnor O'Grady's glowing account of the influencce of IAF's
Community Service Organizations in Hispanic communities in
California.

The "Puerto Rican problem" was big news in New York
City in the early 1950's. The *New York Post* had just completed a
long series of articles on the plight of New York's most recent
immigrants. The *Post*'s reporters concluded: 1. New York's
Puerto Ricans were gravely in need of strong, independent,
responsible leadership. 2. They weren't likely to get it as long
as there was a Mayor's Committee on Puerto Rican Affairs as
presently constituted. 3. Their adjustment to New York life
and the solution of their economic and social problems would
be impeded until they did get leadership.[63]

Puerto Ricans, of course, enjoyed full American citizenship. They began coming to the mainland in increasing numbers during World War II, mostly for jobs. Later they came
also because of overcrowding and unsettled political conditions
in the islands. Over eighty percent of these Puerto Rican
immigrants settled in New York City, where, as New York
State Rent Commissioner Charles Abrams said, they found
"little or no community life, and overcrowding so intense that
family morale and family structure are virtually impossible to
sustain."[64]

In December 1953 Alinsky presented a proposal to the
NYF requesting a three-month grant of $9,000 to determine
whether IAF's kind of community organization could be used
effectively in New York's neighborhoods, particularly those
with large numbers of Puerto Rican families. If, the proposal
said, as a result of his investigation, IAF decided to organize in
New York, Alinsky would submit a three-year budget request
for a community organization in one neighborhood.[65]

Strangely enough, Alinsky was unusually ambivalent
about an IAF project in New York City. In an earlier letter he
wrote to the Macys, otherwise filled with domestic details

about Jean's two Labrador retrievers, a two-week visit by his WASP mother-in-law, and his son David's poor marks in arithmetic, spelling and reading (Jean would have to skip the next trip to California to tutor David before exams), Saul referred to the NYF study: "The Puerto Rican thing cooks between the New York Foundation and the Industrial Areas Foundation and I am afraid that sooner or later we are going to get snafued into that deal."[66]

The New York Foundation approved the grant to the IAF. Saul carried out the investigation personally. He worked at it on and off during all of 1954, spending much more than the promised two months in New York, and one month in Puerto Rico. (He was impressed with the officials in Puerto Rico, less so with their New York counterparts.) Not until July 1955 did Alinsky present the report to the NYF Trustees. It contained first-class data about Puerto Ricans from both ends of the migrant stream.

In the second half of the report Alinsky described in some detail two areas in New York with large Puerto Rican populations, neighborhoods that looked ripe for IAF-style organizations—a large area of the South Bronx, and a smaller neighborhood on the lower West Side of Manhattan, called Chelsea. He referred to several extraordinary New Yorkers he had contacted in the course of the study. He seemed especially taken with the director of the Hudson Guild settlement house, a social worker named H. Daniel Carpenter.

Whatever caution Alinsky's instincts were raising about his organizing in New York, he ignored them. He argued, in his report to NYF, that the IAF was uniquely equipped to organize either of the designated neighborhoods. He said that a three-year organizing budget of $574,767.15 would be sufficient to build an organization in the South Bronx; the Chelsea project would cost only $289,127.46.[67]

Before the NYF study was completed, however, the cast of characters changed: Leona Baumgartner left the New York Foundation to become the Commissioner of Health in the administration of newly elected Mayor Robert F. Wagner. Saul's report was turned over to Dr. Paul McGhee, a consultant to the foundation. McGhee was dean of the Division of

General Education at New York University. He was also
Baumgartner's friend and neighbor in Greenwich Village.

At first McGhee bristled at what he considered the arrogant tone of Alinsky's report to the foundation. But Saul soon
won him over. McGhee was impressed with Alinsky and his
approach to community organizing. The two men became
allies in the pursuit of funds for an IAF organization in New
York City. Alinsky said that their "Saul—Paul" letters sounded
like the "title of a guide book to the road to Damascus put out
by a Catholic book club."[68]

As soon as the word got around in New York, however,
that Saul Alinsky was about to receive funds from the New
York Foundation to organize a neighborhood organization in
the city, a well-connected cabal of social workers began an
intense lobbying effort to block the project. The group was led
by members of the United Neighborhood Houses, a coalition
of New York settlement houses. Alinsky called them the "Committee To Keep Alinsky Out of New York." At first the social
workers raised the alarm that Saul's rough-and-tumble organizing approach would alienate supporters of neighborhood-based
social agencies, and perhaps even stir up ethnic warfare among
whites, blacks and Puerto Ricans in the poorer neighborhoods.
Later, after the Chelsea Community Council was organized,
the neighborhood house group engaged in a full-scale vendetta,
the scars of which remain in New York to this day.

Settlement house professionals disliked Alinsky from his
early days in the Back of the Yards. The director and trustees
of the Chicago University Settlement House refused an invitation to join the Back of the Yards Council. They became, in
time, relentless foes of the council, its programs and tactics.
When Agnes Meyer was writing her series on the Back of the
Yards for the *Washington Post,* she said that the settlement's
complaints against the Back of the Yards organization sounded
like a broken phonograph record. They claimed to approve of
the council's objectives, but not its methods; they said that the
council was biased, always ready to take the side of the residents in community disputes, and that the council's leaders
worked closely with labor unions. Meyer was critical of the
Chicago University Settlement House, saying that it chose to

remain aloof, in "obstinate, righteous isolation, indifferent to the creative activity and the dynamic democracy swirling about their disintegrating institution."[69]

Saul did nothing to help the situation; he never missed a chance to criticize social workers. In *Reveille for Radicals* he blasted members of the profession as professional outsiders, meddlers, do-gooders with little or no faith in ordinary people or in the democratic process. He charged that they did everything they could to prevent the kind of conflict and controversy necessary to make changes in a community. Those who claimed to be "community organizers" among their number were the targets of his sharpest barbs.[70]

The social workers, in turn, attacked Alinsky and blamed him for John O'Grady's attempts to move Catholic Charities away from case work and toward community organization. Under the spell of Alinsky, they charged, O'Grady wrote the editorials in *The Catholic Charities Review* that advanced Alinsky's view that settlement houses were institutions of the past. "The settlements in our turbulent communities of today have a fine program on paper," O'Grady wrote. "They are interested in doing things for people, they know what is good for people. But they can hardly be called community centers. The nearby taverns really are much more like community centers than the settlement . . . very few of the people have ever been inside the neighborhood settlement."[71]

It is easy to understand, therefore, that while Paul McGhee may have been won over to Alinsky's proposal for a New York organization, the majority of the NYF trustees were not. McGhee wrote to Alinsky about the board's reaction to his report: "Off the record, and just because I want to play fair with you, as a friend I will say that I don't expect them to do anything at all about it, at least as an IAF enterprise under your direction."[72]

McGhee realized what Saul didn't—that the New York Foundation was not about to give money to a controversial organizer from Chicago when it was surrounded by an army of social workers who were experts at what they called "community organization." As McGhee explained, "community organization" to a social worker means that a professional "*organizes* the community, assigns jobs to this person or that, involves this or that person on boards, etc., etc. Nuts. What's needed is *participation*."

McGhee was won over by Alinsky's view of local citizen participation, and he understood how different it was from what the social workers meant. He continued: "Although this group is willing to pick up and use this newish term 'participation,' they don't know what the hell it means. Mrs. FDR (Franklin D. Roosevelt) will speak at a meeting and they will somehow get a host of community people to show up and then they call this participation. Nuts again."[73]

The foundation acted on Alinsky's request as McGhee predicted. Faced with a major controversy over Alinsky, the NYF decided to fund a similar proposal submitted by H. Daniel Carpenter, director of the Hudson Guild in Chelsea. Carpenter had sound social work credentials. He had served on the staff of the Hudson Guild for twenty-five years and been named executive director upon the resignation of John Lovejoy Elliott, the Guild's revered founder. Recently Carpenter had set up a blue-ribbon citizen's group, called the Chelsea Committee for Neighborhood Development, to focus attention on problems of housing on the Lower West Side. To the NYF this certainly was community organization.

Actually, Carpenter was an impressive man. Alinsky liked him immediately when he interviewed Carpenter during the investigation of Chelsea as a possible site for an IAF organization. After this meeting, Saul described Carpenter as imaginative and open-minded, virtues Alinsky said were in short supply among the majority of settlement house directors. Saul's friend Julius Edelstein, then an aide to Senator Lehman, said that Alinsky thought "Dan (Carpenter) was the greatest thing since Magic Markers."[74]

Carpenter's proposal to the New York Foundation sounded exactly like an Alinsky project. He even used Saul's name in the proposal's subtitle: "A Citizen Participation Project Prepared by the Hudson Guild (As Suggested by the Industrial Areas Foundation's Report Prepared by Saul Alinsky for the New York Foundation)."[75] To the NYF trustees the Hudson Guild's proposal offered a masterful compromise—a neighbor-

hood project in Chelsea, based on Alinsky's organizing philosophy and managed by the director of the prestigious Hudson
Guild settlement house.

Although Alinsky's name was mentioned nowhere in the
text of the proposal, Carpenter told NYF that he intended to
hire Saul as a consultant to the project. The inclusion of
Alinsky mollified the Lehman/Baumgartner/McGhee faction
of the foundation.

At his first opportunity, Alinsky told McGhee how disappointed he was that the IAF did not get the Chelsea project. He
agreed with McGhee's analysis that neither the foundation
trustees nor the settlement house people understood "community organization" in the IAF's sense. He despaired of being
able to work with the settlement house crowd, but he thought
that probably Dan Carpenter was different. For this reason,
Saul said he was willing to negotiate a consulting role for IAF
with Carpenter.

At McGhee's urging, Saul wrote a memorandum in which
he set out point by point the weaknesses he saw in Carpenter's
proposal for the Chelsea citizen's organization. He prefaced the
memorandum with a statement of his personal respect for the
Hudson Guild's leader. Once that was said, however, Alinsky
delivered a devastating commentary on Carpenter's proposed
organization. He charged Carpenter with putting forward a
"completely different kind of animal from the project recommended in my report to the New York Foundation." Unless
Carpenter agreed to change the proposal to meet IAF's basic
criterion for an independent citizen's organization, Saul said he
would not participate in any way. Getting down to specifics,
he criticized Carpenter for promising to build an organization
that would not antagonize anyone in New York. Alinsky
agreed that an effective organization did not have to go out to
court antagonisms or hostilities with special interest groups
(social workers, politicians, business leaders), that a good organization made a patient presentation of its point of view, but if
discussions and explanations resulted in a continued negative
reaction, then, said Alinsky, "you proceed into action based
upon your belief."

In short, the Hudson Guild's proposal was all wrong,

according to Alinsky. Carpenter did not have the slightest
inkling of what Alinsky meant by a genuine people's organization. It was not just a matter of neighborhood people, as
Carpenter thought, turning up at meetings called by the Hudson Guild's director, wearing his organizer's hat, "but a real
participation in which individuals acquire a sense of belonging,
a sense of dignity, a sense of self-confidence and a realization
which grown-up people must achieve if they are going to step
even halfway out of their childhood, and that is that nobody is
going to take care of their problems except themselves. It
means an organization which is a welding of those interests in
a community crucible heated by a fanning of interests, enthusi-
asms, dreams, passions, ambitions and determinations into a
citizen's pressure bloc—into an articulate representative organization whose strength is recognized by all civic authorities
for what it is and therefore they will respond to this pressure."

Saul was always at his most eloquent in a fight. His explanation of what he meant by community participation and
organization was evidence that he respected Carpenter and
thought it worth a fight to change him. At the end of the
memo, Alinsky went back on the attack, saying "that there was
as much relationship between the Hudson Guild's proposal
and an authentic IAF organization as there would be in a
proposed project on 'The Merits of Reuben's Cheescake, as
suggested by a Report on Community Malnutrition.' "[76]

In his reply, Dan Carpenter adopted Alinsky's tough tactics. He counterattacked with a point-by-point defense of his
plan and managed miraculously to convince Alinsky that they
were really in agreement on the basic elements. He offered to
incorporate all of Saul's corrections in his final proposal. But
he didn't.

The rewritten Chelsea proposal remained a mess from
Alinsky's point of view. Carpenter proposed to direct the project on a halftime basis from his office at the Hudson Guild.
There was no mention of IAF's having veto power over staff
appointments, as Alinsky had requested; instead, Carpenter
agreed to "consult" with Saul before hiring. Alinsky had no
control over the project, its director or its staff—he was strictly
a hired gun. At the last moment Carpenter added insult to

injury when he asked Saul to accept a reduced fee of $4,800 for five consulting days a month.

Nevertheless, Saul agreed to his weakened consultant role. As soon as he signed the agreement with Carpenter, the New York Foundation moved to grant $120,000 to support the Chelsea Citizen Participation Project. An additional $60,000 was pledged by Alinsky's old friends at the Schwartzhaupt Foundation.[77]

From the beginning, Chelsea was Alinsky's most abnormal organizing effort. At every stage of the negotiations he expressed great ambivalence about IAF's participation in the project. When Paul McGhee, who was, by now, impatient to get the thing moving, argued with him that the Alinsky/Carpenter differences were a matter of semantics, Alinsky roared back: "Semantics, shemantics—what I don't like is the smell of the whole thing!" In the next breath, however, Saul reaffirmed his trust in Carpenter, as the "kind of people that I would bet on."[78] Carl Tjerandsen is correct in saying that "Alinsky was not the acme of consistency."[79] For some reason Saul wanted to believe that Carpenter could be brought around.

The IAF's Lester Hunt, who worked a couple of months with the Chelsea organization, thinks that Alinsky at some point had made up his mind to do a New York project. When he couldn't get the funds, he decided to go along with the Hudson Guild and to look upon the IAF's involvement as an experiment in using the IAF approach through a social service agency.[80] (This was the same period when Saul was working with John O'Grady to see if community organizations could be built under the auspices of Catholic Charities agencies. The Chelsea project was approved by the funders between the time O'Grady pulled out of St. Louis and moved into Lackawanna.)

Also, there may have been another, more personal reason why Saul wanted to be near his old friends in New York. His wife Jean was not well. For months she had been complaining about her lack of energy and recurrent spells of dizziness. Partly to cut down on her housekeeping chores, the Alinskys had recently sold their large house in Chicago's Hyde Park and moved into an apartment. At this period, Jean was undergoing a series of medical tests to see what, if anything, was affecting her health. One day, even before the tests were completed, her doctor sent for Saul and told him that he was almost sure that Jean was suffering from multiple sclerosis. He urged Saul, however, not to tell her about the condition as long as the disease was in remission. In the meantime, Jean remained miserable and so did Saul. At the same time, news came that Alinsky's friend, Marshall Field, was seriously ill.

When the Chelsea organization was launched finally in July 1956, the honeymoon between Carpenter and Alinsky lasted only six weeks. On his second visit to New York, Saul found out that Carpenter had hired an assistant director—without consulting him. Like Carpenter, Marjorie Buckholz was a social worker. Saul was furious. It wasn't so much that Buckholz was a woman, though Saul was still not convinced that a woman could do the rough and tumble kind of street organizing in Chelsea's tenements and in its waterfront bars. What made him angry was that Carpenter felt free to ignore Alinsky when the ink was barely dry on their joint agreement.

To add to his injury, a story appeared that same week in the *New York Times* about the Chelsea organizing project. The headline ran, "Block Plan Seeks a Better Chelsea; Citizen's Project Undertaken by Hudson Guild."[81] No mention was made in the story of the IAF's joint sponsorship. The Chelsea organization was presented as totally a Hudson Guild program. "He (Carpenter) was using the IAF to get the $180,000," Alinsky said later. "I think he was just going to flop us off."[82]

When Alinsky threatened to quit, the two foundation executives, McGhee and Tjerandsen, who were unwilling to see the project left entirely to the Hudson Guild, talked Alinsky into staying on. Alinsky agreed only because, outside of Carpenter, the project's staff seemed pretty good; maybe through them he could influence Carpenter. In November Alinsky spelled out in another memorandum his role and responsibility as "advisor" to the project. It was an attempt to keep the record straight with the funding organizations. To the staff members he insisted that they cut down on their interviews with residents and begin to take action on the local issues. They were to send him weekly reports so that his visits could be devoted to advising them, not just listening. Saul even tried to get Carpenter to agree to a New York IAF advisory committee who could counsel the staff if a crisis arose during his long absences. It was really a "watchdog committee" of people he trusted (Paul McGhee, Leona Baumgartner, Trude Lash of the Citizens Committee for Children, and Ralph Whelan of the New York City Youth Board). Of course Carpenter saw through the ruse and refused.[83]

Nothing of significance happened during that first year. The staff members grew more dependent on Alinsky and paid less attention to Carpenter. Saul made no attempt to undermine Carpenter's authority, but it became evident to the staff that Alinsky was the organizer and Carpenter was a settlement house director.

Nearly one hundred local organizations joined the new organization in its first year. Besides the Hudson Guild and a dozen of its affiliated groups, the roster included three parent-teacher associations, the local political clubs, veterans organizations, the General Theological Seminary, seven Catholic churches, one Protestant church, two YMCAs, various ethnic societies, the International Longshoreman's Association, the Bartender's Union, B'nai B'rith and the American Jewish Congress.[84]

The staff remained stalled in their attempts to get some action going around the key neighborhood issues. Alinsky complained that too much of his time each month was being taken up with what he called labor relations: mediating internal disputes between Carpenter and the project's staff.

In the spring of 1957, a temporary executive committee of Chelsea residents was formed. Fr. Robert T. Dunn, a Catholic priest, who was the assistant pastor of St. Columba's Church, moved into the leadership position of the committee. In November the Chelsea organization was launched officially at a well-attended constitutional convention. The delegates elected Father Dunn as the first president of the Chelsea Community Council.

What no one at the convention realized until later, however, was that a decision made a year earlier by the Board of Directors of the Hudson Guild would cause great trouble for the new council. At the meeting at which the settlement house's board approved the Chelsea project, they voted also their unanimous approval for a giant cooperative housing development to be built in the center of Chelsea. The project, called Penn Station South, was sponsored by the International Ladies Garment Workers Union. Even though Penn Station South was federally sponsored housing, Chelsea's poorer residents could not afford to live there.

For four years Penn Station South became the one public issue in Chelsea that overshadowed everything else. The project brought radical changes in Chelsea's residential make-up. More than any factor, Penn Station South spelled the doom of the Chelsea Community Council.

One of Manhattan's oldest and loveliest neighborhoods, Chelsea was laid out by Clement Clarke Moore on his grandfather's estate (Moore is better known as the author of the most famous Christmas poem, "A Visit from St. Nicholas"). The neighborhood is on the Lower West Side of New York; it stretches from 34th Street south to 14th Street, and from the Avenue of the Americas west to the Hudson River.

By the 1950's, when Alinsky arrived there, the quiet, old residential neighborhood, with its nineteenth century townhouses and the gracious campus of the General Theological Seminary ("Little Oxford" it was called by its founder), had changed. Commercial buildings and light industry had pushed into Chelsea. Most of its 61,000 residents were Irish-American dockworkers and newly arrived Puerto Ricans who worked in the city's restaurants and garment industry. Penn Station South would displace thousands of these less affluent residents, and in those days neither federal nor municipal housing authorities worried about relocating evicted tenants.[85]

That is why, even before the Chelsea Community Council could mobilize the residents around an agenda of local issues, Penn Station South split the community into warring factions. Carpenter, his Hudson Guild affiliate organizations and, in general, the better-off residents were committed to Penn Station South. On the other side were Father Dunn and his parishioners, the six other Catholic parishes, and the majority of Chelsea's residents and local organizations. People were against Penn Station South, not because it wasn't fine housing, but because they couldn't afford the rents. Everything the Chelsea Community Council tried to do after the first year foundered on this basic community disagreement.

For a long time Alinsky was unaware of Penn Station South. Once he found out, however, he tried to turn the staff and council leaders away from a last-ditch fight over the project. He told them that the council could do nothing to stop Penn Station South, or anything else, until the organization was big enough to take on the ILGWU, Mayor Wagner and the Federal Housing Authority. But Carpenter would not allow the issue to be put on the shelf; he kept pushing the staff and council leaders to come out in support of the housing. The staff fought him at every turn. Alinsky was disgusted at all this waste of organizing energy on a battle that could not be won. Buckholz remembered Saul shouting at them in frustration during a staff meeting: "Penn Station South, North, East or West, I couldn't care less. I am interested in building a people's organization in Chelsea."[86]

At the community congress in 1958, Dunn was re-elected president. On the advice of Alinsky the majority of the delegates were prepared to adopt a neutral stand on Penn Station South. But Carpenter and his supporters forced the delegates into a long and acrimonious debate over the issue. Finally the council voted not to oppose the new housing but to demand that the city administration and the Federal Housing Authority set up effective relocation procedures and give Chelsea's displaced residents a priority on new public housing in the area. Carpenter and his faction left the meeting in a huff, vowing to continue the battle for the Chelsea Community Council's approval of Penn Station South.

After the congress Alinsky was more convinced than ever that the Chelsea Council was, in his terms, a "loser." Again he tried to resign. Dunn begged McGhee and Tjerandsen to talk Saul out of leaving. The two foundation executives convinced Alinsky to stay by promising to force Carpenter to resign. Saul went off to Italy, but said he would return in the fall.

Nothing changed. The council's membership continued to grow, but there remained only the one issue. At the second annual congress in 1959, Carpenter and his supporters did their best to oust Dunn and take over the council. When Dunn was re-elected, Carpenter stormed out. Two months later, led by the Hudson Guild, nineteen member organizations withdrew from the council, including most of the Protestant and Jewish groups. The battle over Penn Station South now took on overtones of a religious war—Protestants and Jews against Catholics.

Actually the battle over Penn Station South was a class conflict. Thousands of Puerto Rican residents, mostly Catholic, were being displaced, according to one of Alinsky's critics, "with a more heterogeneous population of a higher social class. The Hudson Guild and other non-sectarian, Protestant and Jewish Chelsea groups welcomed the project. . . ." Father Dunn, according to the same critic, was claiming that "the council is concerned with protecting the rights of the present residents and providing the community with adequate housing of all types. . . ."[87]

The religious bigotry was the last straw for Alinsky. He urged Dunn either to reorganize the council completely or to dissolve it. Saul wanted Dunn to dissolve it. The reasons for the Chelsea Community Council had been lost in a firestorm of emotions and bitter partisanship. "Discussion has given way to defamation," said Alinsky. "Logic and democratic debate were non-existent. Communication had ceased. . . . The face of the enemy had ceased to be that of evil and injustice, but instead was assuming the likeness of two opposing camps."[88]

After the Carpenter faction withdrew, Alinsky agreed to send Lester Hunt to help the staff organize the rest of Chelsea's Puerto Rican residents. After a few weeks on the job, Hunt too saw that the council was hopelessly stymied. "It was my analysis," Hunt recalls, "that the organization was at a stalemate because of the wide split in the community. They were going to end up throwing rocks pretty soon if it didn't close its doors. Maybe it could be tried again at another time after the wounds had been healed. . . ."[89]

Before the annual congress in 1960, Alinsky wrote a long memorandum to Dunn in which he argued again for the dissolution of the council. He praised the struggle of the Chelsea residents to take responsibility for their community. They were beaten, he explained, only because of unfortunate timing and a convergence of stronger interests.

At the close of the letter Alinsky told Fr. Dunn and the leaders of the Chelsea Council that someday they would see that it had been worth the risk to fight for freedom, dignity and a functioning democratic society, even though it had ended in a temporary defeat.

The Chelsea memorandum has become an organizing classic. It is full of insights into the complex personality of Saul Alinsky—his own special mixture of tough, pragmatic organizer and warm human being. On the last page he wrote:

> What has already happened has caused the drastic crumbling of the walls which separated many of your organizations and their leadership. When there was no communication, no exchange of opinions, no getting to know others, there was silent suspicion and beneath-the-surface hostility between groups. I suggest such a condition is, in the long run, worse than the open controversy of today. It was a hidden infection, that could not be treated, because it went undiagnosed. Even the religious issue raised in connection with the council's policy toward Penn Station South has been with you in the Chelsea community for many years. It long antedates the Council's beginning.

Saul made reference to the wonderful changes that had happened to Fr. Dunn:

> Until the Council was started you had never been inside a church of another religious faith. You knew few people from the other faiths or from other community groupings. You never worked with a heterogeneous group on a give-and-take basis. The last three years has changed all that.

Alinsky tried to turn Dunn's attention to the future, hoping that the priest would understand that the defeat of the organization in Chelsea was just a temporary setback for the democratic process. "Your city will not always be a French pastry tray to be picked over by 'a higher social class.' It may seem a bit removed now, but your fellow citizens will yet live in decent houses, send their children to good schools, eat well, live in pleasant surroundings, be liberated from their ghetto jails, and, above all, rule themselves, make their own decisions and cut the patterns for their own destinies. But this will only be done, as always, by the organized efforts of the people represented by those whom they have chosen."

There was a final word of pride and hope for the priest who had become his comrade-in-arms through the long, bruising battle. It states well Alinsky's organizing creed: "I am proud to be associated with you in defeat, as proud as I would be ashamed to be connected with those who have triumphed over you. It is a windy world, my dear friend, and the fire blows out again and again, and it must be lit again and again."[90]

The Chelsea community Council was not Alinsky's failure. True, the organizer later admitted that he went against his own best instincts in taking on a project over which he had no control. Even after many years, Father Dunn remembers Alinsky and the Chelsea campaign with affection and pride. He gives high praise to Saul for the time and the effort he gave the council's staff members and leaders. "I admire him greatly for what he tried to do. . . . He wasn't the director, he was only a consultant. What I object to is all these people writing about the Chelsea Community Council as though it were Alinsky's baby. It wasn't his baby at all. . . . If they want to study Alinsky, let them go look at one of the organizations where he was in control."[91] It is difficult to recreate the situation that greeted Alinsky in Chelsea in the late 1950's, but it may be that the organization would have been a success, and that Daniel Carpenter, along with Fr. Dunn, might have become a heroic witness to Saul Alinsky's skill as an organizer. But Penn Station South changed Chelsea radically—almost overnight. Even if it had happened two or three years later, after the Chelsea Community Council had its act together . . .

By the time the council dissolved itself in 1960, Alinsky was involved in a whole new set of urban problems and organizing projects in Chicago. For several years Saul continued to keep in touch with Fr. Dunn. Usually they got together in December, when Saul was in New York for his annual IAF

Board meeting. The two men would meet in a favorite bistro on the West Side for a special Christmas celebration of Wild Turkey bourbon and porterhouse steak.

One Christmas Saul could not make their dinner and wrote to Dunn instead, "All my love and best as always, and it really isn't Christmas without our having our usual walk and drinks and laughter and everything else, so from a distance I do it by proxy and with a big embrace. . . . When I think of some of our mutual acquaintances I am reminded of Hannibal's toast on Christmas Eve, 'Piss on our enemies.' (If Hannibal never said that, he should have.) Affectionately, Saul D. Alinsky."[92] That was Alinsky's epitaph for the Chelsea project.

4.

Back to Chicago

Neighborhood Integration

Except for the headache that was Chelsea, the second half of the 1950's was a good time for Alinsky. His home life was relatively calm. The kids were growing up. The only domestic cloud was his wife's health. Jean's multiple sclerosis was in remission, but she was disturbed continually about her weakness. She took her problems to one psychoanalyst, then another. Saul complained to a friend about the cost of Jean's analysis, yet he made no attempt to tell her about her true condition. He continued to believe, with his doctor, that she would be better off not knowing she had multiple sclerosis, a disease that was incurable and with no specific treatment. Evidently Saul's way with sickness—and death—was to keep moving. Sickness, possible invalidism, death—he treated them as pursuers, like a persistent posse. When his time came, he hoped it would be a surprise, and that he would die quickly.

But while her health allowed, Jean was a good mother to Saul's two children. She tells of Sunday afternoons in the big house in Hyde Park with Saul and the kids. At one stage he decided to read the Bible to Kathryn and David in lieu of synagogue or Sunday school. He wanted them to have a "little religious education" as a part of their heritage. In memory of his childhood experience with the rabbi and the shiny penny, he offered financial rewards to the kids as an incentive to pay attention. He would read a chapter, then question them about it: "For ten cents, who was Eve's father?" Jean says that these

Bible study sessions were often interrupted with gales of laughter.

Dogs, too, were a part of the Alinsky household. When they were first married Jean brought along her dogs, two large Labrador retrievers. Saul and the dogs developed a mutual dislike. It was not helped by Jean's preference for walking the dogs in the early morning when Saul wanted his breakfast. Later, the Labradors were replaced by Pang (short for "Pang-nana," the "Tough One"), an Alaskan malamute, who was friendly and quiet. But Pang was also tough, and Saul liked the fact that his dog could beat up any other dog in Hyde Park. Saul, like Pang, had a tough, hard streak—something he had gained from growing up in Chicago's West Side ghetto.

Saul's travel schedule was a problem for Jean. She never got used to his frequent absences. When the kids were old enough, she went with him, whenever possible, especially on his trips to California. They stayed at Monterey, near the CSO's headquarters. Jean grew to love the beautiful Carmel Valley. She said she felt better in that climate. Whenever she could, Jean dragged Saul off to look at the houses for sale in the valley.

Saul worked closely with Cardinal Stritch in Chicago. The cardinal continued to be interested in how the Church could help preserve the heart of the city and its expanding circle of neighborhoods. As mentioned before, most of Chicago's Catholics came from working class families, and Stritch wanted to keep the current generation in the city, where the large churches and parochial schools had been built by the sacrifices of their immigrant parents and grandparents.

What complicated the city-suburb problem, Stritch understood, was the ever-growing population of blacks and Hispanics moving into Chicago. He depended upon Alinsky and von Hoffman to give him sound advice about what the Church could do within the Catholic community to reduce discrimination and exclusionary housing practices. Though the Archdiocese and the IAF had a long-standing informal arrangement, Stritch's first official commission to Alinsky was for the IAF to do a study of the city's Near North Side. The neighborhood

was part of the Cathedral Parish of the Holy Name, and within
its boundaries lived the majority of the newly arrived Puerto
Ricans. Alinsky used the data of the study to prepare a grant
request for $149,000, which he sent to the Fund for the Repub-
lic ("a wholly dis-owned subsidiary of the Ford Foundation,"
according to its director, Robert Maynard Hutchins) to build a
community organization in the cathedral area. Nicholas von
Hoffman began organizing there while they waited for an
answer from the Fund. When the request was turned down by
Hutchins, Alinsky pulled von Hoffman out and sent him to
organize Lackawanna for O'Grady.

In 1957 Stritch told Alinsky that the Archdiocese would
fund a major study by the IAF of Chicago's racially troubled
neighborhoods. Depending on what the study showed, the
cardinal said he would entertain a proposal for the IAF to
organize these inner-city and transitional neighborhoods. From
the treasury of Chicago's Catholic Charities, Stritch promised
Alinsky $120,000 to fund the three-year study. Saul thought he
could get a matching grant from a foundation. The archdiocesan grant included money to permit the IAF to begin training
Chicago priests to take part in the organizing campaign in the
neighborhoods.[1]

As soon as Alinsky received the first check from Stritch,
he called von Hoffman back from Lackawanna and rehired
Lester Hunt. The energetic Fr. John Egan became the IAF's
first priest-intern. His on-the-job training also gave Alinsky an
additional researcher for the neighborhood study. The IAF's
research division (von Hoffman, Hunt and Egan did the leg-
work; Saul directed the operation) started out looking for a way
to encourage and expedite the integration of the large and
volatile black population into the normal life of the city. Without a deliberate plan to integrate Chicago's neighborhoods,
Alinsky feared that the black slums would continue to over-
flow into white areas, racial violence would increase and white
families (including the cardinal's urban flock) would continue
their headlong flight to the suburbs.

That fall Alinsky and his IAF staff went to Stritch with a
proposal for the organization of a single Negro community on

the South Side. Saul assured the cardinal that he would continue the overall neighborhood study, but he argued that a successful black organization could help test IAF's hypothesis
about integration. The research they had already done into all-
Negro and what were called "interracial communities" (white
neighborhoods being invaded by blacks) convinced Alinsky
that real integration was not happening. He called "wishful
thinking" the hope of local liberals that there would be a
natural and gradual integration of Chicago neighborhoods:
"So-called interracial communities are actually communities in
a state of transition. They are usually called interracial during
the short period when Negroes are moving in and whites are
moving out. On close inspection they turn out to be only bi-
racial communities which are shortly entirely Negro."[2]

The IAF's integration plan was brilliant in its simplicity.
Saul suggested an approach that dealt in terms of whole neighborhoods rather than individual families. It was a variation on
his original Los Angeles plan: Organize an all-Negro neighborhood adjacent to a well-organized white community (or organize the two separately) and let the two organizations learn to
deal with each other as equals. Chicago's black neighborhoods
were disorganized and powerless, overrun with crime and slum
conditions. The welfare costs for a one-on-one approach to the
city's poor and powerless blacks, nearly twenty percent of
Chicago's population in 1958, would be an exorbitant sum.
Each slum neighborhood, according to Alinsky, would require
"five thousand social and kindred workers to take care of
people adequately."

IAF's proposal offered to organize Grand Boulevard, a
run-down all-black neighborhood, adjacent to the eastern
boundary of the Back of the Yards. According to the proposal,
once the Grand Boulevard organization was viable and operating effectively in its own neighborhood, it would be ready to
form alliances with the all-white Back of the Yards Council.
Common interests and issues, shared committees and projects
and all kinds of elbow-rubbing would lead to a limited sort of
integration; the rest would come later.

Better housing in Grand Boulevard, for instance, Alinsky

said, would mean less pressure on the Back of the Yards. A long-range program of cooperation on shared interests would defuse tensions and build the foundation for future residential integration. Stritch was impressed with Alinsky's argument: "The people of the Back of the Yards and Grand Boulevard can never be expected to . . . respect each other because they are of different races . . . but once they have met and worked with and associated with each other they will no longer be able to look upon each other as white and black."[3]

Stritch directed Monsignor Vincent Cooke, the director of Chicago's Catholic Charities, to gather up the money needed to finance the Grand Boulevard organization. One month later, however, Cooke advised Alinsky that Catholic Charities income had dropped precipitously because of the current business recession. The project was postponed for a year. The cardinal assured Saul that the money to continue the neighborhood study was already "in the bank."

According to Nicholas von Hoffman, these "arrangements" between Cardinal Stritch and Alinsky were informal, shake-of-the-hand agreements. In the first years of their collaboration, Saul received no reimbursement from the Archdiocese except the salaries of von Hoffman and Hunt. Later, however, "Stritch put in a lot of money through Cooke of Catholic Charities."[4]

One unforeseen result of the Alinsky-Stritch arrangement was the breakup of Saul's longtime friendship with Bishop Bernard J. Sheil. When Sheil, the IAF's treasurer, heard that Alinsky was working with Cardinal Stritch, he fired off a telegram to Saul and IAF President Marshall Field, "Resignation from the IAF Board effective immediately. Saul, you've sold out to the Catholic Church."[5]

Sheil was an auxiliary bishop in Chicago under four archbishops. He and Cardinal Stritch did not get along. As Sheil grew older, his behavior became somewhat erratic. The kind of courage that allowed him to take independent and unpopular stands on public issues (organizing the packinghouse workers and denouncing Senator Joseph R. McCarthy) tended to isolate him, to some extent, from the official archdiocesan entourage.

The Vatican Connection

Things were quiet on all fronts in the spring of 1958, so Alinsky went to Europe "to visit various adult education and community organizational sites in Denmark, France and Italy for purposes of comparison and understanding of approaches. . . ."[6] The highlight of his trip was a three-day meeting in Milan with Archbishop Giovanni Montini, the future Pope Paul VI.

For years Jacques Maritain had spoken approvingly to Montini of the democratic community organizations built by Saul Alinsky. When Saul announced that he was going to Italy, Maritain set up a meeting between Alinsky and Montini who was, at that time, the Archbishop of Milan. The American organizer and the Italian prelate spent three afternoons in earnest discussion about Milan's political and economic troubles. The Italian Communists were strong and winning the allegiance of the workers. Montini was searching for a way to reverse the exodus from the Catholic Church and from its political ally, the Christian Democratic Party. The archbishop was impressed with Alinsky's understanding of urban problems and his pragmatic approach to political issues but, most of all, with his skill as a popular organizer. Before he left, Saul gave Montini several books, including his own *Reveille for Radicals* and *John L. Lewis.* The archbishop said that he would read the books and then get in touch with Saul about doing an IAF project in Milan.

The evenings in Milan Alinsky spent at a local tavern, in the pleasant company of a Communist official. As he later told an interviewer, "It was an interesting experience . . . Archbishop Montini and a beautiful, grey-eyed, blonde Milanese Communist union offical with whom I explored common interests bridging Communism and capitalism."[7]

Before returning home Saul met in Paris with Count Jacques de Bourbon-Bussets, a highly placed UNESCO official who had visited the Back of the Yards Council in the company of Alinsky the year before. Another of Maritain's connections, Bourbon-Bussets suggested that the United Nations agency might be willing to fund a second European trip for Alinsky.

He mentioned a number of possible European sites for an IAF organization.

On his return to Chicago, Saul spoke somewhat mysteriously about his plans for a European branch of the IAF. He wrote to IAF Board President Gordon Clapp about his tour: "The mission of the trip was fully achieved, and its objective is now packaged and ready for delivery as soon as natural events provide the opportunity."[8]

But nothing happened. The Church in Italy was caught up in selecting a successor for Pope Pius XII. For a time speculation was rife that Archbishop Montini, the protégé of the deceased Pope, would be his successor. Alinsky hoped that the rumors were true. Two days before the papal election, Alinsky wrote to new IAF Trustee George N. Schuster: "No, I don't know who the next Pope will be, but if it's to be Montini then the drinks will be on me for years to come."[9]

As it turned out, of course, a relatively unknown Italian cardinal was elected and took the name Pope John XXIII. The new Pope lost no time in naming Montini a cardinal. Maritain told Alinsky that the new cardinal was reading Saul's books and would contact him soon. In the meantime Italian Church-state politics continued to play like second-rate grand opera. When a letter from Montini arrived in December, it was only a Christmas greeting.

Cardinal Stritch was in Rome when Alinsky arrived from Milan, and the two men spent a day together talking about Chicago. Five days later Stritch was dead. When Alinsky arrived back in Chicago, the chancery officials who were friendly to Alinsky advised him to prepare a full report of IAF's activities for the Archdiocese so that they could present it to Stritch's successor before Saul's enemies could get to the new archbishop.[10] Until Alinsky could renew IAF's lease with the incoming archbishop, he put everything else he was doing on the back burner, including his Italian project.

A month later, Milwaukee's scholarly Archbishop Albert G. Meyer was named by the Pope to succeed Stritch. John O'Grady wrote to Meyer on Alinsky's behalf. In flowery ecclesiastical prose, O'Grady urged the new archbishop to meet with Alinsky, calling the meeting a "blessed opportunity."

Alinsky groaned aloud to Leonard Rieser about the tone of O'Grady's letter: "My reaction to that kind of letter would be, 'If anybody ever asks to see me and his name is SDA have him thrown into the Chicago River.' "[11]

Early in 1959 Alinsky met with Meyer and was assured of the Archdiocese's continued support for the Chicago neighborhood study. With IAF's survival thus assured, Saul turned his attention to, among other things, his proposed "second front" in Italy. This time he asked Monsignor O'Grady, who had good contacts in the Vatican, to set up an appointment with him with high Church officials in Rome. O'Grady wrote to Cardinal Domenico Tardini, the Vatican secretary of state. This letter, too, was an embroidery of ecclesiastical pieties and diplomatic indirection. O'Grady managed to make Saul Alinsky sound like an Irish Catholic—a man who "has given his life to applying the doctrines of the Church, the doctrines Pope Pius XII used to call 'universal brotherhood,' to the ordinary relations of life." In his last paragraph O'Grady threw in a couple of sentences that caught the attention of a Vatican bureaucrat: "Mr. Alinsky works closely," said O'Grady, "with some of our foundations that control large amounts of money. I am sure that he would be glad to help us in securing sufficient funds to carry out in a number of Italian communities the principles to which I have been referring."[12]

Saul was furious with O'Grady's ecclesiastical pussy-footing. He was sure that O'Grady's letter had ended his chances for a serious hearing in Rome. "You must get away from the theoretical approach," he scolded his friend, "and emphasize the fact that on a hard-boiled, realistic straight power operation . . . this is the way it works and that when we apply these principles and practices into a situation such as Italy we know that it will work and it is not an 'experiment' or anything else of that kind."[13]

To make sure that O'Grady said the right things about the IAF's operation on his forthcoming trip to Rome, Alinsky sent him a four page memorandum. In it, Saul sketched the rationale for his plan to organize Italian industrial communities and draw the workers away from the Communist camp. The memo is straight Alinsky. He directs O'Grady to appeal to the prelates in terms of their institutional self-interest—the Church's losing battle with the Italian Communists. He explained briefly how the Communist Party in the Back of the Yards had withered on the vine once the local people began running their own effective democratic organization.

In the meantime, Pope John XXIII appointed a new secretary of state. O'Grady contacted the new secretary, Monsignor Angelo Dell' Acqua. He asked Dell' Acqua to meet with Alinsky in April. Again, what seemed to have attracted the attention of the Vatican bureaucrats were O'Grady's references to Alinsky's contacts with American foundations. Dell' Acqua wrote back to O'Grady. "I was pleased to learn of Mr. Saul Alinsky's generous dispositions and shall be happy indeed if, thanks to his liberality, it will be possible to alleviate the sufferings and improve the conditions of many needy families."[14] Despite the vague nature of the invitation from the papal secretary of state, Alinsky went to Rome, confident that he could clarify his position and sell his proposal when he met face-to-face with the Vatican officials.[15]

Alinsky arrived in Rome sometime around Easter 1960, and stayed about ten days. The weekend before his appointment, he rented a Fiat and drove down into Southern Italy to visit the areas the Vatican officials seemed most anxious to discuss. Saul was appalled by the extreme poverty he saw throughout the area. Back in Rome, after the meetings began, he reported to Jean "a slight chill in diplomatic relations when I rejected having anything to do with working in South Italy." He told the officials, "They don't need a community organization—they need a revolution. They do not have the resources with which to do anything even if organized. The abysmal poverty ... demands a complete program of economic reconstruction with capital from the Italian government and the World Bank. It's a wonder to me they're not Communists."[16]

Despite this rocky beginning, the talks continued. At various times the group that met with Alinsky included officials from the Vatican Secretariate of State, Monsignor Carlo Boyer, secretary general of Caritas International (the worldwide Catholic Charities), several aides of Italian Premier Amintore Fanfani, perhaps the Premier himself, and a number of trade union leaders from the North. It took some time to get down to business. Saul complained to his wife, "It's too early as yet to begin to get an idea if the 'Vaticano' (Saul's Italian) and the IAF do business. So far we exchange ideas as though we came from different planets."[17]

What surprised the politically savvy Alinsky most was the extent to which the Vatican was involved in Italian politics and the inflexible right-wing stands it took on most domestic issues. It reminded him, he said, of the "old pre-war mentalities of embracing Fascism as a defense against a 'Communist menace.' " At some point the meetings moved to Monsignor Dell' Acqua's office. Alinsky said, "Everyone was refreshingly blunt and candid." Dell' Acqua presented Alinsky with a beautiful book of color plates of the Sistine Chapel. That day, Saul decided that the Vatican officials really wanted the IAF to organize a project in Milan, and later, perhaps, other projects in Turin and Rome. They still wanted something done about Southern Italy. The secretary of state agreed to join with the IAF in sending an application to the Ford Foundation (the "first time in history," Saul told Jean).[18]

Saul was on a high that night when he wrote to Jean from his room in Rome's Hotel Metropole: "Since there are so many bridges to be yet crossed, I am reserving judgment as to whether I'll resign (from the IAF) and we will all live here for five years or whether we will spend our summers, Christmas holidays and spring vacations over here."[19]

A few days later he was deeply discouraged again. His old back trouble was bothering him; he complained to Jean that it was stiff and aching. His comparison seemed apt: "The Inquisition couldn't have been worse." It was a rare thing for Alinsky to complain, so he must have been really depressed. "Last night I was so discouraged on the reactions of the labor and political conferences (it would be a cinch to organize against V. [Vatican], but it would be folly at this point and eventually you would end up a captive of the Communists) that after I got back to the hotel around midnight, I went for a long walk down the Via Cavour. . . ." He walked as far as the Coliseum and took shelter in an arch during a rain shower. "I returned wet and tired—as a matter of fact I've been feeling very tired the last couple of days—the old Chelsea feeling. . . ."[20]

By now Saul was convinced that the Vatican officials were afraid to try something new. They were going to stick to their anti-Communist condemnations, even though they knew they were not working. Alinsky had fallen in love with Italy, its people and its age-old culture and traditions. But he could see no help for the Italian people as long as the religious wars continued between the Church and the Communist Party. He complained to Jean, "It reminds me so vividly that all through history the ruling classes have not been overthrown so much by the intelligence and power of those seeking change but by their own shortsightedness. I expected more from the V. and am disappointed."[21]

Back in Chicago, Alinsky wrote to O'Grady that the "Rome Project" was dead. A letter had just arrived from Monsignor Igino Cardinale of the Vatican Secretariate of State. Cardinale said he was writing on behalf of Dell' Acqua, "He has been studying the question from various angles, and all in all I am afraid he has come to the conclusion that considering the present condition of this country, the plan would have scanty chances of success. . . . 'Rather than face a failure with all it involves, it is better not to start at all.' "[22] So ended the IAF's European second front.

Saul Alinsky celebrated his fiftieth birthday as the 1950's came to a close. His teenage kids were almost grown. That year he bought a house in California. Saul wrote to Carl Tjerandsen:

> I . . . finally achieved a personal dream. We own an acre in the Carmel Highlands, just back of Point Lobo, with a brand new tiny little house (it is impossible to describe) to which we will have to add on a couple of bedrooms. It is the second road from Point Lobo, and all I can think of is exactly what it is, and that is the line out of Peter Pan when Wendy asks him where he lives and (if I can remember it loosely) he replies, "Two down from the corner and on to morning." We are nestled in tremendous green pines, redwoods and huge flat-top cypresses with peaks of the ocean between the branches and all this for $12,500![23]

Saul kept his office and a tiny apartment in Chicago. As long as the National CSO continued operating at full steam on the West Coast, he was able to commute from Chicago to Carmel on a regular schedule.

Saul lost two of his closest friends and collaborators in the late 1950's. Marshall Field III died suddenly of a heart attack late in 1956. Alinsky missed sorely Field's friendship, and his advice and strength. Monsignor John O'Grady began slipping fast in 1959; he was under pressure to resign as the head of the National Conference of Catholic Charities. He held on a little longer, then retired, an invalid, to a nursing home near Washington. Saul continued to visit O'Grady when he came to Washington. Fortunately Saul was able to get Gordon Clapp, former director of the Tennessee Valley Authority, to take over the presidency of the IAF Board. A brilliant and kindly man, Clapp became Alinsky's trusted counsel until his untimely death in 1963. The lone organizer had few close friends, and he felt the loss of each one as a major blow.

As for the IAF's far-flung projects, all were doing well—except for the ill-fated Chelsea Community Council. In Chicago, Fr. John Egan, Alinsky's clerical protégé, had been named by Stritch's successor, Cardinal Meyer, to a new archdiocesan post as director of the Office of Urban Affairs. Egan's full-time job was to see to it that the Church in Chicago continued to find ways to serve the urban community. Before Egan even had an office of his own, a couple of inner city pastors began urging him to get Alinsky to build an organization in their troubled middle class neighborhood. After nearly ten years of hard work, Alinsky saw Chicago's Catholic parishes starting to come alive.

But there were storm warnings also. During the interregnum between Stritch and Meyer, the year before, while Saul was in Europe, Fr. Egan and Nick von Hoffman led an attack, with the blessing of the archdiocesan officials, on Mayor Richard J. Daley's showcase Hyde Park Urban Renewal Project. Egan saw to it that there was a barrage of editorials in the *New World*, Chicago's weekly Catholic newspaper. Daley's urban renewal program was attacked as a covert attempt to move

black families out of the Hyde Park area, which was the bedroom community for the University of Chicago's faculty.

When Alinsky returned from Europe, he found himself
and the IAF being blamed for a campaign against the mayor's
urban renewal project that was actually the work of Saul's
employees, Egan and von Hoffman. Saul was angry at the two
of them, especially at Egan who engineered the fight. It was
not that they were wrong about Daley's project being a "Ne-
gro-removal" scheme, but that they had involved the IAF and
the Catholic Church in a battle they could not possibly win.
Hyde Park was not organized, so there was no way its residents
could change or halt the city's plan. Certainly, Egan and the
archdiocesan officials were not going to halt bulldozers by
threatening to excommunicate them.

In October the Hyde Park plan was approved by the City
Council without any trouble, just as Saul had predicted. The
Alinsky-Catholic Church arrangement that came to light during the battle over Hyde Park received a lot of adverse publicity for nothing. Some of the city's Protestant church leaders
began expressing their fears that Alinsky was helping the
Catholic Church to take over Chicago.

Alinsky did not let Fr. Egan forget the Hyde Park fiasco.
One evening, shortly after the city government approved the
urban renewal project over the objections of the Catholic Archdiocese, Alinsky invited Egan over for dinner. When the priest
arrived, he was greeted by a sign hung in Alinsky's living
room. It read: "Lost and Found Department. A pair of trousers
lost in Hyde Park apparently belonging to a Catholic priest
carrying the initials J.E.. Will the owner please claim."

In many ways Chicago of the 1950's was already a Catholic
city. It was the largest Catholic diocese in the United States.
Mayor Richard J. Daley began each day by attending Mass in
his parish church in Bridgeport, an old Irish neighborhood,
near the Back of the Yards. Catholics and Protestants did not
work together; they did not even talk together. The ecumenical
age of churchly openness and dialogue had not yet been ushered in by "good Pope John." Only a couple of years earlier,
Cardinal Stritch had forbidden Catholics, under pain of sin, to

attend the meeting of the World Council of Churches held in nearby Evanston.

Alinsky's politically pragmatic, religiously undogmatic soul could not understand the colossal waste of energy that went into inter-church squabbles. For him the enemy was elsewhere—wherever people suffered from hunger, poor housing, political and economic slavery. To him it seemed more Christian for churches to work together to carry out the Gospel message.

But Alinsky found religious toleration a commodity in short supply in Chicago. Shortly after Stritch died, Saul was eating dinner with Monsignor Edward M. Burke, the chancellor of the Catholic Archdiocese, at Burke's favorite restaurant, Barney's Market Place, on the edge of Chicago's Loop. In the course of dinner conversation Alinsky brought up Burke's announced intention to block the movie "Martin Luther" from being shown on a local television station. Alinsky argued strongly against Burke's action because he said it would do further harm to Catholic-Protestant relations in Chicago. Burke remained adamant. Several rounds of drinks later, Alinsky returned to the argument over the Luther movie. He told Burke that a better way to handle the movie would be to get the TV station to agree to run the film backward: "That way, Luther ends up being a Catholic." For a second the table was silent; then Burke exploded with laughter. He agreed to drop his prohibition of the movie.[24]

Alinsky had won a small victory, but he knew that somehow Chicago's Catholics and Protestants would have to go beyond toleration and start working together to help heal the city's racial wounds and organize its powerless neighborhoods. He was afraid, however, that before that happened, many old suspicions and prejudices would have to be exposed and overcome.

Organization for Southwest Chicago

At precisely this time, out in Southwest Chicago, Monsignor John McMahon, the pastor of St. Sabina's Church, had

come to the decision that an Alinsky-style community organization was badly needed in the white, middle class area that
surrounded his parish. McMahon had been one of the first of
Chicago priests, in the early 1950's, to listen to John O'Grady's
advice about involving his parish in a program of neighborhood conservation. While McMahon figured it was too early to
talk about a community organization at that time, he did set up
an educational program in an attempt to help his parishioners
understand the destructive effects of trying to exclude black
families from their neighborhood.

By 1958, however, conditions on the Southwest Side of
Chicago were growing rapidly worse. For the first time, Mc-
Mahon found that he had the support of the other Catholic
pastors in the area to invite Saul Alinksy to organize a mass
organization to deal with the problems that were hopelessly
splitting the community. McMahon had approached Stritch
before the cardinal left for Rome and received a promise of
archdiocesan support. Later, when Archbishop Albert Meyer
took over and appointed Fr. Egan to the new post of director of
the Archdiocesan Office of Urban Affairs, McMahon began
knocking on Egan's door.

Egan says that the monsignor was relentless in pressuring
him to designate the Southwest side as the first area for the
Archdiocese's program of neighborhood organization. "He is
on my phone every week," recalls Egan; "he's down at my
office. He keeps pounding on the need for a community organization."[25] After a couple of months of these pastoral entreaties,
Egan went to Alinsky and asked him to talk with McMahon
about an organization in Southwest Chicago.

But Alinsky was not enthusiastic. The Southwest Side was
new territory for the IAF; it was not one of the areas his
researchers had studied in their survey of inner city neighborhoods. "Saul was very reluctant to get into a white, middle
class area," says Egan. "He fought against McMahon's proposal
every step of the way."[26] But he was too late to stop the clerical
juggernaut. McMahon had won over Egan and, soon after,
archdiocesan officials Burke and Cooke. All the monsignor
needed now was a nod of approval from the new archbishop.
McMahon and Egan visited Archbishop Meyer as soon as he

was settled in his new office. Meyer was impressed with the proposal. He was interested too because John O'Grady's old friend, Saul Alinsky, was to direct the venture. Meyer directed McMahon to call a meeting of all the Southwest Side pastors and said that he would attend.

The pastors met on January 6, 1959 (twenty years after Alinsky's first meeting with residents in the Back of the Yards), at Christ the King parish, after a dinner hosted by Monsignor Patrick J. Gleeson, one of the most respected of the Southwest Side's priests. The priests told Meyer about the rising tide of violence in their neighborhoods—the frightened residents, the late-night telephone threats, the new vigilante groups, the bombing of homes newly purchased by Negro families. The reports disturbed Meyer to the point that he authorized the pastors to pool regular parish funds to hire Alinsky for a major community organization drive. Before he left the rectory that night, Archbishop Meyer encouraged the assembled priests to go ahead with the plan: "I want you to know that my presence here is an indication of my approval and an encouragement to the priests who have been working so hard in the program (the Cardinal's Conservation Committee), and an invitation to all the priests of the Southwest Side to take part."[27]

With funds and Church support assured, Alinsky agreed finally to take on the project and sent von Hoffman to look over the area. To assist von Hoffman, Alinsky assigned Ed Chambers, who had just returned from Lackawanna, and Joe Villemas, a promising young organizer he had recently hired away from the Welfare Council of Chicago. The three organizers began moving quietly through the neighborhoods and meeting with small groups in the churches. By May the organizers had brought together a representative group of residents. They declared themselves to be the Provisional Organization for the Southwest Community and announced plans to hold a constitutional convention to vote on a permanent organization and elect officers in October.[28]

Whatever reservations Saul had about organizing in this middle class area disappeared as soon as von Hoffman and his assistants began to uncover the dark web of plots and violence that lurked just below the surface of this pleasant suburban-like

section of shady streets and well-trimmed lawns. The IAF
organizers found that the residents were mainly working class
families, only a generation removed from the Back of the Yards
and other immigrant neighborhoods. There were also a couple
of higher income neighborhoods within the Southwest Side
area, with a sprinkling of doctors, lawyers and Irish politicians,
all of whom had successfully completed the climb from the old
neighborhoods. At the eastern and northern borders of the
district, the Southwest Side residents saw an impatient, overcrowded community of upwardly mobile black families waiting to move into their neighborhoods.

Later Alinsky described what the IAF organizers found on
the Southwest Side of Chicago: "At the time the organization
was established, the Southwest Side represented the usual big-
city area that has always been impervious to the promotion of
actual racial equality. The area has been the scene of countless
episodes of organized anti-Negro violence. It was honey-
combed with a dozen varieties of segregation conspiracies,
some brutal and stupidly ineffective, some intelligent and quite
effective in their own way. The community's fears of Negroes
coming in resulted in innumerable bombings, arsons, and other
attacks against persons and property. In the wealthier Southwest Side districts where physical violence had gone out of
style, economic cold war is used by means of buying syndicates
and combines to prevent its falling into the hands of Negro
families."[29]

Shortly before the first meeting of the Provisional Organization for the Southwest Community, the U.S. Commission on
Civil Rights held public hearings in Chicago on the state of
housing discrimination in the city. The commissioners declared Chicago the most segregated city in the Northern United States. At the hearings, Fr. Egan testified in the name of
Archbishop Meyer (Meyer had just been named a cardinal by
Pope John XXIII). Egan made a strong statement that placed
the cardinal and the Archdiocese of Chicago firmly behind a
policy supporting residential integration. He said that the
Church favored organizing the Negroes of Chicago. "We must
have community organization," Egan said, "to ensure that
Negroes do gain access to our communities, but not to the

degree that we merely extend the boundaries of the racial
ghetto." Egan says that von Hoffman wrote the speech, but
that Cardinal Meyer went over it line by line before delivery.[30]
The next day Alinsky appeared before the U.S. Commission
and made a calm and reasoned appeal for a system of benign
residential quotas (he mentioned five percent, for discussion
purposes) for Negro families in white neighborhoods as a necessary first step to break down the growing segregation in
Chicago's housing patterns.[31]

The next day the Chicago newspapers carried the story of
the Civil Rights Commission's hearings. Alinsky's call for a
quota system to integrate Chicago's residential communities
got all the headlines. Pictures of Alinsky and Cardinal Meyer,
together with reports of Egan's and Alinsky's speeches, made it
appear to the readers that the Catholic Church was calling for
racial quotas for Chicago. All hell broke loose in the city.
Alinsky had managed to anger both liberals and segregationists
with his proposal for racial peace.

The news media suddenly discovered that Alinsky's organizers were moving quietly through the neighborhoods of
Southwest Chicago. The message that flashed along the neighborhood grapevines was a shock: "Alinsky is building a mass
organization to integrate the Southwest Side, an organization
supported by the Catholic Church." The so-called neighborhood improvement associations, which were the cover adopted
by the militant segregationists, said that the organization
would put "two Negroes in every block." Harsh warnings to
get out of the area were delivered to the IAF organizers. One
right wing organization in the Brainerd District said that
Alinsky's organizing project was part of a larger Communist
plot hatched in Southern California that intended to foment
racial trouble and neighborhood disruption in large cities
across the United States.[32]

As the October date of the convention drew near, other
charges were made against the new organization. While the
segregationist groups were calling it a Communist plot to force
integration of Negroes on white neighborhoods, some Protestant critics were charging that the Provisional Organization for
the Southwest Community (POSC) was rather a Roman Catho-

lic plot to keep Negroes out of all-white neighborhoods. The
IAF organizers made use of these charges to recruit the rest of
the area's Protestant churches. By late August Alinsky and the
POSC leaders decided that the IAF's connection was a liability
for the budding organization. Alinsky recalled von Hoffman
and announced publicly that the IAF was dropping out of the
Southwest project. The POSC then hired former IAF organizers Chambers and Villemas and began looking for an organizer
who was a Protestant.

D. Barry Menuez, an official of the Executive Council of
the Episcopal Church, was at that time a student at the University of Chicago's Divinity School. One day Gibson Winter, the
chairman of the school's department of Ethics and Society,
called the seminarian to his office. He told Menuez: "There's
this wild man Saul Alinsky who has started organizing again,
on the Southwest Side. He's the one who formed the Back of
the Yards Council. He's looking for a Protestant organizer.
Why don't you go out and talk to him, work for him for six
months, and then come back and write a paper." "It sounded
like the usual university approach to social situations," says
Menuez, "but I needed a job. I had a wife and two kids and
things were tight. So I went out and talked to Ed Chambers.
He took me to see Nick von Hoffman and finally to Saul. I got
the job, and I stayed five years."[33]

From the right and the left, attacks against the organization intensified as the convention drew near. The majority of
the residents were moderates, and they began to be galvanized
into action by the violence and the attacks of the hardliners
against what to them looked like an open democratic process. A
couple of Catholic pastors, initially wary of the organization,
became angry at the fake charges of a Communist plot. They
began showing up at the meetings. On the eve of the convention twenty-seven Protestant and eleven Catholic churches
were paid-up members of the organization.

Three days before the convention, *The Christian Century*, a
national Protestant journal published in Chicago, launched an
editorial attack on Alinsky, the Catholic Church and the fledgling OSC. The gist of the long-time liberal Protestant magazine's attack was a charge that the Alinsky-organized twenty

year old Back of the Yards Council and the newly formed organization on the Southwest Side were part of a national effort to build "racial iron curtains around certain city areas" to keep Negroes out. The editorial described the IAF organizers as undercover agents of a malign conspiracy, "covering their tracks by a snowfall of idealistic pronouncements concerning community betterment." The editorial went on to point out: "In early stages of organization they are especially diligent in securing the sponsorship of churches and other highly esteemed organizations. At the same time a camouflaged power structure is being built—a power structure with hidden purposes, some of which the churches would have difficulty in justifying to a conscience only moderately sensitive."[34]

The Christian Century's editors quoted as their sole authority Walter Kloetzli, the secretary for urban church planning for the National Lutheran Council. Kloetzli had been trying for several months to get the Lutheran churches in Southwest Chicago to withdraw from the new organization. The editors promised to continue to expose Alinsky's dangerous program of "racist subversion of democracy and the church."

At the moment, *The Christian Century*'s editorials helped strengthen the rather fragile ecumenical coalition of the Southwest Side's Protestant and Catholic churches.[35] But the magazine's attacks continued for nearly five years and provided ammunition for those who did not like Church involvement in mass community organizations.

The Organization for the Southwest Community (OSC) was born on October 14, 1959 at a large and boisterous convention. A reporter who was there described it: "In the tradition of the New England town meeting, delegates representing one hundred and one organizations streamed into gaily decorated Calumet High School. They had been sent there by civic and social clubs, churches (one of them already integrated), fraternal groups like the Knights of Columbus, and patriotic clubs. For hours delegates listened to sometimes lofty, sometimes banal oratory. At the end they shouted their approval of a fledgling federation to be known as the Organization for the Southwest Community."[36]

The overriding issue for OSC, according to organizer

Chambers, was integration. The question was whether integration of Negro families would happen peacefully, directed by the residents, or whether it would happen in a violent manner, with families, homes and pleasant neighborhoods torn apart in the process. The problem was not solved by the delegates at that first convention. What they did that day, however, was to organize the majority of the area's residents and organizations to deal with the problem. Only one small Baptist congregation sent an integrated delegation to that first convention. Its delegates had to be escorted into the hall by an armed guard, but the minister and his people came, and they cast their votes.[37] Whatever *The Christian Century* or the segregationists said in their attacks, the people of the Southwest Side voted to solve their problems by means of the democratic process.

Ed Chambers recalls those first days of the OSC: "All we tried to do during the first year was to put together an organization of moderate residents and church groups to get control over this racial transition and stop the violence. Within three or four months we knew who the bombers were, in whose kitchen the tactics were planned—it was like the White Citizens Councils in the South."[38]

The controversy over blacks moving into the area continued to be debated hotly within the organization. While this was going on, however, the various committees moved ahead on the agenda agreed on at the convention. The emphasis was on the conservation of the neighborhoods and residential control over the real estate market. The OSC leaders understood that they had to prove to the majority of the Southwest Side residents that the organization had the power to make needed changes in the community.

During that first year, a Home Loan Fund was started, in cooperation with local banks. The fund made eighty-three loans, a total of $1.2 million. These loans, which required only ten percent down, attracted younger families who wished to buy older homes in the fringe areas.

The Real Estate Practices Committee went after the "blockbusters" and the shady speculators. The committee showed people how the panic-peddlers operated. With the help of OSC, three realtors were indicted for conspiracy and fraud and convicted. The organization was able to force real estate agents to make needed repairs on their buildings. Over five hundred complaints of housing violations were investigated by the Housing and Zoning Committee. One hundred thirty-two of these were filed with the city buildings department for subsequent action. The first OSC Home Show drew enthusiastic crowds.

In October a series of four public hearings were held to prepare the slate of issues for action at the second annual convention. The racial issue was debated at length during these televised hearings, and the factions within the new organization argued their positions for all Chicago to see.[39]

At one point Alinsky discussed the stormy OSC with Leonard Rieser: "This project affords a chance, maybe one out of a hundred, but if the stakes are big enough then I would consider that a pretty good risk, of creating a controlled integrated community. Something has got to be done to break this damnable log-jam, and as I have often said to you before, the idea of so-called existing communities which are integrated are myths—they are either communities in a state of transition, or small islands of idealists, or unusual situations with a single powerful institution such as the University of Chicago in Hyde Park ... but we still do not have a typical kind of community operation which would have sufficient universalities applicable to a great many other communities in the American scene. It is our hope that this may come about in this project."[40]

Chambers remained on as OSC's staff director for two years. He admits that OSC was hard going for the organizers. They were threatened and followed everywhere they went, and their personal lives were investigated by the "Red Squad" of the Chicago Police. But gradually, he said, the democratic process began to work as the factions fought out the issues openly at the monthly council meetings. "Everything was concentrated around the fact of the changing racial scene," Chambers says. "No matter what the issue was—transportation, building codes, zoning, integrated meetings—the votes were always on integration. Three or four hundred people would show up every month to reaffirm that what we were doing was the democratic and Christian way. The right wing and the liberals would battle it out on the floor in those really hot meetings ... and the moderate majority would keep carrying the day for justice and equality and dignity. It was a new day for these people—Protestant and Catholic. The priests, the ministers, the lay leaders, area businessmen—they were constantly making the churches Christian. They had to deliver the troops each month, count up the votes to make sure there were enough—sometimes the votes were very close."[41]

Years later, when Alinsky died, Monsignor John McMahon, now retired, summed up OSC as a powerful democratic struggle by a community to save itself. Despite its failings, McMahon said that OSC was a positive stage in the life of the changing community on the Southwest Side. "We were doing something on a grand scale that had never been attempted before," he said. "It was not an experiment or an attempt to contain any race or nationality, nor a grand integration plan. Basically, it was to save an upper middle-class neighborhood and to give people services and protections which would induce them to stay in the neighborhood and welcome newcomers ... much was accomplished. Changes were less violent, newcomers found they were welcome, and to me personally there was the joy and excitement of working with fellow priests, the laity and clergy of other faiths and the people, and last but not least, of knowing and loving and cooperating with Saul Alinsky."[42]

While Alinsky's organizers were helping the residents to fight segregationists in the Southwest Chicago neighborhoods, another Catholic pastor was watching their progress. He was preparing to ask Alinsky to organize his neighborhood—the rundown, overcrowded, crime-ridden, all-black section called Woodlawn.

5.

The Golden Years

A New Social Movement

The turbulent organizing campaign that brought into being the OSC in Southwest Chicago rocketed Saul and his tiny Industrial Areas Foundation into a new decade. Although he did not know it yet, once he began to help integrate Negroes into Chicago's white residential areas, Alinsky was moving into the national spotlight. At that moment, when he came under fierce attack from the city's rabid segregationists and the editors of the liberal church publication *The Christian Century*, Saul was aware only that something different was stirring just below the surface of the national consciousness.

That first year of the new decade brought forth a surprising assortment of radical actions, taken by university student groups across the country, at the very moment a fresh rhetorical breeze began to stir in the nation's political debates. Alinsky was delighted with these signs of life. Perhaps they were omens that the winter of America's apathy and political conformity was coming to an end.

In January he read a brief newspaper report announcing that the student auxiliary of the dormant League for Industrial Democracy had changed its name to Students for a Democratic Society (SDS) and that the organization was beginning a recruiting drive for new members on the nation's campuses. The next month four freshman students from all-black North Carolina Agricultural and Technical College walked into Woolworth's in downtown Greensboro, sat down at its segregated lunch counter and ordered coffee. Later, that spring, hundreds of students and faculty members at Bay Area colleges and universities signed petitions against hearings to be held in San Francisco by the House UnAmerican Activities Committee. When the students picketed the hearings, the police attacked them with clubs and firehoses. Sixty-three picketers were arrested for disorderly conduct.[1]

In September Senator John F. Kennedy of Massachusetts, the Democratic nominee for President, flew off on his first campaign trip around the nation. He quickly warmed to his theme of getting the country moving again as he spoke to increasingly enthusiastic crowds. "If you think we can provide better schools for our children," he told a crowd in Richmond, California, "and more help for the older, if you think we can develop this state and the resources of the West, if you think it is possible to strengthen the image of the United States throughout the world, then come with us. If you are tired and don't want to move, then stay with the Republicans. But I think we are ready to move."[2]

In the Deep South the Student Non-Violent Coordinating Committee (SNCC) was born in October. The civil rights movement in the South, which had taken a quantum leap under the leadership of the Reverend Martin Luther King, Jr. during the Montgomery bus boycott four years before, jumped ahead again under this aggressive, disciplined student organization that was controlled by a new generation of young black men and women.

Later in the year, the youthful John F. Kennedy was elected the nation's thirty-fifth President. In his Inaugural Address, the new President declared that the "torch had been passed to a new generation of Americans." Certainly, something new was happening in the nation; what it was was not yet clear.

Even presidential campaign reporter Theodore H. White was not sure what it all meant. He called 1960 "a year of national concern—but vague, shapeless, unsettling, undefinable national concern." White said that it was the first time in history that the United States Congress had felt the need to convoke formal hearings on the National Purpose.[3]

Sociologist C. Wright Mills was one who welcomed the

new political revival in the nation. In an article entitled "The New Left," Mills wrote, "Let the old men ask sourly, 'Out of Apathy—into what?' the Age of Complacency is ending. Let the old women complain wisely about 'the end of ideology.' We are beginning to move again."[4]

In the last months of that year, Nicholas von Hoffman, Alinsky's top organizer, was working hard to get an organization off the ground in the all-black South Side Chicago neighborhood of Woodlawn. After months of pre-organizing meetings with people on the neighborhood's streets and in the local churches, pool halls and bars, von Hoffman had gathered a small steering committee, the Temporary Woodlawn Committee (TWO); it was made up of representatives of five local organizations, four black and one Puerto Rican. The issues that were hurting Woodlawn's residents were everywhere. TWO's first action was a protest against the city's allowing the University of Chicago to clear a chunk of Woodlawn to extend its campus without consulting the area residents. There were a couple of other modest actions after that, but nothing yet that was able to spark the interest of a majority of the more than 100,000 people who lived in crowded, run-down quarters in Chicago's Woodlawn ghetto. Even the resourceful von Hoffman, who had organized resistant communities like Lackawanna and Southwest Chicago, was at a loss to know what kind of issue would mobilize Woodlawn's powerless people.

Then, one afternoon in mid-May 1961, he got a long-distance phone call from a University of Chicago student who had been a volunteer at the TWO office. The student said he was calling from his bed in a New Orleans hospital. He was a member of the Chicago chapter of the Congress of Racial Equality (CORE) and one of the first contingent of CORE's black and white "Freedom Riders" who had started from Washington, D.C. a week earlier to integrate interstate bus terminals across the South. He told Nick that he was among the group of volunteers who were dragged off the bus in Anniston, Alabama and beaten by a crowd of Ku Klux Klan hoodlums. The kid offered to bring with him to Chicago some of the other Freedom Riders if von Hoffman would help

CORE stage a rally for the benefit of the Freedom Ride campaign in the South.

Von Hoffman agreed that Woodlawn could use a civil rights rally and told the CORE volunteers to come to Chicago as soon as they were released from the hospital. After he hung up the phone, however, von Hoffman began to have second thoughts. What if TWO and CORE couldn't get a crowd to come out for a rally for the Freedom Riders? "I knew," von Hoffman says, "that there had never been a civil rights rally on the South Side of Chicago that had drawn more than a hundred people—and that was when Emmett Till was lynched." But he was committed now, so he got his TWO organizers and CORE's staff to pass the word around the neighborhood that there would be a rally in honor of the returning Freedom Riders at the hall of St. Cyril's Church on June 1. Von Hoffman scheduled the rally for 8:30 P.M.

Like a good organizer, von Hoffman had the folding chairs set up so the hall would look reasonably full, even if only a few people showed up. That night he was there an hour early; he checked the hall, turned on the lights and then went out on the steps to have a cigarette and wait. Nick remembers what happened next. "At 7:30 this old black couple hobbled up the stairs and asked, 'Is this the place where the Freedom Riders are going to be?' People began coming in twos and threes, up the street and into the hall. By 8 o'clock we had run out of chairs, and by 8:30 we were trying to connect loudspeakers so that people who couldn't squeeze into the hall could hear the proceedings out in the street."

A couple of white observers from the University of Chicago looked more and more nervous as the crowd of black people pressed into the hall and jostled one another good-naturedly for a better view of the Freedom Riders on the platform. There were speeches from CORE officials; then the seven battered Freedom Riders told the story of the long ride and their ordeal at the hands of the Klan. At the end of the rally, von Hoffman says, "one of the Freedom Riders told the crowd: 'We have a song that we sing at the end of all our meetings; it's called "We Shall Overcome." How many here know the words?' Four hands were raised. They began to sing. Everyone in the hall learned to sing it that night."[5]

Late that same night von Hoffman called Alinsky, who was at his home in California. Nick, still shocked at the size of the turnout of Woodlawn residents, told Saul about the rally—the more than seven hundred people who came and overflowed into the street, how the crowd sang "We Shall Overcome" and then passed the hat for $600 to aid CORE's Freedom Rides campaign. "I think," Nick told Saul, "that this is no longer putting together a (neighborhood) organization, but trying to direct a social movement." Alinsky said, "I'll be back tomorrow," and hung up. Von Hoffman didn't sleep that night. He was too busy thinking of ways he could channel this new militancy into building The Woodlawn Organization.[6]

The Churches Unite

TWO was the first attempt by Alinsky—or anyone—to organize an entire black urban community. Alinsky was not sure where to start in this troubled and complex black ghetto. Nick von Hoffman had no idea either when he arrived to do the actual organizing. He recalled later, "I found myself at the corner of 63rd and Kimbark and I looked around."[7]

The catalyst for the Woodlawn organization was, as had been for OSC, a Catholic priest who decided what his rundown parish neighborhood needed were the services of Saul Alinsky. Fr. Martin Farrell, "Doc" to his friends, was the pastor of Holy Cross Church. He was ordained a priest in Chicago the same year Alinsky began organizing the Back of the Yards Council. In the 1950's the priest attended all the meetings of the Cardinal's Conservation Committee and listened to Alinsky and O'Grady talk about community organization and self-help for neighborhoods. Farrell says that all he was waiting for was the day he would have a parish of his own so he could hire Alinsky. When he was named pastor of Woodlawn's Holy Cross Church in 1958, he began pressing Alinsky to organize in Woodlawn. "At first," he recalls, "I kidded him; then I got serious. I told him: 'You'll never be a great organizer until you organize Negro communities. They need it more than anyone else.' "[8]

A few months later the "ghetto grapevine" began saying that the University of Chicago and Mayor Daley were conspiring to bulldoze part of Woodlawn to extend the university campus. When Farrell heard the news, he sent a message to Saul that sounded like a call to the Crusades: "It is quite evident to me that all and any effort for neighborhood betterment must come from the people without any outside help. I call upon you to consider probably the most interesting neighborhood ever in your career. We must have a neighborhood organizer quickly. . . . Woodlawn itself is the most disorganized community in the United States. There is no leadership. On the other hand, I have found many ordinary people in the community waiting for somebody to lead them to effective democratic organization according to American and Alinsky principles."[9]

Soon after he sent the note, Farrell recruited to his cause the new co-pastors of Woodlawn's venerable First Presbyterian Church. Even though the South Side ghetto had moved in and surrounded it, First Presbyterian remained the parish church of many of the University of Chicago faculty members and their families. In response to the needs of its changing community, the congregation had asked the Presbyterian Board of National Missions to send it a pastor who could find a way to "do something about Woodlawn." The result was the pastoral team of Charles T. Leber, Jr. and Ulysses B. Blakeley. They were an integrated, big-city team: Leber, white, came from Detroit, and Blakeley, black, was from Philadelphia; both men were former directors of neighborhood settlement houses. Their only connection with Alinsky came from reading *Reveille for Radicals* in seminary. After a few months in Woodlawn, they realized that they had no idea of how to proceed. Leber said, "We wore out the seats of several good pairs of trousers while attending an uncountable number of meetings held 'to do something about Woodlawn.' "[10]

When they responded positively to Farrell's plan to invite Alinsky in to organize the South Side, the two Presbyterian ministers were acting less from ecumenical zeal than from frustration. Before the three clergymen went to see Alinsky, they talked Arthur Brazier into coming with them. The Rev. Brazier was the young pastor of Woodlawn's influential black congregation, the Apostolic Church of God. The delegation was rounded out by Fr. John Egan, Alinsky's friend and the director of the Cardinal's Conservation Committee (soon to be the Office of Urban Affairs).

Alinsky listened to the clergymen as they made their case for an organization in Woodlawn. When they finished he told them that he would come into Woodlawn only if he were invited by a representative group of the Negro residents of the neighborhood, and if the local churches could raise enough money up-front to keep an organization going for at least two years.

The four Woodlawn pastors went home and called a meeting of neighborhood clergy and representatives of the Catholic Archdiocese of Chicago, the Illinois Synod of the United Lutheran Church and the Presbytery of Chicago. The first issue was to see if they could find financial support from Catholic and Protestant bodies beyond the parish level. The Catholic representatives, long-time supporters of Alinsky, saw no problem in getting money from archdiocesan coffers for an Alinsky project in Woodlawn; Farrell said that the Catholics were ready to pledge $50,000 to start the organizing fund. The Presbyterians were more cautious; they were not sure they could raise that much money from the local Presbytery. The Lutheran delegation, dominated by the hostile Walter Kloetzli, objected strongly to the hiring of Alinsky. Kloetzli, director of urban church planning for the Lutherans, questioned the IAF's ability to organize the Woodlawn community and raised ethical questions about Alinsky's organizing methods. The Lutheran delegation demanded that Alinsky appear before a second meeting of the church representatives to answer questions about his operation.

A few weeks later, when Alinsky met with the churchmen, the group had grown to thirty clergy and lay leaders. Before answering their questions, Saul made it clear that his presence at the meeting in no way committed the Industrial Areas

Foundation to undertake a project in Woodlawn. He had no intention of getting trapped in a religious war; he was seeing enough of that these days in Chelsea. The rest of the meeting was dominated by Pastor Kloetzli. He questioned Alinsky like a public prosecutor, asking for a detailed explanation of the IAF's history and methods. Saul answered each question carefully and completely; his manner throughout the session was thoughtful and respectful. When the churchmen declared themselves satisfied with his explanations and called for adjournment, an angry Walter Kloetzli insisted that he still had a number of questions that Alinsky had not answered. Saul offered to answer his remaining questions in writing. In March Alinsky submitted to the clergy representatives a sixteen page memorandum in which he answered Kloetzli's inquiries one by one. Attached to the memorandum was a sheaf of documents describing the work of the IAF around the country. Again the majority of the churchmen declared themselves completely satisfied with the organizer's explanations.[11]

For months nothing more happened on the Woodlawn proposal. In the meantime, Alinsky and his organizers were busy putting together the Organization for the Southwest Community. Leber and Blakeley continued to talk up a Woodlawn organization with Presbytery officials but found little interest in contributing to the project. As far as the Presbytery leaders were concerned Woodlawn was a Catholic project, and they saw nothing to be gained from a cooperative venture. The ecumenical spirit had not yet begun to blow in Chicago. The local church executives were not prepared to ask for money from National Presbyterian mission funds for an Alinsky project in Woodlawn.

An official of the Chicago Presbytery at the time, Bryant George, a black minister, says that the mood of mistrust about Woodlawn was because the "Catholics were behind it." On his part and that of other black Presbyterians among his circle of friends, there was also a fear that the "ethnic Catholics" (Irish, Poles, Italians, etc.) would use Alinsky's organizations "to contain blacks in a certain part of the South Side, to keep a sanitized corridor between these blacks and their (white) communities which were southwest and east of Woodlawn." At the same time, according to George, there were any number of white Presbyterians who were genuinely afraid of a takeover of Chicago by the Catholic Church: "They were looking dead into the eye of the power of the cardinal of Chicago, and that was considerable power."[12]

But Woodlawn ministers Leber and Blakeley were now as stubborn as Fr. Farrell about getting Alinsky to agree to organize Woodlawn. The two Presbyterians decided that the only way to get the necessary support from their denomination was to reorganize the Chicago Presbytery by replacing the "old guard" leaders with those sympathetic to their cause. Leber says they were helped at the beginning of their task by a couple of Presbyterian ministers who had become involved in OSC on the Southwest Side. These ministers "started sending in to the Presbytery committees reports of what a tremendous experience this was and what real organization was all about."[13]

The reorganization of the Presbytery of Chicago involved more, however, than support for Woodlawn and Alinsky. For months Leber, Blakeley and a tiny circle of younger ministers and lay leaders (Alinsky met with them on several occasions) worked to build up a new orientation to the church's everyday mission in the city and the support structure needed to make it happen. As Leber explained it, they were building a solid base within the Presbyterian polity so that the local church could deal effectively with the matter of Catholic-Protestant cooperation and with what they saw as the major issues facing the churches in the 1960's—race, community life, church survival, urban-suburban tensions and the "whole business of the ghetto in Chicago."[14]

The reorganizers started with the mission committee because it was the focus of what they wanted to do and because one of their caucus members was its chairman. A year later they increased their caucus to fifty ministers out of a total of eighty in the Presbytery. Leber still remembers the excitement they felt over their victory: "We brought in a new Presbytery executive within a year, and the first thing that the new executive did was present to the mission committee a proposal for community organization of Woodlawn, and it went through."

In all, Leber says, it took a year and half to bring the

Presbytery of Chicago around to approving the use of church mission funds for the Alinsky organizing project in Woodlawn. It was not an easy victory, but when it was over the Presbyterian Church in Chicago was ready to move in new directions in carrying out its mission and ministry.

It was during this same period, unfortunately, that *The Christian Century*'s editors, alarmed by OSC and a possible organization in Woodlawn, the Protestant debates over Alinsky and the harsh charges made by Walter Kloetzli, began its attack on Alinsky and the churchmen who supported him. The editorial vendetta that began in October 1959 continued until sometime in 1964.

The Christian Century charged organizer Alinsky and his church allies with attempting to unleash a contemporary version of the Peasants' Revolt in large cities in the United States. One editorial summarized the basic charges against Alinsky: "This program (Alinsky-style mass organization), which is being spread over the Chicago area in successive steps by Monsignor (John J.) Egan with the help of an agency called the Industrial Areas Foundation, works by setting up a superorganization whose real aim is to gain and exercise 'power.' Its method is to send in experts in 'reorganization' who 'rub raw the sores of discontent,' enlarge and manipulate hostilities, discredit trusted community leaders and substitute for them their own handpicked leaders and organizational structures. Presumably the Roman Catholic Church, which produces a large share of the funds for this Machiavellian approach to municipal politics, expects to gain some advantage from it. One way it gains is to use the instrument of power created by the reorganizers to prevent or slow down urban renewal and to stabilize population shifts, in the hope that the church properties and services will be protected from the disastrous consequences of rapid change."[15]

The attacks on Alinsky, the Chicago organizations and the Catholic Archdiocese seem to have been a personal crusade by the magazine's editor, Harold Fey, and his friend Walter Kloetzli, the Lutheran minister who was in charge of urban church planning for the American Lutheran Council. According to Presbyterian Leber, Fey lived in a spacious apartment on the Midway that separated the University of Chicago from Woodlawn. Fey was worried, says Leber, that the deterioration and rot, which he could see from his window, would eventually spill over from Woodlawn into the university area. It would be in his self-interest if the university could get the approval of the city fathers for its plan to bulldoze the decrepit structures on the adjoining section of Woodlawn and extend its lovely green campus farther south. When Fey discovered, instead, that the Woodlawn churches were raising money to bring in Saul Alinsky, a known troublemaker, to organize Woodlawn's Negro residents against the university's urban renewal plan, he took up his editorial cudgels.

Fey was also convinced that Alinsky's popular organizing was a Marxist plot, a way of fomenting urban class warfare. A pacifist, Fey talked about "violence," where the Alinskyites spoke of "people power" and "conflict." There was also more than a little old-fashioned anti-Catholic bias contained in *The Christian Century*'s editorials. The Catholic Church in Chicago in the 1950's was not yet the Church of John XXIII and the Ecumenical Council Vatican II. Many mainline Protestant churches still worried about "neo-triumphalism," says Leber: "The Catholics were going to take over Chicago . . . they were going to use Saul Alinsky to do it . . . Cardinal Meyer was the instrument, and it was going to be the model for the world of the 'New Catholicism' . . . you never heard such stuff."[16] Bryant George agrees that the many Protestant churches were "sort of unreformed at this time too. They saw the city slipping away from them and they were entirely puzzled by it. But they still thought that just around the corner was a change back to the good old days when they were going to pack those (city) churches with white Christians . . . they really needed a few more black churches, but that was it. . . ."[17] Underneath Fey's attacks, Leber still thinks there was an element of snobbery. He didn't want Alinsky and the churches empowering Woodlawn's Negroes, "black, welfare, truck-driving, part-time working cruds who had the gall to attack this magnificent university."[18]

The Christian Century's editorial attacks did not bother Woodlawn's residents; no one there ever saw a copy. But the magazine was passed around among church people and its arguments were hashed over again and again during this time of intense debate within the churches and the larger Chicago community over the propriety, the objectives and the methods of the Alinsky-church-neighborhood coalition. Later, it provided a mine of handy quotations for anyone, anywhere, who was opposed to Alinsky's populist organizing efforts. On the other hand, it was probably the debate occasioned by *The Christian Century*'s campaign that attracted the attention of *Fortune* magazine and one of its best reporters. The furor over Woodlawn brought Charles Silberman to Chicago, and he would do the kind of investigation of Alinsky and his organization that more than made up for the slings and arrows of *The Christian Century*.

Despite what seems extreme provocation, Alinsky refused to debate *The Christian Century*. His only response was a memorandum sent to the IAF's board and supporters which contained a point by point refutation of the magazine's charges. In November 1960, however, Saul gave a speech in Chicago in which he called on the city's church leaders to adopt a more realistic approach to the problem of racial discrimination in the city. Adopting the biblical style of discourse favored by his ecclesiastical critics, Alinsky called for a moratorium on high-level church conferences and high-blown theological rhetoric about racial problems. He said:

The only issue is what we are doing or going to do about it.

We are overdue leaving the mountain tops where men can preach morals and play at being prophets in cool, comfortable safety. We must go down into the valleys and gullies where the atmosphere is hotter, and where the people and the problems are.

Down here in the valleys and low places, where the people and the issues are, we cannot avoid confronting the seaminess of human conditions, hates, and the passions. Here the heat forces us to shed our righteous raiments of uncompromising purity which were so comfortable on the airy mountain tops.[19]

What really convinced Alinsky that the IAF should organize Woodlawn was the positive response shown by the majority of Catholic and Protestant church leaders at the meeting
with him in February 1959. After that, despite the annoying
attacks of *The Christian Century* and the Lutheran resistance,
Alinsky knew that the churches would support an organization
in Woodlawn. During the period when Leber and Blakeley
were wending their way with the Woodlawn proposal through
the Presbyterian bureaucracy, Saul sent a formal request to the
cardinal archbishop of Chicago and to the Schwartzhaupt
Foundation. Cardinal Meyer proved to be the key to raising the
$200,000 Alinsky said it would cost to organize Woodlawn.
With Meyer's original pledge of $50,000 as bait, the Presbyteri-
ans were prepared to ask for a like amount; Saul was asking the
Schwartzhaupt Foundation to make up the difference. Months
went by, however, and there was still no action in Woodlawn.

Then, in July 1960, the University of Chicago shocked the
Woodlawn clergy into taking action. The university's planners
presented formal plans for approval to the Chicago Land Clearance Commission. The ghetto grapevine had been correct. The
University of Chicago was asking permission to clear a mile-
long strip of Woodlawn to extend its campus. The planners
argued that the university already owned sixty percent of the
land and the rest was blighted buildings that could be condemned under the city's urban renewal powers. According to
von Hoffman, the only thing that slowed down the bulldozers
at this point was the chairman of the commission. He became
angry at the pushy tactics of the university officials and tabled
their request for six months.[20]

The Woodlawn clergy realized now that they had to stop
talking and start organizing. At Alinsky's suggestion, they
changed the name of the local ministerial association to the
Greater Woodlawn Pastors Alliance. The change allowed Fr.
Farrell and other Catholic priests to join. With the triumvirate
of Farrell, Leber and Blakeley in charge, the Greater Woodlawn Pastors Alliance officially invited the IAF to organize
Woodlawn and hired Nick von Hoffman to prepare a survey of
the area. Things began to happen once von Hoffman hit the
streets.

In September the money came through. Cardinal Meyer sent Alinsky a check for $50,000. In his letter Meyer said that the check was the first installment of a three-year grant of $150,000 for the Woodlawn project—"an indication," the cardinal wrote, "of the deep interest which the Archdiocese of Chicago has had in the works and programs of the Industrial Foundation for the past twenty years."[21]

Egan says that he and Saul met with Meyer a couple of days later. Alinsky thanked the cardinal on behalf of the Woodlawn residents. "I'll never forget that day," Fr. Egan recalls. "Alinsky got up to leave and Cardinal Meyer rose to walk him to the door. The two men shook hands; Meyer was an imposing man, about six foot six. Alinsky looked up into his face and said, 'Your Eminence, when we get going in Woodlawn, there's going to be a lot of controversy; it's going to get pretty hot at times.' The cardinal met his glance and replied quietly, 'Mr. Alinsky, you and I don't share the same faith, but Christians need never be afraid of controversy or conflict. After all, there's nothing more controversial than a Man hanging on a cross.' "[22]

In October the Schwartzhaupt Foundation granted $70,000 to the Woodlawn project. The Presbyterian Board of National Missions came through with $21,000. Alinsky decided it was enough to guarantee the organization two years of worry-free operation before the local leaders would have to raise their own budget. In November IAF organizer von Hoffman rented a South Side storefront headquarters and hired two young Woodlawn residents to be his organizing staff. He was just in time.

Taking On the University

Just before Christmas, the University of Chicago gave the Woodlawn project an organizing issue it couldn't pass up. Nick von Hoffman got a tip from Fifth Ward Alderman Leon Despres that Julian Levi, the university's urban renewal troubleshooter, was going before the Chicago Plan Commission with a proposed ordinance that would enable the university to circumvent their stalled urban renewal plan and begin clearing land in Woodlawn. The meeting was set for the next night. Von Hoffman got forty people, led by Blakeley and Farrell, to come to the meeting and protest the university's attempt to bypass the city's planning process. Farrell told the commission members, "You are being used by Levi and the University of Chicago. . . . He is now attempting to sneak in and get your approval before you know the desires of the people." The matter was tabled by the commission until proper hearings could be held on the university's plan. When a shaken commissioner was asked later how many people were in the Woodlawn delegation he said, "Hundreds—you might as well say a thousand."

Before the Plan Commission met again in January, von Hoffman called together the five organizations who were represented at the December protest—the Woodlawn Pastors Alliance, the United Woodlawn Conference, the Knights of St. John, the Woodlawn Businessmen's Association and the Woodlawn Block Club Council. Together they set up the Temporary Woodlawn Organization and elected as chairman the Rev. Robert McGee, assistant pastor of the Apostolic Church of God. The Rev. Arthur Brazier, McGee's boss, was designated TWO's "official spokesman." The temporary organization would "assure common action and a single voice for the community of Woodlawn" until the organization could hold a public convention to create a permanent structure and elect officers.[23]

When TWO arrived at the January commission meeting, their delegation had grown to more than three hundred. The odds were considerably improved that the residents' complaints about the university's plan would be listened to by the commission. The result of the hearing was that the Plan Commission, and later the City Council, agreed to protect the right of Woodlawn's citizens to be involved in this and any future planning for their neighborhood. For the moment, at least, the angry university officials had to back off.

Unwilling to lose the impetus set in motion by the urban renewal protest, von Hoffman turned quickly to another issue. He reminded TWO's executive committee of the many complaints he had heard on the street about shady retail practices by some of Woodlawn's local merchants—overcharging, giving short weights and a variety of illegal credit traps. TWO launched a retail campaign it called the Square Deal. It began with a parade of a thousand marchers, right down the main shopping district on 63rd Street. The marchers carried signs which advertised their complaints against the merchants in full color. The parade pictures were featured in the next day's Chicago papers.

The following Sunday, TWO set up a checkout counter, complete with a registered scale, in the front yard of a church near the business section. People brought their purchases from the suspected stores and had weights and prices checked by TWO's special clerks. Results were recorded on a giant scoreboard set up in the church yard. During the week, leaflets were passed out all through the neighborhood, urging people to boycott the offending merchants.[24]

Next, the Woodlawn Businessmen's Association, a charter member of TWO, drew up a code of ethics and established a board of arbitration in cooperation with TWO to handle future consumer complaints. According to von Hoffman, the organization's strategy was intended to correct abuses, not drive out local retailers. As he explained later, " . . . you need his (the merchant's) money which you will get if he fears you, but not if he hates you. You will also get his money . . . if the organization's progress includes objectives that are worth something to him. . . . Purists may find such a procedure intolerable."[25]

The Square Deal campaign and a spate of tenant's strikes that TWO engineered early in its organizing phase drew the attention of many of the people of Woodlawn to the new organization. TWO began to be recognized and to develop prestige within the local community. Newspaper reports of the Square Deal parade, in particular, announced the new organization to the larger Chicago community. Every month, new groups were inducted into the organization. The ghetto, von Hoffman was discovering, was not full of large organizations like the white ethnic communities of Saul's Back of the Yards organizing days. But there were lots of small groups where people gathered to talk and socialize. TWO accepted these small groups as member organizations: beauty shop groups, sports teams, the local janitors' association, sororities and fraternities, choirs, youth clubs, political organizations, even the regulars at the corner pool parlor. "Building a mass organization," said von Hoffman, "is the tedious job of stringing beads on a necklace." Many small groups, even though they had little immediately in common, were brought together by the organizer around common issues. Under Alinsky's supervision, the brilliant von Hoffman added new techniques to the art of organization-building in a black ghetto community. In these small groups he found the natural leaders he needed, and he helped them broaden their horizons and learn large-scale political process. All during this early period, he had to keep reminding himself and the members that their primary objective was not to correct abuses—which were multitudinous in Woodlawn—but to build a power organization through which the people could fight their own battles. "An organization that wields power," von Hoffman taught, "as opposed to the kind that throws an intermittent stick-bomb, must be big, must be broad, must be quasi-institutionalized."[26]

As the organization took shape that first year, several of the individuals and groups who had helped put TWO together jumped ship. The first to go were five disgruntled pastors who withdrew from the Greater Woodlawn Pastors Alliance and TWO and set up an alternative ministerial association. The clerical dissidents charged that TWO and the Alliance were operating undemocratically and using immoral tactics in their attacks on the university and the merchants. They reheated all the arguments made in *The Christian Century*'s editorials and fed them into the local congregational debates about the role of the church in the Alinsky-style community organization.

Shortly thereafter, the United Woodlawn Conference (a charter TWO member) pulled out of TWO. Its members said that they did not feel comfortable with TWO's hard-nosed approach to social reform. They were happy to return to more traditional social service approaches to community involvement. On the other side, one of the local Catholic priests and most of the Puerto Rican members drifted away. They said that they lost interest in TWO because the organization did not pursue a tough enough policy in its Square Deal drive against the local merchants. They were angry because the organization was not pursuing a single-issue fight.

Organizer von Hoffman was not surprised at these defections; he knew from experience that a number of the original groups and individuals would drop out once they realized that the organization's objectives and tactics were not what they expected. "The beginning of every viable organization," wrote von Hoffman, "smacks of being a one-shot affair, for the simple reason that theorists who fiddle around waiting and delaying until they've got a full blown across-the-board organizational program set are never ready to commence swinging into action."[27] The one-shot people soon leave. Others follow because they dislike controversy, or because their own pet projects aren't accepted; sometimes individuals join because a new organization gives them a chance to be leaders. Whatever the reason, when things don't go their way, these people drop out. Good riddance, as von Hoffman saw it—better for them to go before the organization gets involved in a big fight where it will need the strong support of its members. Meanwhile, TWO was adding new members at every meeting.

After the successful rally for the CORE Freedom Riders, von Hoffman and the TWO steering committee called for an intensive house-to-house drive to register Negro voters in Woodlawn. As soon as word got out in the neighborhood that TWO was going to register Woodlawn voters, it ran into stiff opposition from Woodlawn's black political boss, Second Ward Committeeman William Dawson (later a U.S. Representative), a Daley loyalist. When Dawson's threats to withhold political favors from TWO members didn't work, he tried to block the registration. The climax of TWO's voter registration drive was to be a caravan of buses taking three hundred residents downtown to City Hall to register. The day before the voter registration caravan was scheduled, Dawson forced the Chicago Transit Authority to cancel TWO's forty-six chartered buses. Von Hoffman got on the telephone and found a suburban bus company that agreed to provide buses. The next day TWO's "Northern Freedom Ride" carried two thousand black Chicagoans, armed with signs and banners, on an eight-mile ride through Chicago's streets to City Hall for a massive "Vote-in." The buses formed a giant circle around the City Hall complex. Forty-five extra registrars were called in to handle the crowd. The message from Woodlawn to Mayor Daley came through clearly to "hizzoner" in his fifth floor office: "The Woodlawn Organization is here and it is building a new kind of power base among the Negro citizens of the South Side." When they returned to Woodlawn after their Freedom Ride, the TWO leaders found dozens of new groups ready to join the organization. As Alinsky told a reporter at the time: "The most important thing to me about the forty-six busloads of people who went to City Hall to register was their own reaction. Many were weeping; others were saying, 'They're paying attention to us; they're recognizing that we're people.' "[28]

Within a few days, TWO and von Hoffman were ready with a second action they had borrowed from the Freedom Movement in the South—an attack on Chicago's segregated school system. The brilliant strategy used with such skill by tiny TWO pointed up the amazing organizing ability of Alinsky's protégé, Nicholas von Hoffman. In terms of sheer imaginative ways to taunt the entrenched enemy into the open where it became visible and vulnerable to public scrutiny, the public schools campaign showed that von Hoffman was the equal of Alinsky. Advised by von Hoffman, with Alinsky coaching from the sidelines, the school issue gave the TWO leadership an opportunity to take on the lumbering Chicago Board of Education, the guardian of the city's segregated and unequal public educational industry.

TWO began its campaign in the fall at a major public hearing held by the Board of Education. Three hundred TWO members jammed into the hearing room or marched outside the doors. After two hours of patiently waiting to be allowed to testify, the three hundred people walked out angrily, followed by all the reporters who were covering the meeting. The TWO representatives took over the corridor and held a rump meeting. Their testimony was reported in the next day's newspapers and on the television news shows. For the first time Chicago's white citizens heard the complaints of black parents who were worried about the quality of their children's schooling. Most of Chicago had not known before about the double shifts in all-black schools while there were dozens of empty schoolrooms in all-white neighborhoods. Black parents in other sections of Chicago heard mothers and fathers like themselves indicting School Superintendent Benjamin Willis for his "mendacious public relations, his secrecy and his unfeeling interest in Negro children."[29]

At TWO's regular meeting, one week later, the organization's members called for Willis' resignation. "Willis Must Go" became a rallying cry on the city's South Side. The TWO leaders announced a public hearing on the school issue to be held the following week in Woodlawn's Southmoor Hotel. They invited parents of school children and all interested residents to come and be prepared to speak. The TWO leaders promised that the meeting would continue until all who wished had an opportunity to say their piece. Nearly one thousand people attended the hearing. Among the speakers were three public school teachers, with their heads covered with black hoods to protect their jobs from the school administrators. The testimony of the parents and community leaders was damning. The schools in the ghetto neighborhoods lacked the resources to give black kids a quality education. The crucial charges against the school board and its administrators boiled down to two: that the schools in Chicago were intentionally segregated and that the school system's policy of secrecy concealed that fact from the public.

By the next day all of Woodlawn was talking about the school battle. An unrelenting pressure was kept by TWO on the Board of Education. At the next meeting of the Board, and all subsequent meetings, TWO mothers, dressed in black capes, in mourning for their educationally dying children, took up a "death watch" over the deliberations of the school board. Delegations of parents and clergy tried in vain to meet with Superintendent Willis and the president of the Board of Education to discuss specific grievances. Teams of mothers paid visits to nearby white schools to photograph the unused classrooms.

The TWO school campaign brought no immediate victories. What it did, however, was to mobilize black parents to fight for quality education in the ghetto schools. The Woodlawn parents became more involved with their children's schooling than the members of a suburban P.T.A. The school controversy continued to be fought on one front or another for several years. All the time, TWO's reputation in Woodlawn and in other black communities in the city was growing as an organization that could get things done for its members. The awakened Woodlawn residents approached TWO's first convention, more and more aware of their new-found sense of pride and community power.

For months the University of Chicago and TWO remained in a stalemate over urban renewal in Woodlawn. Nothing was happening except a bitter war of words. Alinsky would laugh later when IAF organizations were criticized for using unfair publicity tactics against big institutions; he said that the IAF never approached the level of vitriol poured forth by the University of Chicago's public relations flacks at this period. At one point, Julian Levi charged Alinsky with being anti-Semitic.[30] On another occasion, when the Chicago newspapers refused to print questionable material about Alinsky and the IAF, the university had the charges published in *The Maroon*, the student newspaper.

The same week that TWO held its first convention, the Chicago city planners presented an overall plan for the entire Woodlawn area. Included in the plan was the controversial extension of the university's south campus into Woodlawn. The plan was the city's response to TWO's demand, more than a year before, that the university not be allowed to begin "urban renewalizing" Woodlawn without its slum clearance project being part of a comprehensive renewal design for the whole area. In their haste to break the university-TWO impasse, however, the city planners ignored the other half of TWO's demand, namely, that planning for Woodlawn involve careful consultation with community residents. When asked whether they were guided by the opinions of the Woodlawn residents in preparing their plan, one of the city's consultants replied, "There is nobody to speak for the community. A community does not exist in Woodlawn."[31]

TWO reacted quickly to the city's plan and its built-in attempt at social engineering for the ghetto. "We don't want to be planned for like children" was the gist for TWO's news release. With the assistance of the Woodlawn Businessmen's Association, TWO hired an outside firm of city planners to prepare a critique of the city plan.[32] The planners worked for weeks with TWO members to develop an alternate urban renewal proposal. TWO's plan ("A People-Oriented Approach to Urban Renewal and Planning") was published in full in the neighborhood newspaper. Rehabilitation of sound buildings and spot clearance of vice areas (especially a block known as "Baby Skid Row") and hopelessly deteriorated buildings was favored over the indiscriminate slum clearance of the city's plan.

At TWO's convention, delegates voted overwhelmingly for a toughly worded resolution that condemned the city's attempt at social planning and demanded self-determination for the Woodlawn community: "The best programs are the ones that we develop, pay for and direct ourselves. . . ."[33]

The city planners and the university officials were prepared to ignore TWO and proceed with their plans. Months passed without any movement on either side. TWO did what it could to put pressure on Mayor Daley to arrange a summit meeting between the university and TWO. When the mayor continued to hesitate, the TWO officers leaked word that the organization was planning a massive "sit-down" in the middle of busy Lake Shore Drive during rush hour. Alinsky then stepped in as the "good cop" in the scenario and asked the TWO leaders to call off the demonstration in favor of a visit to the mayor. On July 11, 1963 seven hundred TWO members went to "visit" the mayor at his City Hall office. (Remember that this was a tactic that had not been used before—especially by a black community.) When Daley realized that TWO was not going to go away, he quickly forced the reluctant Chancellor of the University of Chicago to meet with TWO's representatives. With the mayor looking on, the two sides agreed on a compromise that called for construction of low income housing on vacant land before existing structures were torn down, and a Woodlawn citizens' planning committee to be set up to oversee the urban renewal program, with TWO members getting the majority of the seats. When the citizens' committee was named, Mayor Daley personally phoned to ask the Rev. Blakeley to chair it.

TWO's leaders and members celebrated their signal victory. They had saved Woodlawn from the bulldozers and, at the same time, had set an important precedent for citizen participation in the nation's expanding urban renewal program. The next day the organization's leaders began work on a TWO-sponsored not-for-profit corporation to build federally financed low and moderate income housing on the largest site in the renewal area.[34]

TWO Settles In

The battle for Woodlawn was not finished, of course, but in two years TWO had proved to its community and to all of Chicago that it was a viable organization, able to deal with the mayor, city agencies and the University of Chicago—and win. While it was true that Woodlawn was still a slum, it was now an organized slum whose people had power, hope and the services of the Woodlawn Organization. One reporter wrote of the Woodlawn victory:

> A few years ago no one would have predicted that slum Negroes would grasp the banner of Negro leadership from the hands of the professionals who had always carried it. Through their urban renewal battle, Woodlawn Negroes have championed the cause of downtrodden urban Americans, white and colored alike, by forcing urban renewal into the form intended by Congress. Designed to eliminate slums by providing slum dwellers with better housing, this noble aim was perverted to serve the over-privileged, the upper-middle-income tenants, and real estate promoters, evicting the poor it was supposed to benefit and thereby worsening their living conditions. . . . Urban renewal has been put back on the right track in this Chicago slum which had the courage to fight for urban renewal for the people and by the people.[35]

Outside the ghetto in Chicago, TWO was becoming so well known for its controversial tactics that even some of its friends were worried that the organization might be going too far. At one point in the "Willis Must Go" campaign against the Chicago Board of Education, even the faithful Cardinal Meyer questioned Fr. Farrell about TWO's harsh treatment of Superintendent Willis. Meyer told Farrell, "I don't like what TWO is doing to Willis." Farrell replied, "Your Eminence, there are arguments on both sides in this battle, but I'm on the black side." Then Farrell explained the issue and the tactics to the cardinal. Afterward Meyer said, "Father, I never heard the black side of it before. Stay on it."[36] The Chicago school campaign was a good example of how a tough, complicated political battle over basic issues could be reduced by outside (not always uninvolved) observers to a simple ethical equation of means and ends. For an embattled minority, however, fighting for its rights in a non-violent manner, tough, even outrageous tactics, like TWO's personalized attack on Superintendent Willis, may have been the only effective means available. In this issue, and others, Alinsky argued that abstract, "mountain-top morality" was often not morality at all.

At TWO's first convention on March 23, 1962 (more than two years after Alinsky first met with the Woodlawn clergy), more than twelve hundred delegates representing ninety-seven community groups met at the Southmoor Hotel to constitute The Woodlawn Organization and elect officers to take over the organization from the temporary steering committee. It did not go unnoticed that Mayor Richard J. Daley attended the convention as Alinsky's special guest. Daley had the expert politician's instinct for shifts in political power. His presence at the convention meant that Woodlawn and TWO were fast becoming a significant focus of black political power on Chicago's South Side. The mayor served notice on TWO's new leaders that he would deal with them when he had to.

What the new mass-based citizens' organization meant for Woodlawn's residents, and for Daley's political machine, was the beginning of a redirection of the flow of political power and influence away from the ward organization of the South Side's black political boss, William Dawson. Woodlawn's residents began going to TWO with their neighborhood complaints and requests, not to the largely unresponsive ward organization. Dawson understood what was happening; this is why he tried to block TWO's Freedom Ride of new voters to City Hall. Daley, too, understood what TWO might do to his South Side organization, so he made a friendly appearance at TWO's convention. The key element for Alinsky in democratic government was "responsibility." While Dawson and the other black political leaders had been primarily responsible to the Daley organization, which returned them to office again and again, now TWO's members were saying: "You must be responsible and responsive to us, your constituency. If you do not do what we, the organized citizenry, want, then we will vote you out of office at the next election." Like James Madison, Alinsky didn't want more government necessarily, just more responsive government, with all the possible checks and balances operating.

The man elected as president of TWO was a remarkable young black leader, the Rev. Arthur M. Brazier, pastor of Woodlawn's Apostolic Church of God. An imposing man, Brazier was a popular preacher and a theological conservative, the quintessential black pastor. For a long time he had tried to remain in the background of TWO by letting his assistant, Robert McGee, represent him in the leadership of the organization. But von Hoffman had his eye on Brazier from the start. He saw the young minister's extraordinary public presence and capability for leadership. The organizer spent a lot of time with the pastor, bringing him along and answering his doubts about political action and the role of the Church in the civil rights movement. Fr. Farrell was also impressed with Brazier and saw him as another Martin Luther King, Jr.—a model for urban black leadership in the North.[37]

With TWO's first convention drawing closer, von Hoffman brought Alinsky and Brazier together in a well-orchestrated luncheon session at the Palmer House's swank Empire Room restaurant. It was a memorable meeting, with both Saul and Nick working on Brazier to get him to run for the presidency of TWO. They told him that he had the talent to be the top black leader in Chicago, and that, as the leader of TWO, he would get the kind of experience and exposure he needed. Brazier was interested, but said that his church responsibilities would not allow him time to run TWO. Alinsky offered his twenty-four hour personal consulting help and said that he and von Hoffman would write all Brazier's speeches. After the luncheon, Alinsky agreed with von Hoffman that Brazier was a superb presidential candidate. At the March convention the young pastor was elected easily to the top spot in the organization. Later, when the Woodlawn Organization moved into the national spotlight, Brazier added to his local reputation as a strong, competent, attractive leader.

The second year of TWO's operation was less exciting because there were fewer dramatic battles. The struggle with the University of Chicago and the city administration over urban renewal for Woodlawn turned into a kind of urban trench warfare, a long, excruciatingly slow campaign, with few decisive battles. Time was surely needed by the burgeoning organization to consolidate its gains, to train its members and to learn how to function for its community as a multi-purpose democratic organization. But it was necessary to keep moving all the time. What Alinsky knew from his years of organizing experience, von Hoffman was now learning—that mass citizens' organizations must either keep moving forward on a variety of issues or they begin to disintegrate. The organizer is the one who has to keep everything going at once, like the harried juggler entertaining the crowd between circus acts. His assistants were two inexperienced young blacks from the neighborhood. TWO's leaders, outside of Brazier, were the "little Joes," used to running small operations. All of them were voluntary part-timers, with full-time jobs and family responsibilities. As a result, the organizing of Woodlawn took over von Hoffman's life. He lived only three blocks from TWO's office; his apartment became TWO's all-night annex. At one time, even Nick's wife was working at TWO's headquarters. Saul demanded of him, as he did of all IAF's organizers, weekly written reports that covered all facets of the organization's activity. When Saul was in town, he and Nick had late-night sessions at Alinsky's home. Time for sleep and family life was the usual victim.

It should be remembered that Woodlawn's black community was a unique challenge for the IAF. Alinsky had no experience in organizing a black ghetto. Von Hoffman in Woodlawn was in much the same situation as Alinsky had been twenty years before in the Back of the Yards. Later, Nick was really writing about how he felt when he arrived, alone, that first afternoon at 63rd and Kimbark in Woodlawn: " . . . the organizer who comes into the community for the first time is internally in a precarious position. He is afraid—or at least he should be if he has got any brains which he doesn't want beat out. . . . He doesn't know the people, and we are all vaguely afraid of people we don't know. If he is white . . . in a Negro community he is doubly afraid. He is afraid because he is the bearer of . . . new ideas. . . . They may mean trouble. . . . The organizer's mere presence in the community is a tacit insult. . . . He is saying in effect to the people, 'You are so dumb that you need me to think your way out of the mess you're in.' "

The odds on an organizer succeeding in such a venture are not good. That is his other fear. "The organizer is also afraid," von Hoffman wrote, "because a failure is a crashing blow to his ego or his self-respect. . . . In his own eyes, he is being tried as a person, as a huge test of his own worth. To fail is to be adjudged a capon, a sexless, impotent thing by one's self, or so I always found it."[38]

Nicholas von Hoffman didn't fail in Woodlawn. In thirty months he organized the Woodlawn Organization, an effective community organization that Charles Silberman described later that year as the "most important and the most impressive experiment affecting Negroes anywhere in the United States."[39]

Shortly after TWO's second convention in the spring of 1963, Nick von Hoffman resigned his position as staff director of TWO. He was exhausted. A few months later he left the IAF and went to work as a reporter for the Chicago *Daily News*. At first Saul hoped that Nick would come back after he was rested, but he didn't. For Alinsky, von Hoffman's leaving was a sore blow. "He was the best organizer who ever worked for me," Alinsky said.[40] By that he meant that von Hoffman was the most like him—a brilliant organizer, a master tactician, an intellectual, yet a man of action, with a keen instinct for what it takes to get people to act politically on their own behalf.

When Saul reported von Hoffman's resignation to the IAF Board, he told them that he had been grooming von Hoffman for the post as IAF's associate director, prepared to succeed him as director, should the need ever arrive. Whether or not Alinsky had explained his plan to his top organizer is unclear. In terms of career planning, the thirty-three year old von Hoffman decided it was time for him to move on.

To help Nick prepare for the second TWO convention, Alinsky had transferred Ed Chambers from OSC to the Wood-lawn staff. Farrell says that Chambers was a talented organizer, but in a different way than von Hoffman—a mechanic, an expert at putting the pieces together, the guy who got the everyday tasks done, the dues collected, the meetings called, always around when the leaders wanted to talk about their fears and problems. Chambers was able to move smoothly into the staff director position vacated by von Hoffman. For the next two years Chambers helped TWO's leaders solidify the organizational structure and take charge of the day to day operation.

The relative ease with which Alinsky was able to survive the loss of von Hoffman is an indication of how well his IAF team was working in the early 1960's. One reason for this was that Fr. Egan, as soon as TWO was off the ground, was organizing another group of churches, this time in Northwest Chicago. After a bit of salesmanship on Egan's part, a North-west clergy caucus was ready to invite Alinsky in to organize the neighborhood. When Saul tried to put them off by telling him that he had no organizer to send, Egan was prepared with a promising organizer recruit.

The Northwest Community Organization

The prime mover behind what has been called the "Gold-en Age of Community Organization in Chicago" was Monsi-gnor John J. Egan, the director of the Archdiocesan Office of

Urban Affairs. In his early forties at the time, Egan was an example of the social justice-minded priests who graduated from Chicago's St. Mary of the Lake Seminary in the two decades before Vatican Council II. Bright, urbane, enterprising, sociable, the Irish-American priest had learned about the problems of city and suburban families as the head, for thirteen years, of the Cana Conference, a program for married couples that emphasized the meaning of everyday Christian living in contemporary society. When Egan met Saul Alinsky in the early 1950's the young priest was interested in finding flesh and blood ways to bring to life for Chicago's younger Catholic families the Church's social teachings about work, poverty, education, family and community life. At that time Alinsky was looking for a way to involve the churches in his plan to reorganize America's city dwellers in mass-based organizations. It was a match made in heaven. Egan recalls their first meeting: "Saul and I had a three hour conversation. . . . He was saying, 'You should be working with me.' "[41] It was two years before they got together again, at Monsignor O'Grady's famous dinner at Chicago's Blackstone Hotel when Alinsky and von Hoffman met and fought over the best way to organize the Puerto Ricans in Woodlawn. For the next seven years Egan worked closely with Alinsky; he organized the churches of Chicago to support Alinsky's organizing of the city's neighborhoods.

In the summer of 1961, while von Hoffman was organizing the Freedom Rides in Woodlawn, Egan was meeting with the Catholic priests on Chicago's Near North Side in the old neighborhood of West Town. The priests there were worried about the future of the neighborhood. Most of the residents were Catholic. About sixty-five percent were of Polish descent, the rest a mélange of Irish, German, Slavic, Croatian, Latvian, and Lithuanian, with a sprinkling of blacks and Puerto Ricans. In the approximately five square miles that made up West Town, there were twenty-two Catholic churches, a handful of Protestant and Orthodox churches, and three bishops (Ukranian, Greek and Polish National).

One observer described the area as a "dying community. . . . An area which seems to have many of the ingredients for wholesome and lively community life—about 30 schools (public and parochial) . . . churches, four hospitals, six settlement houses, accessible shopping, the best location of any Chicago community for public transportation, more than a dozen banking institutions, and finally over 160,000 people forming a richly varied ethnic mosaic—this area is suffering with deep and ominous ills."[42]

What worried the churchmen most of all, Egan discovered, was the persistent rumor of the past couple of years that a large section of West Town was already targeted for the urban renewal bulldozers; the cleared land was then to be rezoned for industrial use. After a couple of sessions with the priests, Egan had them convinced that they needed the services of Alinsky to organize their community. But when Egan came with a proposal for the Northwest Side, Saul was not interested. He did not want to get involved in white neighborhoods, now that he saw what could be done in a black ghetto like Woodlawn. Besides, he told Egan, "I have no organizers to send and . . . there's no money for a new organization."[43]

After the disappointed Egan left Saul's office, he went to see Cardinal Meyer. The next week the cardinal met with the West Side pastors. At that meeting he authorized them to raise a two-year organizing budget from regular parish funds. In two months they had raised $53,000 and had pledges for an equal amount for the next two years.

Once the money was taken care of, Egan sent thirty-eight year old Thomas Gaudette to a meeting with Alinsky. The ensuing session proved to be nearly as explosive as Saul's first meeting with Nick von Hoffman. Gaudette was a vice president of the Admiral Corporation in charge of transportation, which meant that among his other duties he organized the company's sales meetings, training conferences and high level get-togethers. Tom and his wife Kay were Catholics (he was a graduate of the Jesuits' Boston College), they had six children so far, and the couple were deeply involved in the life of their neighborhood and their parish church. Gaudette was a leader of the local Chatham Community Council and a vice president of the Association of Community Councils, a coalition of old-line neighborhood associations. Saul was unimpressed with Gaudette's organizing credentials.

Alinsky cross-examined him in his best unfriendly manner (the one Saul kept for interviewing brash, young organizer candidates). Gaudette remembers his arrogant questions: "How old are you? Are you married? How many kids? Do you love your wife? How is your sex life?" Tom says he answered calmly, but could feel his temper rising. When Alinsky ran out of questions, he dismissed Gaudette with a wave of his hand: "You are too old to be an organizer; you have too many kids and you sound to me like some damn lay missionary."

Tom Gaudette was not an impressionable twenty year old recruit. He had been a collegiate champion hockey player, an amateur boxer, a combat pilot in World War II, who led the crew of his shot-down bomber out of enemy territory to safety. Gaudette looked like a tough guy—well-built, with a strong chin, a broken nose and a Jimmy Cagney voice. His French-Canadian-Irish temper finally burst its bounds and he told Alinsky what he could do with his God-damned organizing job, called down on his head a litany of colorful curses and stormed out of the office. Two minutes later a chuckling Alinsky had Egan on the phone, and he was telling the priest how impressed he was with Tom Gaudette. The next day Alinsky called Tom and asked him to come back to his office for a serious discussion. The two men talked about the problems of West Town and what kind of effort it would take to organize it. Saul told Gaudette that if he would quit his job with Admiral, he would hire him for half his present salary. Gaudette went home to talk with his wife. Kay told him that she would be proud to help him to do the job. He called Alinsky back that night and accepted his offer.[44]

The next day Saul surrendered to Egan and agreed to organize the Northwest Side. "I never thought they'd get the money," Saul said, "so what the hell can I do?" On November 1, 1961 Gaudette became an IAF organizer for $7,000 a year. He began putting together the Northwest Community Council. To learn Alinsky's approach he enrolled in the IAF's famed on-the-job-organizer-training program. Gaudette explains how it started: "Saul said to me, 'Tom, I want you to go out there and meet the people and the clergy and see what their problems are and let me know. Good luck to you.' "[45] Actually, there was a little more to it than that: lots of reading (everything from Tom Paine to Tom Prendergast) and visits to Back of the Yards and TWO. He had to send in the weekly reports demanded by Alinsky of all the IAF organizers. The weekly reports not only kept Alinsky abreast of what was happening, but also forced the organizer to reflect carefully on what he was doing. The rest of the time Gaudette was on his own, trying to figure out what had to be done, making lots of mistakes, learning to fly—like Ross, von Hoffman, Chambers and others before him—by the seat of his pants. At least once a week Gaudette went to Alinsky's house, late in the evening, for one of Saul's free-wheeling staff discussions. Egan says that those bull sessions with Alinsky and his organizers were wonderful. The discussions ranged widely, from concrete organizing problems in Woodlawn or West Town ... to whatever— music, architecture, fiction, history, politics, theology—all done with wit and Alinsky's brand of rough, Socratic give and take.[46]

Gaudette hired two staff members to help him. Craig Heverly was a divinity student at the University of Chicago who was attracted to the IAF by what he had heard about Woodlawn; Edward Dziewulski, on the other hand, was a local resident, a married insurance salesman with four kids (Gaudette described Ed as "about my age, angry as a son-of-a-bitch, a big, powerful Polish guy who knew everything about the neighborhood"). Working together, the three fledgling organizers welded together a solid, exciting organization out of the fractious, multi-ethnic neighborhood on the Northwest Side. It did not go smoothly, however; as soon as Gaudette began visiting the Protestant clergy, Walter Kloetzli's friends appeared with the same old charges of Communist conspiracy and Catholic takeover. Despite these critics, ten Protestant congregations sent delegates to the first convention of the Northwest Community Council (NCO) in 1963. One Presbyterian minister who made an emotional attack on Alinsky on the floor of the Presbytery received a note the next day from a clerical colleague. The note said, "Dear Bob, After all, we have alcoholics and prostitutes in the church; why not Saul Alinsky?"[47]

The key organizing tool used by the organizers was provided by the heavy-handed opposition of the local political leaders. The old ethnic neighborhood was a hotbed of political apathy before Gaudette came along. People had long ago given up trying to fight the political machine. The first time the NCO leaders went to see the committeeman, who held all the strings on the Near West Side, he told them to get lost. When Gaudette went alone to put a little heat on the committeeman, he told the organizer that he owned the neighborhood and nothing was going to happen unless he okayed it. At the next meeting of the NCO, the leaders asked the committeeman to address the Council. When people began questioning him, asking him why he never did anything and why he never showed up except at election time, he denounced them angrily as a bunch of Communists and stalked out of the meeting. The Council then bypassed the local leader and took about a thousand members to the next meeting of the Building and Zoning Committee of the City Council. They protested the rezoning of the area for industrial use. The committee agreed to the demand of the aroused citizens. Afterward, the people were bused back to St. John Cantius Church for a coffee and cake victory party. Heverly, the young organizer, reported, "I sensed a kind of awe and a very happy surprise among the people that they had been able to gather this many people and win an uncontested victory."[48]

The famous IAF incident of the "garbage tactic" took place in the early days of NCO. When a ward leader ignored the Council's request for increased garbage collection in a crowded area, the organization leaders hired a truck and solemnly deposited a ton of Chicago garbage on the sidewalk in front of a neighborhood tavern owned by the politician's wife.[49]

There were no miraculous cures, however, of the Northwest Side's deteriorating housing stock and its changing population, but the people were learning how to control their own lives and community. They were working together for the common good despite their ethnic and religious differences and the old feuds. Two years after he started organizing NCO, Tom Gaudette was asked by an interviewer what the organization had accomplished. Gaudette's answer is a classic description of an Alinsky-style organization. He said: "I don't know how many houses have been rehabilitated . . . but I can tell you about individuals, how they've changed. Once they were fearful, scared, hesitant. It was impossible to do anything. The people were apathetic, without hope. Then all of a sudden they were not afraid, not fearful. By God, they say, we *can* whip the enemy."[50]

Alinsky and the Churches

For a brief moment in early 1962, Saul Alinsky was directing the largest and most experienced staff of organizers he ever had (actually, "directing" is too strong a verb to describe Saul's kind of supervision which was decentralized yet disciplined—a triumph of charisma and modern communication). Some of his organizers were on the IAF payroll; the others were paid by the organizations but maintained a close consulting relationship with Alinsky. In California, Fred Ross was working with the CSO; Cesar Chavez was the CSO's director/organizer; Dolores Huerta was directing the Women's Educationals under an IAF grant from the Schwartzhaupt Foundation; Joseph Meegan was still the director of the Back of the Yards Council; Nicholas von Hoffman was organizing TWO; Edward Chambers was directing OSC; Richard Harmon was a staff organizer of TWO; Tom Gaudette was organizing NCO; John Egan, from his post in the Archdiocesan Office of Urban Affairs, was the liaison between the cardinal archbishop of Chicago and the IAF; D. Barry Menuez was a staff organizer of OSC; Lester Hunt, after organizing in Chicago, Butte and Chelsea, was leaving IAF to go to graduate school (he kept in close touch with Alinsky and was tempted to come back to the IAF a couple of times in the next ten years). Saul did no direct organizing after the Chelsea debacle. For the next ten years, his was the role of the organizer's organizer. He began also to develop a new sideline as educator and public figure.

According to Jack Egan, the early 1960's in Chicago were the "Golden Age" of Alinsky's mass community organizations. Besides the active, independent, twenty year old Back of the Yards Council, Chicago enjoyed the active services of OSC, TWO and NCO, which formed a rough line of organized neighborhoods from the changing Southwest Side, through the South Side ghetto, to the besieged neighborhoods of the Near Northwest Side. At the beginning of 1962 Alinsky saw IAF's Chicago organizations forming parts of what he called the "Pattern Project." He explained what he meant in IAF's *Annual Report.*

> This program represents a new departure in the field of community organization in that organizations initiated and developed within a particular community for specific issues no longer constitute the terminal point of the operation. Here a project (TWO, with NCO to follow) is conceived and organized, not only for its effects within the community, but as an integral part of a planned pattern of a series of projects wherein the functioning interrelationship of each project to the other is the essential objective and force for attacking certain major issues as in this case, that of residential segregation. We believe that this holistic springboard offers the only hope for possible success.[51]

The Chicago "pattern" of local organizations was a refinement of Alinsky's basic concept in *Reveille for Radicals* of well-rooted, independent neighborhood organizations forming coalitions based on shared community interests and with the necessary clout to influence city and metropolitan political structures and decision-making.

The Catholic Archdiocese of Chicago and the neighborhood parish priests continued to be the backbone of IAF's organizing efforts. The man who did the recruiting, the money raising and took charge of the care and feeding of the Catholic network was the adroit Monsignor John J. Egan. The Protestant churches (with the exception of the Lutherans) continued their internal debates over Alinsky's intentions and methods and over the role the churches should be playing in political affairs. While the debates continued, the Protestant churches were actively supporting the organizations in their neighborhoods with money and members. The Rev. Edgar Chandler, the director of the Church Federation of Greater Chicago (the Council of Churches), took the lead among the denominational executives in developing a supportive position for Alinsky's organizing at the metropolitan level. His assistant Douglas Still wrote a position paper with the help of Presbyterian ministers David Ramage and Bryant George and others. The statement was worked over for months, but when it was finished, it gave a sound theological basis for the churches' involvement with Alinsky's organizing as an effective approach to their mission to the powerless, poor, and racially segregated people in the city's neighborhoods. The Church Federation document contained a set of criteria to be used in judging what was a "good community organization." It appealed directly to the churches of Chicago to participate: "If there is no formal organization with the potential to meet the established criteria, it (the local congregation) should take the lead in starting one. If there is more than one formal organization in the community, the following standards may help the congregation in deciding which to join. If there is only one, the church should join and work for the goals set forth in the following description."[52] Later, when some of the Protestant leaders moved into national denominational offices, they brought with them from Chicago a well-developed theological and ethical position on the urban mission of the churches and on the community organizing of Saul Alinsky.

The close working arrangement between Alinsky and the Christian churches in ecumenical coalition became the model for the IAF's approach to organizing communities in the 1960's and 1970's and continues to operate today. Alinsky's support from the Church began with the parishes in the Back of the Yards; John O'Grady, Cardinal Stritch and Egan developed a pastoral and ethical base for the church-community partner-

ship in the 1950's; it became an ecumenical effort in the 1960's
and 1970's. At one point in the mid-1960's Egan and the officials of the Church Federation set up a new ecumenical structure in Chicago, the Interreligious Council on Urban Affairs,
in an attempt to bring into the church coalition those Jewish
religious bodies who were interested.

A couple of years later, a Chicago church leader wrote to a
colleague in Rochester, New York when Alinsky was preparing to organize that city's riot-torn black community. The
churches were being asked to support the organizing project,
and the Presbytery executive wanted some advice. The Chicago minister, the Rev. Donald Benedict, the executive director
of the Chicago City Missionary Society, Church of Christ, told
the Rochester minister that he had been, in the past, a critic of
Alinsky's controversial organizing methods. Now, he said, "I
really feel that this is the only way in which the ghetto communities can be organized." He called the participation of church
members in this kind of organizing "essential." Benedict did
not mince words; he said that the Protestant community in
Rochester would be polarized between those who are for and
those who are against Alinsky. He warned that the churches
would lose a certain amount of financial income because of
their involvement. On the other hand, he said, the project "will
provide a creative tension in which some of the basic doctrines
of the faith can be brought into focus." The ministers would
have to work hard during the organizing to keep an open
dialogue within their congregations about the issues and the
on-going controversy. Benedict said that the churches of Rochester were in for a rocky time, but that the results would be
worth the pain. "In the last analysis," he wrote, "it is only as
those disadvantaged people gain power that they will begin to
take constructive steps in their own behalf. They will make
mistakes and they will not be gentle, but in the long run I
personally have faith in their integrity and wisdom. Their
power may finally corrupt as does all power, but at least it will
offer a balance to the present corruption of the power that
forces them into their present position in our society."[53]

Despite his commitment to what Alinsky was trying to

do, Cardinal Meyer wondered at times if the Church was doing the right thing. It was difficult for Church leaders who were dedicated to peace, charity, patience and the established order (except in just wars) to accept a situation of oftentimes bitter civic conflict and raging controversy supported by the churches. Meyer gave the keynote address at the second NCO convention in 1964. He spoke about the role the Church must play in community struggles, like those they were involved in on the Northwest Side. "I'm sure that the spiritual leaders of the community and their people," the cardinal said, "cannot be indifferent to a work such as this kind, because in this way we give practical exemplification, practical demonstration of our understanding of the great commandment of love."[54] Egan says that despite occasional doubts, Meyer never withdrew his support from the organizations because he saw that they were really organizing poor, powerless, ignored people to help themselves. Later, before his untimely death, Meyer told Egan: "I have never regretted (the support of the community organizations) even though I was criticized for it by some of my own priests when they heard about it. 'God,' they said, 'how we could have used that money to keep our boilers going ... to give it to a man like Alinsky to organize a community organization. ...' "[55]

In the final analysis, Egan says the early 1960's were the "Golden Age" of Church-community cooperation in Chicago because in a time of civic crisis Alinsky brought to the frustrated people in the churches and to the troubled people in the neighborhoods the tools they needed to create democratic power, pride in themselves and the political skills to take control of their lives and communities. Nobody could have done it alone; it took the churches and the neighborhood people—and it required Alinsky and his organizers as the catalyst. Many years later, Monsignor Egan still gets excited, his voice rising in intensity as he talks about this period: "We had fifty or sixty (Catholic) pastors—not just young assistants—pastors who were involved in raising the money, attending the meetings, picketing and marching with their people. Those men had a sense of history, a sense of neighborhood, a sense of church;

they knew without Vatican II telling them that it is where the church should be, where the church *was* church: out fighting for justice for the people—bad housing, rats biting kids, a neighborhood clinic, going down to City Hall and fighting for and with their people. Many of these priests said that during this time the liturgy meant more to them and their sermons took on a new life because they had been dipped in reality during the week. . . ."[56]

Chavez Moves On

While all this organizing was going on in Chicago, Fred Ross and Cesar Chavez continued to build the National Community Service Organization in California. By 1960 the CSO was a successful statewide network of urban Mexican-American community organizations. Thirteen years before, when Ross started the first CSO in East Los Angeles, less than ten percent of California's large Spanish-speaking population was registered to vote. In a few short years, the statistics had grown more healthy: 40,000 of the older generation of Mexican-Americans (people who had lived in the United States for many years) had become citizens; 227,000 new voters had been registered and now voted regularly. (Ross says that nearly 450,000 were registered by CSO workers by 1962).[57] In 1947 no Mexican-American held elected office in California; by 1960 there were more than a hundred elected officials. The long-standing complaints of police brutality, discrimination in housing and municipal services in the barrio communities diminished as the local CSO chapters made their political clout felt. In the first year of the new decade, the National CSO boasted of twenty-eight chapters operating in California and Arizona, with four full-time organizers led by Cesar Chavez, all paid by CSO funds.

In the late 1950's Alinsky's old Chicago friend Ralph Helstein was the president of the United Packinghouse Workers of America (UPWA). His union had won elections to represent packing shed workers in the rich citrus growing area in Southern California around Oxnard. But the citrus growers refused to negotiate labor contracts with their workers. Instead, they were hiring the "braceros"—migrant farm workers from nearby Mexico who continued to come across the border under the protection of a U.S. Government program set up to supplement domestic farm workers during World War II. Now the braceros were being hired illegally by the growers at lower wages and under poorer working conditions than American workers would accept. The growers were determined to prevent the unionization of the farm workers.[58]

Helstein offered to pay the national CSO $20,000 if Chavez would organize a CSO chapter in Oxnard. He had in mind a Back of the Yards strategy where the local community organization would build support for the union. In little more than a year Chavez built Oxnard into the strongest CSO chapter in California. The issue around which he organized was jobs for local workers and the right to organize themselves into a union. In a long, bitter fight Chavez and the CSO leaders were able to bring federal and state authorities to stop the growers' illegal use of the braceros. It was in the midst of this two-year organizing campaign that Cesar Chavez became aware of the worsening plight of the American farm worker—what Edward R. Murrow was to call in the 1960 CBS television documentary the "Harvest of Shame." When Chavez left Oxnard, he felt that the time was ripe to begin organizing the nation's farm workers. His experience with the UPWA organizers, however, convinced him that the conventional unions could not do the job. He returned to the national CSO with the objective of convincing the leaders to let him begin the organizing of California's farm workers. Alinsky and Ross backed him in the new venture, but only Dolores Huerta, among the top CSO leaders, fought alongside him in his attempt to redirect the CSO. The Chavez proposal started a great internal debate within the CSO.

The villain in the piece was Saul's old adversary, "organizational institutionalization." Alinsky explained what was happening in a letter to Carl Tjerandsen: "As you may or may not know, the CSO's have been becoming more and more 'respectable' over the past five or six years. There has been a steady invasion of middle-class Mexican-Americans, who saw in the CSO a platform for status and for a certain degree of power as well as the fact that many of the founding leadership of the CSO have, through the course of time, become middle class themselves. Part of this ... was due to the fact that their effectiveness and success resulted in the political authorities awarding top-paying political plums to CSO leaders. ... Once the big fat check comes in, it very quickly germinates nice big middle-class attitudes."[59]

The fight over organizing farm workers came to a climax at the National CSO Executive Board meeting, just before the annual convention in 1962. Alinsky came out from Chicago for the board meeting and witnessed Chavez and Huerta and a small group of dissident delegates as they managed to wring approval for the farm worker project from the board. Alinsky said he was "shaken" as he saw the strength and skill shown by Chavez and his supporters, many of whom were graduates of the CSO Educationals. He described the parliamentary battle to Tjerandsen: "I saw the strange spectacle of leadership getting up on the floor, leadership which had been completely unknown in CSO circles as recently as three or four years ago. ... They proceeded to change completely the policy of CSO to a militant workingman's almost revolutionary ideology, which in fact is more militant than the ideas which germinated the original CSO." After the board meeting, Saul asked one of Chavez's insurgents what this more militant policy might do to the CSO. The young man said, "If CSO cannot do this job (organize the farm workers), then it should die; it did the first job that it was set up to do, and why should it just keep hanging around doing nothing but 'perpetuating its own identity?' "[60]

By the time the CSO convention was held in March, however, the anti-farm worker leaders were back in charge. The convention delegates voted down Chavez's proposal. They said that they were a civic organization, not a labor union. Dolores Huerta and Ross were in tears. The only one who appeared calm was Chavez. At the end of the convention Cesar stood and announced to the assembly that he was resigning from the CSO.[61]

With no job and no money, Chavez was forced to take his family to Delano where his wife Helen's family lived. There, at least, their kids would not starve. Then, a month or so later, an excited Fred Ross reported to Alinsky: "A small dust devil is starting to streak across the Valley of the San Joaquin. . . . It's Cesar. He has just completed the job in Delano and made the initial contacts, all solid, in the other valley towns. He's steadily winning his biggest fight—fear on the part of the workers. In addition to the Mexican-American workers, he's getting Negroes, Filipinos and Anglos involved. He's going to pull it off, Saul. . . ."[62]

In an abandoned theater in Fresno, California, Chavez, Huerta and the CSO dissidents met with one hundred and fifty farm worker delegates and their families on September 30, 1962 to found a new farm labor organization. At first they called themselves the National Farm Workers Association. Later, after writing a new chapter in the history of organized labor in the United States, they changed the name of the union to the United Farm Workers of America.[63]

Crisis in Black and White

During the summer of 1964, overcrowded ghettos in Northern cities began exploding in widespread rioting, arson and death. These race-related urban uprisings hit first in Cleveland, New York City (Harlem and Bedford-Stuyvesant), New Jersey, Rochester and Philadelphia and continued in other cities through five "long, hot summers" from 1964 to 1968. The nation seemed stunned, unable to understand what was happening and, what was worse, unsure of what anyone could do to remedy the situation.

One bright spot in that first year of blood and fire was the publication of Charles E. Silberman's book, *Crisis in Black and White*. An editor of *Fortune* magazine, Silberman in his book introduced Americans to Saul Alinsky and to The Woodlawn Organization (TWO) on Chicago's South Side. The author described TWO as a successful experiment that proved that people—even people living in a black urban slum—can take care of themselves and their communities if they are organized and work together. The timing of the book's publication was just right. Millions of frightened Americans were asking, "What can we do to stop the rioting?" Silberman's book gave them an answer: "Go and talk to Saul Alinsky. He knows what to do."[64]

Crisis in Black and White helped to make Alinsky a national institution in the middle and late 1960's. On the day that the book appeared in Chicago's bookstores, Saul, with a big smile on his face, told Lester Hunt, "Our stock just split three for one. . . ."[65] After more than a quarter century of organizing America's neighborhoods, Alinsky became an overnight success. Influential groups from a dozen cities, from Brooklyn to the Bay Area, arrived at Alinsky's tiny Michigan Avenue office to enlist his services for restless black ghetto neighborhoods. Alinsky became a popular lecturer on college and university campuses. Catholic and Protestant churches brought him in to give workshops on community organization to clergy and lay leaders.

Alinsky loved his new-found fame. The audience of young Americans he had looked for with his *Reveille for Radicals* after World War II was now packing into college auditoriums to hear him speak—two decades later. The church groups he had courted so assiduously during the 1950's were now beating a path to his door. Even the social scientists who generally ignored Alinsky's rough-and-tumble urban populism showed signs of taking him seriously.

When the urban ghettos exploded in the latter half of the 1960's, all kinds of agencies and organizations, including the federal government, became involved in trying to fix the cities. With his unmatched people-organizing skills and his experience, Alinsky probably could have parlayed the Industrial Areas Foundation into a million dollar business. There were government contracts to be had, well-paid consultancies with cities and corporations, and "think tanks" with large foundation-supplied budgets. Many social scientists and social workers, with far less ability than Alinsky, did just that.

But Saul had no more use for the new anti-poverty "experts," with their expensive programs, than he had for the juvenile delinquency professionals long ago in the Back of the Yards. Alinsky continued his lone organizing ways—independent, frugal, demanding, and always ready to criticize government, churches, unions, corporations, suicidal militants, anybody who raised people's hopes without giving them effective means to change their lives.

But those individuals and organizations who showed a genuine interest in making the democratic process work in their communities Alinsky and his tiny band of organizers were ready and willing to organize.

6.

Alinsky in Smugtown

A Long Hot Summer

Early in 1964, Alinsky was in conversation with groups in Kansas City, Mo., Gary, Ind., and New York's Harlem about providing IAF organizers to build black organizations in those communities. In Kansas City a solid ecumenical coalition of Catholics, Presbyterians and Episcopalians had already raised most of the money for such a project. At the last minute, however, the Episcopal bishop, worried about conservative critics within his church, asked for time so that a committee of the diocese could evaluate the IAF's methods and projects in other cities. By the time the committee presented its wholly favorable report a year later, Saul was up to his neck in Rochester, New York and had no experienced organizer to send to Kansas City.

In many ways the black community organization that the IAF engineered in Rochester between 1965 and 1968 was Alinsky's most sophisticated project. The "Flower City," as it was called in the Chamber of Commerce brochures, proved to be the laboratory in which Alinsky and Ed Chambers, Saul's top organizer since von Hoffman quit, developed the new directions the IAF would follow over the next decade.

It all began during the long hot summer of 1964. The Rochester newspapers reported that it was one of the hottest, stickiest, meanest Julys in the city's history. The spark that turned the already overheated city into a conflagration was struck at a street dance on Joseph Avenue, in the center of the poorest section of the black ghetto. On Friday night, July 24, a

176

group of women calling themselves the Northeast Mothers Improvement Committee sponsored a street dance to raise money to purchase playground equipment for a city-built neighborhood tot-lot.

Shortly before midnight, police were called to arrest a drunk who was allegedly molesting a woman at the dance. When the white policemen began to club and kick the drunken man as they dragged him to the patrol car, the crowd of about two hundred blacks surrounded the officers and shouted threats and insults. Someone threw a bottle at the police car, the police radioed for help, and the battle was on. Before the three nights of ghetto violence were over, four persons were killed, three hundred and fifty were injured, one thousand were in jail, property damage soared into millions of dollars, and fifteen hundred National Guard troops were patrolling the city streets with fixed bayonets. A reporter described the disturbances as the "most violent outbreak of disorder ever to hit Rochester."[1] New York columnist Jimmy Breslin described the unfamiliar sight of armored personnel carriers with heavy machine guns lined up in a city park where children usually played.[2]

The city was in a panic, and public officials were stunned. Mayor Frank Lamb spoke for the majority of Rochesterians when he told an NBC reporter, "It is unbelievable that such a thing could happen in Rochester." In the midst of this chaos, however, one group of private citizens recovered from their shock and came together the next afternoon at the home of the city's premier aristocrat and churchwoman, Georgiana Sibley. The group was made up mostly of Protestants, clergy and lay members of the Rochester Council of Churches and its Board for Urban Ministry. After that meeting, the church leaders held a press conference and called for immediate restoration of civic order. They went over the head of the city's Democratic mayor to ask New York Governor Nelson A. Rockefeller to send in the National Guard. Then they called in members of the Negro clergy to help plan a response to the city's torn black community. Out of these discussions emerged a small group of church leaders with a plan that was to change the face of Rochester in a number of ways over the next few years.[3]

To almost everyone who knew Rochester in the 1950's and 1960's the riots of 1964 were incomprehensible. "What do these people want?" was the question most frequently asked that summer. The "Flower City" was a prosperous and comfortable community. Perhaps the best symbol of people's lack of awareness of the growing racial unrest was Rochester's new network of expressways. Executives could leave the downtown offices of Kodak or Xerox by way of the Eastern Expressway and be home in one of the lovely suburban towns in twenty minutes. The rapidly growing arc of poor black neighborhoods circling the business district was only a momentary blur to the business leaders as they drove by at fifty miles an hour on the Expressway.

In the 1960's, moreover, the city's economy was booming. Rochester was blessed among its neighbors in the Northeast with high technology industries like Kodak and Xerox and some eight hundred other manufacturing companies that were busy turning out great quantities of optical goods, dental equipment, machine tools, men's clothing, processed food, beer and automotive products. Few cities in the United States could boast of Rochester's employment stability.

At the same time, complex and subtle population changes had been creeping up on the city for a decade. The movement of white residents to the suburbs was at floodtide, while the city's non-white population was expanding in the central city. The 1950 U.S. Census listed 487,632 people living in Monroe County—332,488 of them living in the city. By the 1960 census the county population had risen to 586,387, an increase of twenty percent. The city population had dropped to 318,611 in the same period.

Hidden in those figures, moreover, was the growing non-white population, mostly black inner-city dwellers—from 7,937 in 1950 to 24,184 in 1960—an increase of over two hundred percent. A special county census completed a few months before the riots showed a 1964 population of 33,492 non-white. The Rochester Bureau of Municipal Research projected a non-white population of 45,000 by 1970 (actually there were about 52,000 by then, including 6,000 Hispanic-Americans).

The riot areas contained over 25,000 non-whites in two

city wards. The figures give no clue, however, to the living conditions in the ghetto—high mobility, increasing population density (slum clearance was destroying the ghetto housing stock without replacing it), high rents, substandard housing, poor health care and an overall unemployment rate of thirteen to nineteen percent. And these were boom times in the local economy. While the city, whose proud boast was "Rochester Means Quality," was feeling the pains that come with metropolitan growth, its black citizens caught up in the "revolution of rising expectations" were feeling a special discomfort. The Reverend Franklyn D.R. Florence, a young black minister from the South, explained the unique frustration felt by blacks who had moved from Florida and South Carolina to Rochester because of its prosperity and stability. "When you've already reached the Promised Land," said Florence, "where do you go from there?"

As the summer of 1964 faded away, however, without any further ghetto disturbances, so did the news headlines, the white community's fear, the special reports, and the probing editorials. The city became calm again; it began to look like business as usual. The one exception was the Protestant church caucus. The white and black church leaders were working hard on a plan to offset another long, hot summer.

The smooth shift into action by the church caucus—in great contrast to other influential groups in the city—was more than a sudden outpouring of the traditional Christian "peace and good will toward men." Four years earlier, the Rev. Richard N. Hughes, the director of the Federation of Churches (later renamed the Council of Churches) had appointed a committee of local clergy and lay persons and charged these men and women with finding ways to aid the member churches working in Rochester's inner city. Over the next couple of years the committee grew and became a permanent division of the Rochester Area Council of Churches. Renamed the Inner City Board, its members carried out a thorough study of the problems of Rochester's black wards. That study was a unique exercise of "practical ecumenism" on the part of the mainline Protestant churches—a "this worldly," cooperative church mission to the community of Rochester, with a special care for the city's poor and powerless people. The board's efforts were something more than the usual cooperative church planning. U.S. Protestant churches had been doing cooperative planning since the 1920's. H. Paul Douglas described it as a "combination of ecclesiastical eugenics and planned parenthood." The Inner City Board was, however, a genuine ecumenical structure for planning, funding and exercising new kinds of church missions throughout the Rochester area.

By 1963 the board was looking for a full-time executive director. They chose Herbert D. White, a young, enterprising Presbyterian minister, a graduate of Union Theological Seminary, with intensive post-graduate experience in the inner cities of Baltimore and Buffalo. With the help of Eugene Tennis (associate pastor of the prestigious Third Presbyterian Church and White's classmate at New York's Union Seminary) and Stewart Moot (a Rochester attorney and clerk of the local presbytery), White began steering the board in the direction of a more active involvement in the whole city. He stressed that Rochester was the center of a metropolitan network of churches, with large resources of people, funds and educational structures. In 1964 the board changed its name again to reflect these comprehensive metropolitan concerns; it became known as the Board for Urban Ministry (with the singularly unhappy acronym of BUM). Under its revised constitution, BUM was made up of two representatives (one clergy, one lay) elected by each denomination. The reorganized board was ecumenical, an independent body able to receive and spend funds, yet supported and shielded, when necessary, by the parent Council of Churches. The BUM structure, unwieldy at first sight, proved itself well designed for its task under fire. The Board for Urban Ministry was a triumph of organization by its members, sophisticated attorneys and experienced church bureaucrats.

The Board for Urban Ministry sponsored an urban training course for Rochester's young and restless middle-management men and women, those destined to be the future "movers and shakers" in Rochester, according to White. When a small Baptist congregation in the inner city could no longer afford to hire a pastor, the Board found them a young black minister and paid his salary. The board members (at first they were all

white—from white churches) were unsure what they could do
directly to deal with the problems of the black neighborhoods.
After a long discussion, they decided to approach the ghetto by
hiring an organizer to work with the white neighborhoods
contiguous to the expanding black section. The organizer's job
was to prepare the white neighborhood for a peaceful integration of black newcomers. BUM asked the Xerox Corporation to
help fund the project. By the middle of 1964 White and the
Board for Urban Ministry had a solid organization, with the
metropolitan network of churches behind them and the beginnings of a budget for urban ministry. Few cities in the United
States had anything approaching this kind of ecumenical
church structure.

Then, early on Saturday morning, July 25, BUM's director, Herb White, was awakened by a telephone call:

"Herb, have you listened to your radio this morning?"

"No, why?"

"All hell is breaking loose downtown. There's been a riot
going on since last night. The whole place is in a shambles."

White leaped out of bed. While he was dressing, he wondered what a black riot would do to the board's well-laid plans.
He said that he didn't know whether to be angry at the rioting
blacks for screwing up the new cooperative mood in the city or
to be elated that the riots gave the board a big issue and a
license to act.

BUM's members and supporters dominated the church
caucus that met on Saturday afternoon at Mrs. Sibley's home.
They moved quickly to take the discussion away from the
social service types who wanted to set up first aid stations in
the ghetto and to organize a Battle-of-Britain-type evacuation
of black children to the country. White, Tennis and the Council of Churches officials, however, convinced the others that
the first job was to see that order was restored to the ghetto
streets, and then to aid the black clergy to minister to the angry
and frightened black community. White remembered later how
surprised he was at the silence of the black clergy who sat,
worried and uncomfortable, listening to the whites discussing
their future.

After peace was restored by the National Board, BUM

raised the money to help the black ministers bring in a team of observers from the Southern Christian Leadership Conference. Martin Luther King, Jr. sent a delegation of his top aides, led by James Bevel and Andrew Young. The young SCLC ministers helped keep things calm on the streets during the rest of the summer. The SCLC ministers took over the pulpits of the black churches. They encouraged the black congregations to organize themselves and fight for their rights in the non-violent manner the SCLC used so successfully in the South. But Rochester's city streets proved to be another matter. The restless young men and women of this Northern ghetto, faced with no jobs and no future, showed no interest in the SCLC rhetoric of non-violent action. The usual reaction of the street youth was "Man, what is all this Jesus shit?" As fall approached, the SCLC team returned to the South. Their help was significant, however; the young black ministers helped keep the ghetto "cool," thus buying the city time to come up with something before the next summer. Even more important was the contribution they made by convincing many people in the church community—black and white—of the importance of the black community's organizing itself to control its own neighborhoods. Young and Bevel told Franklyn Florence about Saul Alinsky and his work in building The Woodlawn Organization. They gave Florence and White copies of Silberman's book *Crisis in Black and White*. White was excited by Silberman's description of Alinsky's organizing of Chicago's South Side. He bought a couple of dozen copies of the book and gave them out to his board members and to the directors of the Council of Churches. The Board for Urban Ministry and the black clergy discussed whether they should invite Alinsky to organize Rochester's troubled black community. Meanwhile, at Third Presbyterian Church, a group of young white liberals were using Silberman's book as a study club text. In the wake of the July riots, the Rev. Franklyn D.R. Florence, the pastor of the Reynolds Street Church of Christ, emerged as a key black leader. For a time, after the SCLC team left town, Florence continued to wear the denim work shirt and bib overalls that were the SCLC uniform of the day. He was a close friend and confidant of Malcolm X who visited Rochester several times during this period. Like Malcolm, Florence adopted the title of "Minister" instead of the traditional "Reverend." His dress and title were unimportant, however; what was important was that Florence came out of the riots as an important new black leader in the city, and he was ready to act.

The church leaders in the Council of Churches looked on the idea of a community organization for the city's blacks as a moderate suggestion. They agreed with those city residents who said after the riots, "If all those Negroes are unhappy and unemployed and have no leadership, then let them get some decent, intelligent leaders and get their house in order." City Hall was still becalmed, unable to decide whether to spend a lot of money on specially trained riot police or wait for the results of a study of the riots' causes being done by the City Manager. In the meantime, the city fathers were not talking to the blacks. White and his board kept in touch with City Hall through Vice Mayor Mario Pirrello, a friend of Gene Tennis. Sidney Lindenberg, the director of the Baden Street Settlement House in the riot area, was upset with the black clergy and the Council of Churches for bringing the SCLC into what he considered his agency's "turf."

Otherwise, things remained calm on the ghetto streets as another of Rochester's long, cold winters approached. BUM's Herb White and Minister Florence agreed, however, that nothing had changed for the ghetto residents since the riots. Even in snowy Rochester it would not be long before the heat of summer returned.

The Invitation

In early October, the wheels began moving when White contacted Alinsky about the possibility of the IAF's coming to Rochester. Alinsky agreed to meet with a delegation from Rochester at his Chicago office in November. The Presbyterians on the Board for Urban Ministry took the initiative and began looking for funds. White and Paul Long, Jr. (the associate minister of Third Presbyterian Church) wrote a funding proposal that the Board for Urban Ministry could send to the national denominations. In preparing the proposal the two local ministers worked closely with two national church officials, Robert Stone of the National Council of Churches' Commission on Religion and Race and George Todd of the Board of National Missions. Todd, later on the staff of the World Council of Churches, became the principal organizer of the national interdenominational urban ministry caucus (often called the "Urban Mafia") that supported most of Alinsky's community organization projects from 1964–1972. White figured that a grant from the Presbyterians would act as the pump primer for similar grants from the other denominational bodies. The proposal, as approved by BUM in October, requested an "allocation of $15,000 for use by the Board for Urban Ministry . . . for the purpose of attracting funds and conducting a campaign such as Saul Alinsky has instigated in Chicago."[4]

In no way was the BUM proposal a radical document. It stressed the class unrest behind the July disturbances and the legitimate grievances on the part of the city's "have-not" population. Taking this tack with the church funders, rather than emphasizing racial strife, proved to be a brilliant move by the proposal writers. The concern of the churches was stated in terms of the powerlessness and lack of leadership among the poor blacks of Rochester: "The riots gave evidence above everything else that the ghetto resident possesses no vehicle or organized structure which is his own, through which he may gain not only the opportunity to obtain for himself a degree of self determination, but also dignity and respect as a human being."[5]

The delegation that went to sell Alinsky in Chicago (besides White, the members were Richard N. Hughes and Marvin Chandler, Council of Churches' executives; Canon St. Julian Simpkins, an Episcopalian pastor; Constance Mitchell, Third Ward County Supervisor; H. Richard Siciliano, Presbyterian Synod of New York; Paul Long, Jr.; and Fr. Joseph D'Aurizio, Rochester Catholic Charities—three blacks and five whites) returned with positive impressions. Alinsky was encouraging, but told them that the IAF required two nonnegotiable conditions before a Rochester project could be considered: a minimum of $100,000 in the bank for a two-year

project, and a written invitation from a significant segment of
the black population in the city. Alinsky promised to meet in
January with the black and white churches in Rochester. On
his return to the city, White concentrated BUM's efforts on
fund raising and getting the black ministers to organize a
formal invitation to Alinsky. Everything was in place when the
Board, in December, voted to raise $100,000.

White said later that the events at this period bore out
Alinsky's principle that power (the ability to act) follows organization. Because the Council of Churches and its four year
old Board for Urban Ministry were well-organized, the
churches in Rochester were prepared to act quickly and effectively in the severe community crisis in 1964. A second factor
in the church mobilization was the availability of Silberman's
book, *Crisis in Black and White*. That book was read more than
the Bible or the *Wall Street Journal* by the urban ministers that
fall. The availability of pertinent information on Alinsky's
methods, objectives and projects, written by an editor of the
respectable *Fortune* magazine, was crucial to the success of the
enterprise. Studying *Crisis in Black and White* also prepared the
caucus of church men and women to deal with the controversy
that erupted in the city when Alinsky's advent was announced.

What made Rochester different from Chicago and the rest
of Alinsky's projects was the absence of Catholic Church support. Nothing was heard from Catholic Charities after D'Aurizio returned from the Chicago meeting. (The initial probes for
Catholic support were made to Catholic Charities because the
diocese had no structure comparable to the Board for Urban
Ministry. At the time, White commented on Catholic Charities'
failure to respond to the Alinsky project: "Catholic Charities
. . . is self-conscious enough to know that its ties with, and
financial dependency on, the Community Chest and the Council of Social Agencies lend an institutional conservatism which
at that point and time inhibits it as a structure from lending its
initiative to our effort."[6] Saul's old friend Monsignor John
O'Grady had been right to worry about Catholic Charities
becoming too dependent on the United Fund.) The Catholic
Diocese of Rochester in 1964 had its own internal problems,
and chancery officials showed little interest in the city's black

community, the Council of Churches or social action. A handful of inner city church priests were keeping in touch with White and the black clergy in the hopes that they would be included in the new organization.

When Saul Alinsky came to Rochester for the first time in January 1965, he was a feisty fifty-six (about the same age as John L. Lewis was when he organized the CIO), a self-confessed professional organizer, who was at the height of his career. Thanks to the current Northern "black revolution" and Silberman's prose, Alinsky's IAF had, for the first time, money in the bank, more invitations than it could handle, four experienced organizers, and a growing national reputation. As for Saul's personal life, his health was good and he was enjoying a new-found celebrity status and a jet-set lecture schedule. His kids were grown; he had a house in Carmel and an apartment in Chicago. The only dark spot in the picture was Jean's health. Within the last year, his wife's multiple sclerosis, which had been in remission, returned in full force to cripple her. Saul finally told her what he had known for seven years—that she had multiple sclerosis and that it was incurable. Jean says now that she had suspected all along that this is what she had but that she did not say anything in hopes that she was wrong and her health would improve. But now as she felt herself growing worse, she began taking out her frustration on Saul. He came and stayed with her in Carmel every month, wrote letters to her almost daily when he was away, and saw to it that she received excellent medical care. But Jean's condition continued to deteriorate, and so did their marriage. Saul's two best friends, Marshall Field III, and Gordon Clapp, were gone (Clapp had died within the year). Saul's closest friend was his ex-organizer, Nicholas von Hoffman, now a reporter at the *Washington Post*. There were always lovely and interesting women in Saul's life. He was discreet, but he showed no interest in practicing celibacy.

After it was announced that the Board for Urban Ministry was trying to raise $100,000 to hire the IAF, the local news media began an investigation of Alinsky. They found plentiful evidence that Alinsky and his organizations were controversial. In the course of his book Silberman had taken a couple of

swipes at the University of Chicago and, in particular, the head
of its department of sociology, Professor Philip M. Hauser
(Alinsky and Hauser had similar roots: they were the same age,
had grown up in Chicago's Near West Side Jewish ghetto, their
fathers were tailors, and both men were sociologists and graduates of the University of Chicago). By an unhappy coincidence,
however, Hauser chose to launch a counter-attack against Silberman just five days after BUM announced it would bring
Alinsky to Rochester. The Chicago sociologist wrote a long,
carefully reasoned article in the Chicago Sunday *Sun-Times* in
which he soundly criticized Alinsky's use of conflict as a major
element in his approach to community organization. Hauser
was a member of the dominant Parsonian school of social
theorists. These sociological divines preferred community
change, if necessary at all, to operate through an orderly process of balanced political consensus. In his book Silberman had
charged Hauser with believing that Negroes in Chicago, and
throughout the United States, would eventually find their
place in the urban picture as did the European immigrants who
came to the city before them. Time and education would solve
the problems of the blacks. In turn, Hauser criticized Silberman's defense of Alinsky and said that the organizer's deliberate use of community conflict would retard rather than speed
the political consensus essential to Chicago's Woodlawn, or any
other black urban ghetto. (A bit later, Alinsky told White that
all the discussion about conflict versus consensus was "silly":
"After all there is always conflict before consensus and consensus is always good providing that consensus is for integration,
decency, opportunity, justice and democracy. They have a hell
of a lot of consensus among the Southern whites, but somehow
or other I just don't buy it regardless of that 'great' Chicago
sociologist.")[7] As his parting shot in the *Sun-Times* article,
Hauser said of Silberman, who was the Alinsky authority for
the Rochester church leaders: "On the face of it, any simple,
instant solution is suspect. That by Silberman (in *Crisis in Black
and White*) is an especially ingenuous, simplistic and misleading
one."[8]

Rochester's morning newspaper, the *Democrat & Chronicle*,
lost no time in reprinting the entire Hauser article. The

city's premier radio station WHAM followed with a series of
vitriolic editorial attacks on Alinsky and his local church spon-
sors by their news director, Richard Tobias. The alarm was
thus sounded. Rochester became distraught. The city where
old-fashioned "noblesse oblige" toward the less fortunate was
the rule, where the Community Chest was invented, where
social agencies abounded, that peace-loving city was about to be
invaded by a known social agitator, a troublemaker, a modern-
day Attila the Hun. Most disturbing of all to the majority of
Rochesterians was the news that the Protestant churches were
raising money to bring this rascal to the Flower City.

The owner of radio station WHAM warned the Council of
Churches that he would cancel the Council's weekly broadcast
of church services if Alinsky came to Rochester. The Rev.
George Hill, a Baptist pastor and member of the Council of
Churches board of directors, answered Tobias' hysterical editorials in an impressive set of equal-time broadcasts. Hill's inter-
pretation of Alinsky's work was so convincing that the attacks
by the local news media slowed considerably. The threat by
WHAM to cancel the Council of Churches' programs drew
forth an unexpected ecumenical ally in the person of Fr. Henry
Atwell, the respected editor of the *Catholic Courier-Journal*, the
weekly diocesan newspaper. Atwell threatened to withdraw
WHAM's popular Sunday morning program, "Morals Behind
the Headlines," which featured the *Courier-Journal*'s associate
editor, Fr. Richard T. Tormey. "If the other churches are
going to be muzzled," Atwell wrote, "for voicing their convic-
tions . . . then we'd rather not have our voice carried on air-
waves warped so contrary to this nation's tradition of
freedom."[9]

During this period of intense community controversy over
him, Alinsky came to Rochester to meet with white and black
church leaders. At a session with key church men and women
at the Episcopal diocesan headquarters, Alinsky answered
questions calmly and fully, as he had done earlier in Chicago
during the Woodlawn controversy. He made a good impression
on the church men and women. The Board for Urban Ministry
picked up important church allies after that session. White,
Long and other BUM members continued their money raising

for the project—a total of $47,000 was pledged by the end of
January. Board members went out to speak to church groups
every night—explaining, convincing, answering charges made
against Alinsky by the local media, and building a base of
support in the local churches. By the time of its February
meeting, the Board began to sound mildly optimistic: "Press
publicity on Alinsky has actually been good for the cause. A
president of a local firm is reported to have urged the Board to
go ahead and ignore opposition . . . stating that we must accept
opposition. The Church of Jesus Christ (Franklyn Florence's
black congregation) has become a voice in the Rochester community, pleased that the Council of Churches is 'doing something.' "[10]

Marvin Chandler, the tall, black Baptist minister who was
the associate director of the Council of Churches, worked closely with the black clergy to organize the official community
invitation to Alinsky. The black clergy organization, the Rochester Area Ministers Conference (RAMC), was the typical
loosely knit ministers' fellowship—conservative theologically,
evangelistic, its members anything but social activists. But the
riots had shocked the black ministers. They were disturbed also
by the attitude of the young blacks who rejected the Christian
non-violence preached by the SCLC ministers. The community
crisis pulled the RAMC members together in a search for new
leadership and direction. They listened carefully as Chandler
and Florence explained what an Alinsky-style community organization could do for Rochester's blacktown. After Alinsky
met with the group, the ministers agreed to organize the black
community's invitation to the IAF. They circulated petitions
through their churches and sent their members out to collect
additional signatures from black organizations in the city's
twin ghettos. Thousands of black Rochesterians signed their
names to this petition: "We . . . do hereby invite Mr. Saul
Alinsky and his Industrial Areas Foundation to Rochester,
New York. We are willing to work together to make Rochester
a better city for all citizens. We feel that we represent a cross-
section of the community."

There were still pockets of resistance to Alinsky, however,
especially among younger blacks. Sentiment was growing that

only "black power" could change things. "Why do we need," they asked, "a white guy from Chicago to tell us how to organize?" Fortunately the situation was saved by the city's nervous white power structure. Faced with the advent of Saul Alinsky and the growing mood of black militancy, Rochester's business leaders who were the powers behind the Community Chest/United Fund and the Council of Social Agencies suddenly invited the National Urban League to set up a chapter in the city. Although the Urban League had been denied entrance to Rochester by these same leaders before the riots, they now allocated $40,000 to help the Urban League set up shop. This move caused the city's black ministers to speak out for the first time publicly against the paternalism of the Rochester leadership. On the evening television news, Minister Florence denounced the Urban League incursion as an attempt by the city's "white bosses" to undercut the black community's self-determination.

After that, all resistance in the black community to Alinsky ended. The combination of the virulent attacks on Alinsky by the news media and the Urban League incident convinced the doubters. The ghetto telegraph broadcast the message: "If this Alinsky dude can scare the white folks so bad, he must be just the man we need."

In March Alinsky signed a contract with the Rochester Area Council of Churches and the Board for Urban Ministry to build a "community organization based on the principles and practices of the Industrial Areas Foundation in the predominantly Negro communities of Rochester, New York."[11] The city now made up its mind that there was no way to stop the Alinsky invasion, so things calmed down for a while. The Board for Urban Ministry helped its cause by circulating up-to-date information on other IAF projects, some recent articles sympathetic to the IAF[12] and an excellent newspaper interview with BUM's White and Council of Churches' director Richard N. Hughes on why the churches were inviting Alinsky to Rochester.[13] Even the up-to-now-hostile Gannett newspapers helped the Board's cause by sending two of their best reporters to Chicago to report first-hand on Alinsky's work in Woodlawn. Calvin Mayne did a three-part series for the evening *Times-Union* and Warren Doremus presented two hour-long documentary reports on WHEC-TV. White reported to Alinsky that Mayne's articles "progressed from adequate to better in the three days."[14] BUM, pleased with the Gannett reports, sent a note of congratulations to the two reporters for their "support to the cause of improving human relations."[15] The church activists were learning another Alinsky principle, "There are no permanent enemies."

The period of truce with the local news media and the reasoned, informative approach of the Council of Churches and the Board for Urban Ministry helped decrease community fears and aided the fund drive in the local churches. The calm lasted for several months, time enough for the IAF organizers to move into Rochester and begin organizing. Later the lid would be blown off again.

Rochester's octogenarian Catholic Bishop James E. Kearney was asked at this time by the Council of Churches' leaders to issue a statement of support for the Protestant churches. The Catholic Chancery Office said simply: "The Diocese does not feel it is in a position to comment on the necessity or value of inviting Alinsky to work in the inner city area. It is understood the decision to invite him was made by the Board for Urban Ministry of the Rochester Area Council of Churches, an organization whose dedication and zeal in the area of human rights cannot be questioned." Rochester's Catholic bishop was taking his usual stand on matters of civic controversy—a kind of diplomatic inactivity. Catholic support would come at a later date under Bishop Kearney's successor.

The FIGHT Organization

On April 1, 1965 Alinsky's top organizer, Edward T. Chambers, moved from Woodlawn to Rochester. With him was a young black organizer–trainee from Chicago, Ronald Jones. Accompanied by Minister Florence, who was slated to be the chairman of the new organization's temporary steering committee, the organizers rented a storefront office on Prospect Street in the Third Ward and started organizing Rochester.

There was no time for "hanging out" in true Alinsky-style, learning about the community in a leisurely fashion. Chambers had only three months to organize the city's black community before the July sun would return to set the ghetto streets ablaze. The editors of the Rochester newspapers had warned Saul Alinsky that the city of Rochester would hold him responsible for the next summer's riots.

In organizing Rochester's black community, Chambers, an eight year IAF veteran, followed the approach von Hoffman used in Woodlawn. Here, however, time was of the essence. The first convention was scheduled for June 11. Before it could do anything in Rochester, the new organization needed a license to operate and duly elected leaders to allow it to exercise a measure of democratic control over the fractured black ghetto. A peaceful summer was the organization's primary objective.

For his staff Chambers hired three local blacks whose names were suggested by Florence. The black ministers helped the organizers put together the temporary steering committee. All of them, organizers, staff and committee members, fanned out across the ghetto, day and night, to talk to people about the issues and sign up the organizations for the June convention. The name agreed on by the steering committee for the new organization was *FIGHT* (an acronym that stood for *F*reedom, *I*ntegration, *G*od, *H*onor, *T*oday). The name proved to be an asset in recruiting. Besides the churches, which were the backbone of FIGHT, the organizers signed up every assembly, gathering, and company they could find in the ghetto. Block clubs, sororities, fraternal societies, apartment house tenants, barber and beauty shop regulars, youth gangs, pool hall habitués, card clubs, bowling leagues—all were signed up, dues were collected and each group was told how many delegates it might send to the convention. Individuals living in the ghetto who wanted to join but did not belong to any of the member groups were encouraged to gather a few of their friends, choose a name and apply for membership. One ghetto Catholic parish was able to come up with only one group interested in joining, the Mothers' Wednesday Afternoon Bible Study Circle.

One of Alinsky's organizing principles was that there are

no disorganized communities, that the two terms are contradictory. The organizing strategy used in Rochester by Alinsky and Chambers, with Florence their willing apprentice, was to disrupt the settled patterns of the city's Negro community by drawing together its old and new organizations, its new and old leaders, into a different pattern. The resulting new constellation—an organization of organizations—would weld the black community into a reorganized force, powerful enough to act for its constituents within the city's structures and institutions.

In building urban curbstone organizations like TWO and FIGHT, Alinsky proved he understood a great deal about how organizations are built. Academic social scientists are willing to admit that they know little about how organizations come into being. Most organizational studies focus on how existing organizations behave, not how they originate.[16] Professional organizer Alinsky had spent over thirty years building effective voluntary organizations in many community settings. His approach and principles (more like guidelines, really) deserve serious study by political and social scientists. Alinsky's blend of political instinct and organizing experience in dozens of urban communities continues to assist local communities within the democratic enterprise.

The first convention of the FIGHT organization was ready to proceed on time. The organizing phase leading up to the June 11 convention was a virtuoso performance on the part of Chambers, Florence and FIGHT's tiny staff. The weather on the evening of June 11 turned out to be perfect for the annual crop of high school senior balls—and FIGHT's first convention. The gymnasium of the Rochester Institute of Technology was a crazy quilt of bustling people, brightly colored banners, balloons and delegation signs, blazing lights, a high school band and all the other sounds connected with an assembly of excited people. Reporters counted over fifteen hundred people—twelve hundred voting delegates and lots of visitors. One woman said that it reminded her of a hundred block parties rolled into one.

As people came into the hall, they were surprised to find segregated seating arrangements. Only credentialed delegates and organization members were allowed on the floor of the convention. All white visitors were relegated to the bleachers. This was FIGHT's way of reminding friends and foes alike that it was an organization of black citizens. Only about seventy-five white delegates were seated on the floor. They were individuals who belonged to organizations in the ghetto and had been sponsored by a black resident. In the FIGHT constitution, to be adopted later that night, it would say that only white people who actually lived in the ghetto and belonged to a member organization could be delegates at future conventions (this is how the two white priests from the Third Ward's Immaculate Conception Church remained members of all-black FIGHT).

Some of FIGHT's liberal white allies were miffed by their exclusion from membership and by the convention's segregated seating arrangement. The organizers did not want the friendly whites to smother the infant black organization and destroy FIGHT's chance to organize real "black power" in the city. During the convention the delegates, in a move to mollify their white supporters, approved a resolution that stated: "FIGHT recommends to those whites who want to work and fight for equality and justice to form an independent organization called 'Friends of FIGHT.'" The resolution called for close coordination of activities by the two organizations and offered to share with its white friends "FIGHT's know-how and assistance in developing an autonomous organization controlled by whites." The concept of a "Friends of FIGHT" organization was a new one and showed the master hand of Alinsky, whom Florence referred to in his speech as the "Stratetician." At one stroke FIGHT's call for an organized white ally reassured its black critics that the organization would really be a black organization and set the stage for a unique black-white community coalition.

The convention adopted the constitution with only minor changes. The most instructive debate was over the organization's name. Some delegates suggested "LIGHT"; others wanted "LOVE" or "PRIDE." But the consensus of the convention was definitely "FIGHT," and all efforts to soften the name or the strongly worded resolutions were handily defeated.

At the rear of the hall Alinsky was a silent observer. At an afternoon press conference, however, he made several comments calculated to encourage the blacks to stand up for themselves and guaranteed to set the teeth of white Rochester on edge. He described the city as a "Southern plantation transplanted to the North." He said that Rochester's blacks were treated as chattel by the city's business leaders, a necessary evil for low-paying, non-skilled work. What angered city residents the most was Alinsky's calling Rochester "Smugtown-USA," a name he stole from the title of a delightfully satirical book, written a few years before by Curt Gerling, a long-time Rochester newspaperman.[17]

The program that the delegates passed for FIGHT's first year was a tough agenda for community action. It stressed equal employment opportunities in local industry, demanded of the city fathers equitable law enforcement in ghetto neighborhoods, warned local politicians against using law enforcement positions as a "springboard to state office," and advised city planners that FIGHT intended to participate fully in the Third Ward Urban Renewal program.

Minister Franklyn D.R. Florence was elected FIGHT's first president by a wide margin. He promised that the organization would take action on the issues chosen by the convention. He praised the democratic process at work in Rochester's black community. To those who opposed FIGHT he warned that the new organization's "convention is rightly a cause of fear and trembling, because those who fear the people prefer paternalism to democracy."

The first FIGHT convention was a brilliant success. People who were afraid to come out of their homes a few months ago turned out in great numbers to vote for a self-run program for the black neighborhoods. Black Rochesterians, long inured to political apathy, went home that night buzzing with excitement about what they were doing as a community. They felt good about themselves—elderly delegates, young men and women, working people, clergy, professionals, even the black politicians. If even a portion of the energy in the RIT gym that night could be harnessed in the interests of the black community, the leaders knew that there would be no need for any more riots. It is noteworthy that in the months that followed that first convention, white Rochester's favorite attack on FIGHT's legitimacy was put in the form of a question, "Whom do they really represent?" Alinsky said that the eight percent of eligible black adults who were delegates to the convention was about the same percentage represented by the Continental Army in the American Revolution. Patrick Anderson, in an article written a year later, gave this answer: "Just how many people FIGHT speaks for is debatable, but even its critics admit that it represents the Negro community to a degree never before achieved by any organization."[18]

Despite their successful convention, the FIGHT officers understood that this was just the beginning. Before the city's 40,000 black citizens would be admitted to equal participation in the city's power structure, a long campaign would have to be fought. As Alinsky reminded them: "Power is not given, it must be taken." A few days before the convention, FIGHT's members were reminded how easily the powers-that-be can squelch groups that step out of line. One of the ghetto-based settlement houses voted to join FIGHT. When it was reported by the press, the agency received a letter from local Community Chest/United Fund manager Richard P. Miller. He warned the settlement house's board of directors in ominous terms that no Chest money could be used to support Alinsky. The settlement house board voted immediately to withdraw its membership from the new organization. After that the other social agencies in the ghetto did not bother to apply.

Following the Alinsky blueprint, FIGHT's first year was spent in building the organization. Nothing dramatic happened, just lots of hard work. The organization's members were learning the art of political action. As complaints about slum landlords poured into FIGHT's office, the leaders sent the Housing Committee to negotiate changes with the offending property owners. To further encourage compliance, FIGHT organized a mobile guerrilla force that went to the suburbs on Sunday morning to picket the homes of the recalcitrant landlords. The black picketers carried signs that said, "Did you know that your neighbor is a slumlord?" When City

Hall appointed the federally mandated directors of the local anti-poverty agency, Action for a Better Community (ABC), no blacks from poor neighborhoods were appointed. The ABC Board met for its bi-weekly meetings over lunch. Twenty or so members of FIGHT's Poverty Committee attended each ABC meeting and brought their own box lunches. After a few crowded sessions in a small meeting room in the heat of summer, the distracted ABC chairman asked the City Council to appoint three FIGHT representatives to the Board. When the city's Third Ward Renewal Project was announced, FIGHT held a series of information sessions at local churches to discuss the city's plan with the residents who would be affected. Over a thousand residents of the Third Ward testified on the neighborhood impact of the urban renewal plan at a special, FIGHT-organized hearing before the City Council. As TWO had done earlier, the black organization hired an architectural planning firm to develop, with the aid of Third Ward residents, an alternative plan that made substantial changes in the city's proposal.

The real test of whether FIGHT would live or die, however, happened on the ghetto streets during that first summer of its existence. The newly formed FIGHT Youth Committee worked closely with the black gang leaders and the younger militants. The efficient ghetto telegraph provided the FIGHT leaders and staff with an early warning system of potential trouble spots as they roamed the streets on warm summer nights. Minister Florence's squat figure was a familiar sight on the street corners and in the chicken and ribs joints where the young bloods gathered. He was usually accompanied by a couple of his lieutenants (or "bodyguards," depending on which reporter wrote the story for the next day's newspaper). When the call went out that trouble was brewing on Clarissa Street or Joseph Avenue, Florence and his band would quickly appear at the scene. Florence's deep voice could be heard mediating between the edgy police officers and the angry street people. It was a grueling task, but it worked. The streets remained calm all summer. FIGHT gained a reputation among the ghetto residents for being able to handle almost any kind of trouble in the black community, and to do it with very little fuss.

All through that first year FIGHT used the ghetto issues to build its army. The organization's leaders concentrated on black affairs. They paid little attention to the larger white community except when necessary to safeguard black community interests. FIGHT's critics were puzzled by the new organization's lack of militancy. When the Watts district of Los Angeles blew up in August 1965, Rochester's FIGHT was busy training its members to exercise a different kind of black community power. Minister Florence was the personification of the emerging style of leadership that Stokely Carmichael and others were calling "Black Power." Short and stocky, Florence had a preacher's bass voice that could project many shades of oratorical eloquence. He was an imposing man, one of the "natural leaders" Alinsky's organizers were trained to discover. With blacks, Florence was warm, attentive, funny, gentle— especially when people came to him with their troubles. But he could he as hard as steel when he had to be, as his FIGHT colleagues soon discovered. With whites, at least in public, he was aloof, unsmiling, authoritative; when anyone questioned him, he reacted with an infuriating arrogance. In confrontation with officials and others in positions of authority, he had only to appear with his heavy jaw pushed forward and his eyes hidden by dark glasses to reduce his opponents to stammering fury.

On the lips of Florence and the FIGHT leaders, "Black Power" meant black solidarity. The phrase, as they used it, had none of the messianic and ideological overtones it had on the lips of Stokely Carmichael or Eldridge Cleaver. Florence wanted all Rochester to know clearly that the black community was no longer the ward of the city's welfare industry, that blacks were building their own organization, and that they were demanding attention and respect for local black interests from a city with the reputation for crushing its opposition with kindness. The FIGHT watchword was "Respect, Rather Than Respectability." The paternalistic put-down practiced by Smugtown's influentials never worked on Franklyn D.R. Florence.

Friends of FIGHT

Meanwhile, on the other side of town, the white Friends of FIGHT were organizing themselves. After the contract with IAF was signed, Alinsky told White that one of the reasons he decided to take the Rochester job was the good working relationship he observed between blacks and whites in and around the church caucus. Friends of FIGHT used that good feeling to build a third community structure within the FIGHT-Church coalition. The organization was made up of fairly well-to-do middle-management types—white men and women who wanted to do something about Rochester's problems, especially racial segregation and black poverty.

Some insight into what motivated these "young and restless white liberals" (White's description) was found by Alinsky in reading *Smugtown—USA*. Author Curt Gerling described the pattern a young man must follow if he planned to become a success in Rochester. "Some believe the formula as unburdensome as getting a job at Kodak," he wrote, "and learning to pat the proper posteriors. . . ." The up-and-coming young man would need a few more assets, Gerling said, "some education . . . a few clean shirts, well kept nails and a Hickey-Freeman suit (a Rochester firm)." The most important requirements he saved for last: "It may be painful to your normal sensibilities, but you have to learn in your early days to be as unoriginal as possible and to conform to the Rochester prescription—facelessness."[19] The individuals who organized Friends of FIGHT, like the members of the church caucus, had no intention of following the traditional Smugtown formula for civic and social success.

The first impetus to form Friends of FIGHT came from Paul Long's adult study group at Third Presbyterian Church. They were the ones who spent the fall and winter after the riots reading and discussing Silberman's *Crisis in Black and White* and Alinsky's *Reveille for Radicals*. Early in the FIGHT organizing campaign, Long invited Minister Florence to address the group. He came in his SCLC-style denim overalls. The Presbyterians asked Florence what they could do, as whites, to help FIGHT. He told them to raise money to support FIGHT's activities. They thanked him, but after he left, they agreed among themselves that they were not interested in holding raffles and bake sales for FIGHT. They were not the usual church study club. In their number was an attorney from one of Rochester's top law firms (Eastman Kodak and the Gannett Company were among the firm's corporate clients), an accountant, an engineer and a university professor. They knew that getting involved with FIGHT's activities might destroy their careers. To handle this problem, the group decided that any member who found his job in jeopardy could take a no-questions-asked leave of absence from the organization; as far as the public was concerned, however, it would be a formal resignation. Once they worked out this escape hatch, they were ready to organize. Thirteen men and women signed a formal letter to FIGHT in which they asked to be recognized as "Friends of FIGHT."[20] The FIGHT convention voted to accept the Friends of FIGHT organization as official allies.

Alinsky encouraged this black-white coalition. He had serious doubts that the new mood of black power or any possible coalition of poor people could do much to change conditions without strong support from the middle class white majority.

The leaders of the church caucus, especially BUM's White, were delighted with Friends of FIGHT and saw it as a way to move the Protestant support for FIGHT into a broader community coalition. Herb White, who was as "natural" an organizer as Alinsky ever had, talked Paul Long, then the acting pastor of Third Presbyterian Church, into taking the presidency of Friends. Long had been the guiding spirit of the study group and was a key member of the church caucus.

The charter members of Friends of FIGHT represented a broad slice of middle class Rochester. Included in the group were John B. McCrory, an attorney and BUM chairman, Estelle Wurth, a Jewish community volunteer worker, Louis Martin, the associate director of the University of Rochester Library and Catholic, Kodak senior staff members Richard Leinbach, a design engineer and Protestant, Bert Buettner, a chemist and Catholic, Ben Phelosof, an attorney and "non-religious" Jew, William C. Evans, businessman and Unitarian, and Rabbi Allan Levine. At one of the first meetings of the

group, when they were trying to figure out how to put together a membership organization, Long asked IAF organizer Ed
Chambers to talk to them. Chambers listened to their ideas
about supporting FIGHT's agenda but argued that they should
develop a broad agenda of middle class issues as well. He
understood what they did not—that being Friends of FIGHT
at this early stage in the life of the black organization would be
a frustrating experience for the resourceful and articulate
white liberal members. The steering committee ignored Chamber's warning, however; they organized around a single objective: "to engage the white community to give support,
cooperation and assistance by whatever means are appropriate
to the organization FIGHT and its purpose. . . ."

Later events proved that Chambers was right. The relationship between Friends and FIGHT was extremely tenuous
for a long time. The black leaders were suspicious of the well-
to-do whites—fearful of being smothered by them and up-
staged by their activities. For many months Florence kept them
at arm's length, sent them conflicting signals when they did
communicate, and became upset whenever Friends of FIGHT
received more attention from the news media than FIGHT
did. Despite the off-and-on relationship, however, Friends of
FIGHT remained true. In its first two years the organization
grew and extended its influence throughout the Rochester
community. When FIGHT found itself in a life or death struggle with a major corporation, the black leaders were glad to
have the help of their Friends.

Negotiations with Eastman Kodak

The biggest battle of Alinsky's organizing career took
place in Rochester. When it was over, the IAF was moving in a
new direction and into another decade. It began with a one-
sentence resolution passed by FIGHT's delegates at its second
convention in July 1966. The resolution directed that "Eastman
Kodak be urged to initiate a Step-Up program." The Step-Up
program was a modest employment program developed by the
Xerox Corporation to train hard-core unemployed ghetto resi-

dents for entry-level industrial jobs. Xerox was a Rochester company that was in the midst of its first decade of rapid growth in the manufacturing and leasing of copiers and duplicators.

When Xerox, which was considered something of a maverick in local industrial circles, decided to set up its program to hire and train chronically unemployed persons, Personnel Manager Henry Brenner asked FIGHT for help. An industrial psychologist, Brenner wanted the FIGHT leaders to interpret the job training program to ghetto blacks and send the company likely candidates. He also requested the black leaders to interpret black culture and ghetto problems to Xerox's managers and supervisors. At first Minister Florence was suspicious, ever alert to the Rochester version of Greeks bearing gifts, but he decided to cooperate. The Step-Up program was begun early in 1966 with eighteen trainees recruited by FIGHT and the New York State Employment Service. The program was a success from the start. All but two of the recruits ended up with entry level jobs in Xerox. It made Florence and Chambers wonder if the Xerox program could be duplicated on a larger scale within Rochester's healthy industrial community.

From the beginning of the FIGHT Organization's existence, the leaders recognized that the over-riding local issue was jobs for blacks. In 1966 Rochester industry was advertising for workers in the United States and Canada—10,000 openings for skilled workers was the figure quoted. The city's unemployment was a fraction over one percent.[21] But most blacks did not appear in the statistics. A post-riot report by the Monroe County Human Relations Commission said that unemployment in the black ghettos ranged from 8.6 to 35.9 percent. Added to this was the pervasive problem of underemployment among blacks: "Of the employed males, over forty-two percent were at the bottom of the occupational pyramid, as laborers and service workers. Over fifty-six percent of the females were employed as service and private household workers."[22] Blacks in Rochester wanted a chance for steady, well-paying jobs with good fringe benefits at Kodak, Xerox and Bausch and Lomb.

At its second convention, FIGHT announced that it had received a federal grant to set up and run a jobs center to train unemployed persons for civil service jobs (especially in the U.S. Post Office). Weeks before the center was ready to open, hundreds of black men and women had applied for the program. When the center began operations in September, Florence and the FIGHT leaders felt that the time was right to talk to the top officers in the Eastman Kodak company. In 1966 Kodak, the city's premier industry, employed over 100,000 persons worldwide, and 41,000 Kodak employees lived in Rochester. Twenty-five percent of the families in the metropolitan area had at least one member working for the film products company.

The FIGHT officers met with Kodak President William S. Vaughn and other top executives at the company's headquarters. Florence read a short proposal to the company officers. In it he asked Kodak to set up a job training program for five hundred to six hundred unemployed persons, to be run for an initial eighteen-month period. Like the Xerox Step-Up program, the Kodak trainees would receive regular wages and benefits and, when they completed the training, would be hired in entry-level jobs with the company. FIGHT offered the services of its staff and members of its Employment Committee to help Kodak recruit and counsel the trainees. The FIGHT proposal was simply a copy of the Xerox program, with a larger number of trainees and a target date. The Kodak officials appeared interested, if somewhat ill at ease. Florence and Vaughn scheduled a second meeting. The FIGHT officers left Kodak's corporation offices in high spirits.

To understand what followed, it is necessary to understand the position Kodak held in Rochester. In its annual report for that year, the company reported that its fringe benefit package averaged $3,500 a year for each employee. Generous benefits help explain why no labor union had ever been able to organize Kodak employees. In addition to taking good care of its workers, Kodak also took good care of Rochester. Kodak founder George Eastman and his partners had given Rochester its Memorial Art Gallery, the famed Eastman School of Music, the Eastman Theater—home of the Rochester Philharmonic Orchestra—the Eastman School of Dentistry and many of the campus buildings of the University of Rochester.

Kodak was by far the largest corporation donor to the annual United Community Chest of Rochester. (Local legend has it that the first Community Chest in the United States was founded by Kodak founder George Eastman.) It was this same community-minded company that was now being approached by a little band of black ministers and inner city residents asking for a major revision of the company's training and hiring policies.

At a second meeting on September 14, Kodak and FIGHT exchanged documents—FIGHT's job training proposal and a Kodak statement outlining its present hiring and training program. The atmosphere was friendly and more relaxed. Vaughn told Florence that both documents would be discussed. Florence quipped, "A company which can photograph the other side of the moon ought to be able to mount FIGHT's proposed program." Vaughn suggested further meetings to work out a cooperative arrangement. Florence said that FIGHT was ready to meet the next day. The meeting ended amicably. It turned out, however, to be the last friendly meeting between the top officials of the two organizations for nearly a year.

The problem was that Vaughn decided to turn the subsequent meetings over to a team from Kodak's Industrial Relations Department. These men were authorized to discuss only Kodak's current employment program and how FIGHT could cooperate in it, along with other community groups. Florence kept pressing them to discuss FIGHT's proposal for six hundred on-the-job trainees. The Kodak representatives became increasingly nervous. At one point the Kodak spokesman began a statement with a reference to "You boys. . . ." Minister Florence bristled immediately and told the Kodak team, "Go back to your bosses and get clarification on just what we agreed upon as the target of our discussion."[23]

There were more meetings after that, but it was apparent that the Kodak management had no intention of discussing seriously, much less implementing, the kind of job program FIGHT was talking about. Florence tried to keep the door open with an offer to "refine" FIGHT's proposal in further discussions with Kodak management. Nothing happened, however, until Vaughn sent Florence a letter in which he cut off further discussion of FIGHT's proposal. He said that the black organization was demanding an "exclusive" arrangement (nowhere mentioned in the FIGHT proposal) and that Kodak could not discriminate by granting any outside organization an exclusive or monopolistic arrangement in recruiting, hiring or training Kodak employees.

The Kodak officials never understood what FIGHT was trying to do. They saw the black organization as a potential troublemaker that would try to inject ghetto politics into the internal affairs of the profitable private company. On the other hand, FIGHT saw itself as unique—the "only mass-based organization of poor people and near poor people in Rochester," asking giant Kodak to take a dramatic step to remedy the critical state of black unemployment in the city. Florence argued, "If Kodak leads, others will follow." Kodak didn't understand this or was afraid to deal seriously with FIGHT. In his letter, President Vaughn closed the door firmly on FIGHT. That should have been the end of it, but it wasn't. Kodak management also didn't understand that Alinsky's organizations don't go away. Alinsky told the black leaders that unless FIGHT could get Kodak to reopen serious discussions and agree to increase job opportunities for blacks, the young organization would be seen by the black community as just one more failed hope. It took Kodak a couple of months to realize that it was involved in a "do or die" situation on the part of the FIGHT organization.

The FIGHT-Kodak struggle showed Alinsky at his best. He was in and out of Rochester every couple of weeks. All through the fall the organization's strategy was to keep pressure on Kodak to reopen negotiations with FIGHT on some variation of its proposed job training program for unemployed, unskilled workers, especially ghetto blacks. At the bi-weekly FIGHT meetings Minister Florence reported on Kodak's continued refusal to meet with the black organization's leaders. Florence argued with sweet reasonableness that the city's white leadership had called upon the black leaders after the 1964 riots to take control of the ghetto communities to prevent further disturbances. FIGHT had done just that, Florence said, but if civic peace was to continue, it was necessary to provide stable, good-paying jobs for the hundreds of unemployed, young blacks. "Business as usual," he warned, "will not solve the problems of jobs." FIGHT would not march and demonstrate as black groups were doing around the country, Florence said, but the organization would insist on negotiating what its constituency wanted with the public and private organizations and institutions in the city.

In late October Kodak officials announced that the company had hired an outside firm of employment consultants, the Indianapolis-based Board for Fundamental Education to assist in training about one hundred job applicants and employees. The next morning the FIGHT officers arrived at Kodak's personnel office with a busload of fifty unemployed persons. The local TV news cameras recorded the long line of blacks being turned away after being told by the nervous personnel people that the program was already filled with current employees. Florence reported that night to FIGHT's members: "It's a fraud. It's a trick—an out-and-out public relations con." At Temple B'rith Kodesh on the city's south side, Alinsky told an audience that the move was typical of Kodak management's arrogance and self-righteousness. The company was willing to hire an outside firm, rather than cooperate with the black citizens of Rochester. Later that night, at the Rochester airport, the departing Alinsky was asked by reporters what he thought about Kodak's race relations record. Alinsky sneered, "What have they done? The only contribution Kodak has made to race relations is their invention of color film."

Florence began pressing harder on Kodak. Blacks poured into the FIGHT meetings and overflowed the church meeting halls. A resolution introduced at the next meeting sounded a tougher position: "Between December 1 and December 15 an immediate meeting will be arranged with Kodak, or the brothers will come to break the giant Kodak, and make Rochester the Selma of the North." (Florence was referring to the great marches held in Selma, Alabama, from January to March of 1965, when thousands of blacks and whites marched under the leadership of Nobel Peace Laureate Martin Luther King, Jr.)

Meanwhile, a series of unofficial conversations were in progress between John Mulder, a Kodak assistant vice presi-

dent, and the Reverend Marvin Chandler, the associate director
of the Rochester Area Council of Churches. Mulder was a
respected community leader, the president of the city's Council
of Social Agencies and a member of Third Presbyterian
Church. His wife was an early member of Friends of FIGHT.
He was the assistant general manager of Kodak Park, the
company's main manufacturing center. Mulder and Chandler
agreed that Kodak would have little trouble in implementing
FIGHT's request. The two men went together to talk to Kodak
President Vaughn. As a result of that meeting, talks were
reopened between a new FIGHT team headed by the soft-
spoken Chandler and a Kodak team of production supervisors
led by Mulder. Vaughn told Chandler and several FIGHT
officials that he was turning the entire matter over to Mr.
Mulder and, according to Chandler, the Kodak president expressed his confidence that Mulder had "some program ideas
he was certain we would find helpful."[24]

On the following Monday, the FIGHT and Kodak negotiators met at a downtown motel. For two days the two sides met
and worked out an agreement. They agreed that there was no
question of an "exclusive arrangement" with FIGHT, a point
the company had raised earlier. FIGHT agreed also to a flexible position on the number of trainees, depending on economic
contingencies. The eighteen-month target date in FIGHT's
proposal was discussed at length. Chandler recalled that it was
one of the Kodak officials who said, "If I were one of the people
we're talking about, I would want to feel that my name would
be at least considered within a specified time period. It would
give me hope." Both sides agreed finally on a twenty-four
month target for the initial program.

Chandler said that he borrowed a typewriter from the
motel office and typed out a statement that reflected the agreement reached by both sides. Before Mulder signed, Florence
asked him if he had the authority to sign the agreement for
Kodak. When Mulder said that he was authorized, he and
Florence signed the document, which became known as the
"December 20 Agreement." It was 2:00 P.M. At 4:00 P.M. the
same day, FIGHT held a news conference and announced that
an agreement had been reached with Kodak. Mulder confirmed

the announcement.[25] The next morning's *Democrat & Chronicle* quoted John Mulder as praising the "objectivity and sincerity with which the FIGHT negotiators approached this matter." He said that the sessions had been a "very enjoyable and revealing experience." In his turn, Minister Florence praised Kodak for its "vision" and said that the agreement "points the way to other industries in this community." That night FIGHT's store-front headquarters overflowed with well-wishers. Christmas was only a few days away. Florence said that Christmas 1966 would be a feast of hope for Rochester's unemployed black citizens.

On State Street, however, at Kodak's executive offices a different mood prevailed. Louis K. Eilers, the man who would become Kodak's new president in two days, was furious when he heard the news of the pact with FIGHT. He sent for John Mulder and, according to a newspaper account, "expressed the greatest displeasure" that Mulder had signed anything. Unfortunately for Mulder, Vaughn was out of town. After dressing down Mulder, Eilers called a meeting of the company's executive committee. The officers voted to abrogate the document as unauthorized by Kodak management. Mulder's job was in grave jeopardy after that meeting.

On December 22 the full board of directors of the Eastman Kodak Company met to elect Eilers company president. The directors voted also not to honor the December 20 Agreement. Eilers waited until the company's statement was released to the newspapers before he told Mulder of Kodak's decision. The Kodak announcement was terse: "The person who signed the papers did not have the authority to make an agreement. The company regrets any misunderstanding."[26]

That evening a crushed John Mulder went to Marvin Chandler's home where the FIGHT officers were gathered for a celebration. With tears in his eyes Mulder told Chandler and the others about the company's action. Florence called Eilers at his home for an explanation of the move, but his wife said that the Kodak president could not be disturbed. Together Mulder and the FIGHT officers watched the eleven o'clock newscast. Kodak's cancellation of the agreement with FIGHT was the lead story.

The black community was thrown into consternation by the news. The FIGHT leaders were shattered after their months of patient negotiation with Kodak. Late that night Chambers recalled that a dejected Minister Florence came to his apartment. He was ready to quit. Chambers talked to the FIGHT president all night. By morning Florence had recovered and was ready to take up the fight. At dawn the two men went to the FIGHT office and began calling the organization's clergy supporters. Later in the morning, at a meeting at Florence's church, the FIGHT president asked the priests and ministers to take up Kodak's action in breaking the jobs agreement within the context of their Christmas sermons. It was time, he said, for a new strategy and tougher tactics.

This FIGHT-Kodak controversy deserves study as a detailed example of Alinsky's use of conflict in an organizing situation. FIGHT did not start out to use tough tactics, make harsh demands, or set up demonstrations. During the months when the talks were stalled, Florence told the Rochester community repeatedly that FIGHT's demonstrations were not to be looked for in the streets, but at its regular meetings and annual conventions. The FIGHT organization was not a bunch of black protesters, he said; it was a mass organization representing—as no other group could do—the city's growing black community. What Alinsky looked for when a new organization like FIGHT was ready to take on a major campaign was a community situation that could be made to yield maximum advantage to the organization. The main issue in Rochester's black community was the need for jobs in a city that was advertising all over the Northeast for skilled workers. At the same time FIGHT wanted recognition by Rochester's power structure as the only organized power bloc within the city's black community. FIGHT, therefore, made a straightforward bid to negotiate a job training program with the top industrial power in the area. Kodak was the acknowledged leader in Rochester industry. What FIGHT did was eminently reasonable. The black leaders asked the film company to act in terms of Kodak's publicly stated policy toward minority hirings, cooperate with FIGHT ("the only mass-based organization of poor people and near poor people in Rochester"), and take this dramatic step in reducing ghetto unemployment and its attendant despair. In so doing, FIGHT was recognizing Kodak's unique place in Rochester's power structure: "If Kodak leads, the others will follow." When Kodak turned its back on FIGHT, therefore, it was not the end of the battle; it was only the beginning.

After the "Christmas Massacre," Alinsky came to Rochester. He, Chambers and Florence laid out a FIGHT-Kodak battle plan that was a rematch of the biblical struggle of David and Goliath. The main objective was not to let the Kodak officials retreat into the executive suite where they could ignore FIGHT and wait for public opinion to bury the pesky black organization. Eilers met with the FIGHT officers once more, but it was strictly pro forma—he was surrounded by the company's attorneys. He was not moved to further discussion, even when Florence offered to scrap the agreement and start over. A second meeting was canceled by Eilers. Instead, Kodak published a two-page advertisement in the local newspapers which gave the company's side of the dispute. It repeated the charge that FIGHT was demanding an exclusive arrangement and outlined Kodak's "Five Point Plan" for minority hiring which was merely a rehash of company programs already in effect. The ad was a not-so-subtle appeal for support from the city's majority community.

The churches began to feel a backlash from those who were opposed to Alinsky and to FIGHT's war against Kodak. The Council of Churches lost about $20,000 of its budget. The Board for Urban Ministry found itself with a tough fight to raise a third year's budget for FIGHT. Not only were the churches involved in the controversy, but families and old friends all over the city found themselves in heated arguments over the merits of the Kodak-FIGHT dispute. The newspaper in which the Kodak ad appeared carried a tragic story about the suicide of a local minister. The Rev. Lee Beynon, pastor of the well-to-do First Baptist Church, had hanged himself in his church's basement. Beynon had been the president of the Council of Churches when it voted to bring Alinsky to Rochester. Since then he had been under constant pressure from some members of his congregation who were bitterly opposed to

FIGHT. When the Kodak-FIGHT controversy began to heat up, Beynon and his family started receiving threatening phone calls at all hours. The pressure and worry proved too much for the kindly and sensitive pastor.

FIGHT gathered its network of allies for a long campaign. The Friends of FIGHT and the Board for Urban Ministry members went out every night and on weekends to carry FIGHT's side of the story to white church groups and civic organizations. Friends of FIGHT published a newsletter to keep its influential membership up to date on what was happening. This community-wide communications network worked with great efficiency all through the Kodak-FIGHT battle.

Bishop Sheen Arrives

Just before Christmas, FIGHT found a new ally in the person of Bishop Fulton J. Sheen, an international radio and television luminary. Sheen came to Rochester to replace the aged Bishop Kearney as bishop of the Catholic diocese. Sheen was well known for his money raising efforts on behalf of the world's poor in his previous post as the director of the U.S. Catholic Society for the Propagation of the Faith. Within a week of his installation as Bishop of Rochester, Sheen granted an audience to the FIGHT officers. He listened intently to Florence's description of black unemployment and what FIGHT was asking Kodak to do. The bishop promised to do whatever he could to assist them. Before they left, Florence presented Sheen with a black and white FIGHT button. After that, visitors to Sheen's office noted the FIGHT button that rested prominently at the foot of the crucifix on his desk.

A few days after Kodak overturned its agreement with FIGHT, Bishop Sheen announced his first staff appointment. P. David Finks, a young priest from a ghetto parish, was appointed to a new "cabinet level" position as Vicar for Urban Ministry. The priest was one of the few white members of FIGHT. The morning Sheen announced the appointment he invited the FIGHT leaders to the chancery office to hear the news first-hand. The announcement was dramatic, in the Sheen style: "The ancient Exodus has become modern, a flight from and a flight to. The result of a crowd straining to get in, and another crowd stumbling to get out, produces what might be called the inner city. As I look at it, I can see Christ weeping over it as he once wept over the inner city of Jerusalem." The bishop made reference to the contemporary mission of the Church: "to participate in Christ's sufferings in the world, and to have even a kind of lover's quarrel with those members who would not feel the pain of the stripes on the backs of others."[27]

According to Sheen's announcement, the newly appointed vicar was to be his personal delegate, vested with full authority in dealing with problems of the inner city—"housing, education, employment, health, social justice, equality and the sharing of the common heritages of American well-being and Christian civilization." Sheen concluded by saying that this, his first appointment as the Bishop of Rochester, was evidence of his "sweet impatience to serve those who are most in need." The FIGHT officers were delighted with the bishop and his new vicar.

After lunch Bishop Sheen and the Vicar for Urban Ministry walked the half-mile from the chancery to the headquarters of the Gannett Company, Inc., the owner of Rochester's two daily newspapers. He was ushered up to the offices of Paul Miller, the president of Gannett, publisher of the Rochester newspapers and president of the Associated Press. Assembled in Miller's office were the top executives and the editors of the Rochester *Democrat & Chronicle* and the *Times-Union*. Sheen repeated his announcement, introduced the new vicar and offered to answer questions about the new post. After a short exchange of pleasantries, Sheen waved off Miller's offer of a limousine to return him to the chancery. The bishop flashed his telegenic smile and swept out, leaving the Gannett executives somewhat overcome. It was a warm and flawless performance.

The next morning the news of Sheen's appointment was carried on the front page of the *New York Times* (the headlines read: "Sheen Appoints a Vicar for Poor"; "Sheen Names Critic of Kodak as Vicar"). The timing was providential for FIGHT. Within twenty-four hours the national news media began arriving in Rochester to tell the David and Goliath story of FIGHT and Kodak to the rest of the world.

A week later Bishop Sheen spoke at the annual dinner of the Rochester Chamber of Commerce. It was his first civic appearance in his new diocese. All the city's leading figures were in attendance. The Eastman Kodak delegation was led by William S. Vaughn, the Chairman of the Board. In his colorful style Sheen talked about tensions in community in which the "principals may be abrasive, but their principles are holy and on God's side." He did not mention FIGHT or Kodak by name, but praised Rochester's technical excellence: "Look what we do: We help clothe the world; we photograph the world; we make precise the imprecisions of the rest of the world; we multiply copies for the offices of the world; we help teach the world music; we help cure the sicknesses of the world. . . . There is not a single problem in the technological field which we cannot solve." Sheen ended by describing the city as a beautiful woman whose beauty is marred by a pimple on her nose. "The whole world is looking (at her)," he said. "The searchlight in on the blemish. . . . If we just put our heads together . . . we could wipe out the blemish on our nose in two years." His message to the Rochester leaders was clearly understood, if not universally appreciated. The following Sunday morning Kodak's Vaughn was asked by his pastor (a FIGHT supporter) how he was feeling. Vaughn answered dryly: "I'm feeling well, except for this pimple on my nose."

As Rochester's long, cold winter settled in the FIGHT leaders began practicing the art of what Alinsky called "mass political jujitsu," a series of hit-and-run guerrilla tactics intended to goad giant Kodak into attacking tiny FIGHT. Alinsky's use of non-violent (at least, on the part of the community organization) guerrilla tactics was a key element of his organizing approach. He gave credit for these basic "rules" of urban combat to his old organizing mentor, John L. Lewis. The genius of these tactics was their capacity to force the enemy into hurting himself with his own superior strength. FIGHT could not hurt Kodak in Rochester, but it could bait the company into reacting in such a way that it hurt and embarrassed itself before the worldwide audience of its customers.

Bishop Sheen was the immediate key to the news media (Alinsky, too, was always good copy). Once he gave his support to FIGHT's cause, the national press and television reporters came to town to cover the Kodak-FIGHT-Sheen-Alinsky story. Kodak, used to a favorable press and unused to controversy, played its part well. When the national journalists came to interview Kodak's new president (Florence referred to him as "Doc" Eilers), he sat in his luxurious office, surrounded by the trappings of corporate power, and complained about FIGHT's drive for power and its war against community institutions. The reporters had just come from an interview with Minister Florence in his cold, drafty storefront office where they had to sit on folding chairs borrowed from a church. The reporters did not miss the contradictions involved in the two organizations. The black organization's underdog status came across with special clarity on the evening TV news. Eilers' most telling slip came when he referred to Kodak's "Five Point Plan" as the "white hope for Rochester" (one national magazine entitled its article critical of Kodak, "White Hope for Rochester").

According to the company's statistics, Kodak had 1,200 to 1,500 black employees. For the next couple of days, *New York Times* reporter John Kifner and the *New Republic*'s James Ridgeway stationed themselves at the doors of Kodak's buildings at closing time and counted black faces. They found few. Nicholas von Hoffman, the former IAF organizer who was now a reporter for the *Washington Post*, wrote a description of the FIGHT-Kodak impasse that poked fun at the machinations of the photographic products company ("Picture's Fuzzy as Kodak Fights FIGHT"). When CBS and NBC news crews came to town, FIGHT and its friends staged a series of media events to keep the networks supplied with pictures. A rally was held at FIGHT's Job Training Center, one block from the ghetto street corner where the riots began a year and a half before. The crowd was large, noisy and good-natured. The black ministers took turns preaching, "telling it like it is."

Before introducing his special guest, Minister Florence reminded the crowd of the serious nature of the struggle. He said that Kodak and its local allies were out to destroy FIGHT and the Council of Churches and "all with the backbone to stand up against white paternalism." Then he introduced Stokely Carmichael, the youthful head of SNCC (the Student Non-Violent Coordinating Committee). Carmichael, slim and smiling, promised a black boycott of Kodak products across the country. He set the crowd laughing and cheering when he prophesied: "When we're through, Kodak will see him (pointing to Florence), and he'll say 'Jump,' and they'll say, 'How high?' "

At high noon the next day, well-dressed white pickets, calling themselves "Laymen in Support of Involved Clergy," marched in front of the executive offices of the Gannett Company which owned Rochester's two daily newspapers and a local radio and TV station. Their picket signs and the interviews they gave to reporters made clear the connection between Gannett publisher Paul Miller's editorial attacks on activist clergy and Kodak's breaking the jobs agreement with FIGHT. An hour later, still in time for the evening news, student pickets marched in front of the offices of University of Rochester President W. Allen Wallis, a Kodak director and an outspoken critic of FIGHT. Still later, NBC News followed the new Catholic vicar on a walking tour of the riot-scarred Third Ward.

The Council of Churches chose this opportunity to run a full-page advertisement in the local newspapers that supported FIGHT's position. Under the title "Can Kodak and FIGHT Agree?" the Council said: "Because we feel that the December 20 Agreement embodies a sound, creative program which would be beneficial to the whole community, we urge FIGHT to endorse and support Kodak's existing programs and we urge Kodak to endorse and support FIGHT's proposal to reach the hard core unemployed." It carried the full text of the disputed agreement, something Rochesterians had not seen. The text showed that Kodak's charges that FIGHT demanded an exclusive arrangement or a takeover of management prerogatives were patently false. As soon as the ad appeared, the attacks on the churches began anew. Three directors of the Council of Churches resigned, two of whom were Kodak employees. In the midst of this latest controversy, Rochester's "grande dame," Mrs. Harper Sibley, Sr. (her home was the meeting place of the church caucus during the 1964 riots), was elected president of the Rochester Area Council of Churches ("I believe," she said in accepting the battle-scarred mantle, "in the good faith of the different people involved no matter how much they disagree").

Another weapon Alinsky wielded in this kind of a community struggle was laughter. "Your opponents can put up with a lot of brickbats," he said, "but they can't stand being laughed at." He was beloved of reporters because of his always quotable remarks. When they asked him for his reactions to personal criticisms made by University of Rochester President Wallis (ex-head of the University of Chicago's Business School), Alinsky pretended to confuse Rochester's Wallis with Alabama Governor George Wallace (at that time a national symbol of resistance to desegregation). When the reporters corrected him, Alinsky smiled and said, "Well, I guess there isn't much difference."

Minister Florence was an apt pupil of the man he called the "master stratetician." In his speeches the FIGHT president began making ominous references to what FIGHT might do if Kodak remained intransigent. His threats of outrageous demonstrations were directed as much at keeping up the courage of the black community as they were meant to disturb and anger the white community. When a number of black families were made homeless by ghetto fires, Florence suggested that FIGHT take them for temporary shelter to the George Eastman House (the Kodak founder's mansion had been turned into a photographic museum and library). "You know the place," Florence told the delighted crowd, "the shrine, where the master lived and slept."

Another threatened action against George Eastman's legacy shocked the sensibilities of almost everyone. It was a measure of how powerful they thought FIGHT was that Rochesterians took this threat seriously. It was based on another Alinsky principle: "It is not how much power you have as what they think you have. . . ." FIGHT spread a rumor that the organization was planning on buying a large block of tickets for a concert of the Rochester Philharmonic Orchestra at the Eastman Theater. Before the concert, FIGHT would gather up a crowd of blacks and feed them a gigantic dinner of beans— with obvious results during the performance. The "Bean Concert" was never carried out, but FIGHT's people laughed for weeks over all the possibilities of Smugtown's elite suffering the terrors of a black "Stink-In."

The spring offensive in Rochester was a good example of Alinsky's populist political genius. He taught his organizations that, in a democracy like the United States, citizens working together can invent an almost infinite number of outrageous and effective tactics, all perfectly legal (e.g., bean dinners and attending symphony concerts), aimed at bringing an opponent to the bargaining table. His long experience showed him that nothing glues people together for a fight like shared laughter in the face of the enemy and the deflating arrows of calculated impoliteness. Nothing confuses power wielders, Saul taught, like a group that can move outside the enemy's experience with an array of unexpected tactics. Alinsky's critics never really understood this kind of non-violent, decidedly controversial brand of guerrilla warfare.

A Proxy Campaign

In Rochester, however, as spring approached it was clear to Alinsky, Chambers and the FIGHT leaders that, despite Kodak's annoyance at FIGHT's importunity, the company was capable of sitting out the siege behind its public relations Maginot Line. Some way had to be found to bring pressure on Kodak from outside Rochester. Sometime earlier, Chambers had raised with Florence the idea of FIGHT's purchasing a few shares of Kodak stock so that its officers could bring their case against the company in person at its annual stockholders' meeting.

A few weeks later, Herb White and other church leaders were talking about Kodak's intransigent stand. Suddenly Third

Church's Eugene Tennis suggested a proxy fight. White liked the idea: "What could be more in keeping with the American way?" They began tossing the idea around: "How about a national proxy campaign? Churches, national denominational bodies and sympathetic individuals could sign over their proxies to FIGHT and come to the Kodak meeting to back FIGHT's cause." The idea grew. They could see the drama in Minister Florence's standing up before Kodak management and directors armed with thousands of proxy votes and demanding that the company honor its signed agreement with the black community.

At the same time, Alinsky was in Chicago preparing a speech for the annual meeting of the Unitarian-Universalist Association in Denver. He said that the idea of a proxy battle for FIGHT just popped into his head, and he decided to try out the idea on the Unitarians. The church delegates liked the idea; they agreed to sign over their proxies to FIGHT and promised to send a delegation to Kodak's annual meeting in April. Their favorable reaction got Alinsky's juices going. On the plane back to Chicago, he began spinning out the implications of the major church denominations, most of whom had large institutional holdings of Kodak stock, all joining in a national proxy campaign against Kodak. The papers would love it. He was not interested in trying for a company takeover or even in running a couple of insurgents for the board of directors. What Saul wanted was a national uprising of Kodak shareholders on behalf of FIGHT's program of jobs for blacks. That was the kind of publicity, he figured, that would scare the hell out of Kodak.

Alinsky returned to Rochester to discuss with FIGHT his plan to address the church meetings. He was surprised to find them discussing a proxy fight. Saul told the leaders that the theme of his one-man lobby was, "Save your sermons; give us your proxies." FIGHT told him that their annual meeting strategy was to be called "Focus on Flemington," after the little town in New Jersey where Eastman Kodak was incorporated and held its annual stockholders' meeting. The campaign came together quickly. FIGHT and Friends of FIGHT sent out a letter to the church denominational bodies, asking them to join FIGHT's "Focus on Flemington." The letter stressed the nature of the Kodak struggle: "The morality of the issue is directly to the point for Christian churches who wish to champion the cause of the poor, who must lead the nation in its confused and halting search for constructive solutions to the problems of poverty and racial discrimination." Alinsky went on the road for the next four weeks to visit the national church bodies on behalf of the proxy campaign.

Alinsky was in high spirits. Within a week he had talked to Robert Kennedy, who was then the junior U.S. Senator from New York. Kennedy promised to do what he could to put pressure on Kodak from Washington. Saul had visions of Washington hearings and Congressional investigators looking into Kodak's affairs. The more he thought about the stock proxy battle, the better he liked it. All kinds of citizens' groups could use it to deal with corporations—environmentalists, consumers, union members, anti-war groups. The development of the stock proxy tactic in the FIGHT-Kodak stand-off is a good example of how Alinsky and his organizers planned their strategy and tactics. There was no master plan that could be made to fit different situations. New tactics came out of the everyday action. People sat around, usually late at night, over a pot of coffee or a drink, and they discussed the issue at hand. Then somebody would say, "How about this idea?" The others would add details to the plan or reject it. The plan began to develop. The leaders tried it out at the next day's regular staff meeting. Enthusiasm grew. People discussed it. The opponents heard rumors and saw hints of a new campaign in the news stories. The enemy knew that the organization was cranking up another attack, but they didn't know the details. So they began to worry. The stage was set for overreaction. The elephant might trample down the jungle, trying to get the mouse. Good citizen organizations operate this way. It's exciting, fun and sometimes dangerous. When Alinsky was running the show, it was also completely legal.

As April 25, the day of Kodak's annual meeting, drew closer, proxies began to pour into FIGHT headquarters. When Florence tried to get a list of Kodak stockholders from the company's office in Flemington (something he was entitled to according to New Jersey law), he was turned down. FIGHT brought suit against the company for withholding the lists from a legitimate stockholder. By the time of the Flemington meeting, FIGHT and its supporters were prepared to turn it into a giant media event.

The weather was perfect on April 25—a Kodacolor day of bright blue skies, scudding white clouds, and rolling green hills that framed the Hunterdon County High School where the stockholders gathered. The FIGHT contingent rode overnight from Rochester in a convoy of eight chartered buses. Other delegations arrived in Flemington from Eastern universities and from black communities in New Jersey, New York and Pennsylvania. The protesters were greeted by more than a hundred New Jersey State Police, on hand in force to protect the peace.

A few minutes before the Kodak meeting began, Minister Florence led a small FIGHT delegation into the school auditorium. About forty Friends of FIGHT shareholders were already dispersed throughout the audience. As soon as Kodak Chairman William S. Vaughn called the meeting to order, Minister Florence rose to his feet and, in his trombone voice, demanded to know from the Board of Directors, "Are you going to honor the December 20 Agreement with FIGHT? Are you going to keep your word with the poor?"

The packed audience of well-heeled Kodak shareholders and employees shouted for the security guards to throw out Florence and his band. The FIGHT president held his ground as the crowd roared, and Chairman Vaughn ruled him out of order. Florence was told that he would be allowed his turn to speak during the question period at the end of the meeting. "No!" shouted Florence. "We will give you until 2 P.M. to honor that agreement." He signaled to FIGHT's supporters, who rose from their seats all over the hall and filed out. The all-white crowd accompanied the walk-out with boos, catcalls and rude gestures.

Outside the auditorium Florence and the others joined the eight hundred picketers who were marching silently in front of the high school building. They carried freshly painted signs prepared that morning in the basement of a nearby church ("Kodak Snaps Shutter on Negroes," "Kodak Underexposes

600 Black People," "Kodak Is Out of Focus"). As soon as reporters and TV crews, who followed FIGHT out of the auditorium, were in place with their equipment, Florence led the crowd to a large flatbed truck parked near the auditorium. To the cheering crowd Florence gave a blow-by-blow description of what had transpired inside the meeting and told them he would return at 2 P.M. for Kodak's answer. Fruit punch and bologna sandwiches were passed out to the large crowd. People found shady spots on the lawn and settled down in small groups to eat the spartan lunch and wait for the drama's next act. Except for the watching State Troopers and Kodak security guards, the scene looked like a school picnic.

At precisely 2 P.M. the FIGHT officials re-entered the auditorium to receive Kodak's answer. The reporters trooped back into the meeting with them. Florence marched to the front of the hall and asked Vaughn again, "Are you going to honor the agreement? Yes or no?" Vaughn's answer was subdued, "No, sir, we are not." Florence and the FIGHT delegation turned and walked out to a renewed chorus of boos from the audience. To the waiting crowd of FIGHT's supporters, Florence said: "Racial war has been declared on black communities by Kodak. If it's war they want, war they'll get." Then Florence announced to the crowd and to the national news audience that FIGHT was calling a massive meeting in ten days that would bring together church and civil rights organizations to plan this war on Kodak. He described a massive pilgrimage to be held in Rochester in July: "On the anniversary of Rochester's riots," Florence thundered, "thousands of people will process down State Street to Kodak's headquarters, and we will hold a candlelight prayer service to show the feelings of the nation's poor about companies which don't honor their agreements." Back in Rochester, the picture of Florence on the evening news, delivering his chilling message, threw the whole community into a nervous tizzy.

In May John Mulder was dropped quietly from the Kodak Board of Directors and stripped of his company vice presidency. The story that circulated at the time was that Eilers had fired Mulder for signing the agreement, but Mulder refused to accept dismissal, and Vaughn came to his defense. Mulder remained in his position as assistant general manager of the Kodak Park Works until his retirement from the company in 1974. John Mulder has chosen to remain silent about what happened in the aftermath of the agreement with FIGHT. But subsequent events showed that Mulder did the right thing. As IAF's Ed Chambers said later: "Mulder was authorized. That's for sure. Otherwise, they would have fired him and taken away all his benefits. Kodak doesn't fool around."

The tension in Rochester grew as FIGHT's June convention neared, with the promised July 24 national pilgrimage soon to follow. At this time Alinsky reported to the FBI that someone had broken into his Chicago office and his home in Carmel and had stolen a number of his personal papers. In Rochester Florence received threatening phone calls. Even the Kodak officials began to see that an honorable settlement was a necessity. The Flemington demonstration and Alinsky's pledge to continue the proxy fight convinced the company that the FIGHT organization was a formidable foe.

A few weeks later, in a series of secret negotiations, Kodak and FIGHT made peace. The negotiator who brought the two sides together was Harvard Professor Daniel Patrick Moynihan (now U.S. Senator from New York). Moynihan knew Alinsky and admired him. A close friend of Moynihan's was L. Story Zartman, a member of Kodak's legal department. Zartman asked Moynihan to bring the two sides together. Moynihan was able to convince the company officials of Alinsky's integrity and set the stage for a resolution of the long struggle.

A Community Celebration

At FIGHT's third annual convention in June, Florence strode to the podium to the cheers and applause of the packed convention hall. For the last two days the "ghetto telegraph" had been saying that Kodak had made peace with FIGHT. Florence's opening words brought the cheering delegates to their feet, "We spell black power in Rochester with capital letters—F.I.G.H.T." He held up a telegram and said that its message was the business of the convention. Then he called upon the Rev. Marvin Chandler, FIGHT's chief negotiator, and asked him to read the telegram from Kodak President Louis K. Eilers. When Chandler came to the part where Eilers said, "Kodak recognizes that FIGHT, as a broad-based community organization, speaks in behalf of the basic needs and aspirations of the Negro poor in the Rochester area," the audience cheered for some minutes.

When the smiling Chandler finished reading the telegram, Minister Florence added his postscript. "We have a deal for jobs," he declaimed in his best preacher's style. "We have a new relationship. We have an understanding." Here he paused, then chuckled softly as he continued. "I just have to say it—we have an *agreement*." The delegates cheered. He concluded, "When people make up their minds to be persistent, results can be had. And FIGHT has results." Later that night he told a reporter what the two-year-old FIGHT organization had achieved: "Black men and women today can walk taller in this community."

The conclusion of the FIGHT-Kodak pact marked the end of the organizing phase of the black organization. It had won a major community battle and, with that victory, the recognition by the city that the organized black community was a force to be reckoned with in Rochester. Chambers, Alinsky's organizer, stayed with FIGHT until the end of the year. The organization used its hard-won power to set up new housing and economic development programs for the black community. The most interesting of these programs was the establishment of a small, community-owned machine tool factory—FIGHTON, Inc., in which black young people would get experience in industrial management and supervisory responsibilities. The Xerox Corporation provided a team of executive, engineering and marketing experts to develop FIGHTON, Inc. Friends of FIGHT donated its legal and business expertise to the new FIGHT venture. That organization, now that FIGHT did not need the full-time services of Friends, began developing an organization of middle-class whites, with an agenda of issues affecting the whole of metropolitan Rochester.

Once the long and bitter Kodak campaign was done, however, the church coalition that had held together for three years

to support FIGHT began to unravel like an old sweater. Shortly after the Flemington meeting, the Council of Churches'
officials broke with FIGHT and its own offspring, the Board
for Urban Ministry, over their opposition to Florence's threat
of a national demonstration in Rochester on the anniversary of
the 1964 riots. The Council of Churches leaders said they were
afraid that the pilgrimage "would lead only to a dead end,
attended by many risks." This weakening of the united front of
the Protestant churches was not as serious a blow to FIGHT's
cause as it would have been earlier—before Flemington or
before the money had been collected for a third year of
FIGHT's support. In addition, the Catholic diocese was now
fully represented in the church caucus in the person of Bishop
Sheen's urban vicar.

During that summer the Catholic and Protestant agencies
formed a new ecumenical entity, the Joint Office for Urban
Ministry, on Rochester's Main Street, midway between the
Third and Seventh Ward ghettos. It was the first such ecumenical agency in the United States. As FIGHT and Friends
of FIGHT continued to grow and become self-sufficient, the
urban ministry leaders were free to assist other local city and
suburban communities now interested in organizing themselves. The success of this ecumenical venture in black and
white community building brought one pastor to observe that
the Church's problem was probably "under-utilization" in social action, rather than the over-utilization so often charged by
its critics.

The Rev. Herbert D. White, who led the Board for Urban
Ministry all through this period, looked back at these events a
few years later. "I think you can say that from October 1964 to
roughly Flemington in April 1967, the organized Church really
did stand up over and against the surrounding culture." He
went on to say that it was all done by an amazingly few people,
with small influence and less money (the $135,000 raised by the
churches to hire Alinsky and support the black organization
for three years was a minute fraction of the millions of dollars
spent locally on the anti-poverty programs, most of which
vanished without a trace). White summed it up, "All of this (the
reorganizing of the black community and its fight for recogni-

tion and jobs) was initiated by non-power-structure community people, a few clergy and lay persons who were sophisticated
enough to operate within church structures, but not very sophisticated about how to operate in other kinds of structures.
They did it. And it was done by good old solid American civic-
minded citizens—nobody with a hell of a lot of power—and by
a bunch of blacks. Talk about the private sector. I think that
Rochester is the prime example of what the unmonied voluntary sector can do—if it wants to."[28]

On the tenth anniversary of the Rochester riots, William
S. Vaughn, now retired from Kodak, looked back on that time
of civic crisis. Vaughn quoted Shakespeare's line about the
sweet uses of adversity; then he said, "I've got to give credit to
FIGHT and those people not only for propelling us, projecting
us or shoving us into a more acute realization of the problem—
even though they overdramatized it—but in getting us to do
something at an early stage." Of Alinsky and his organizing
methods, Vaughn still had reservations, but not as many as one
might think. He concluded his retrospection with these words,
"Maybe that's what it took in those days, however much I
abhor the methods and methodology of Alinsky and his gang.
... In certain situations, maybe that's the only way to get
things done."[29]

In the mid-1970's, however, the FIGHT organization died
a lingering death. "Natural causes" was the coroner's verdict—
weak heart, poor circulation and hardened arteries. How did it
happen?

In June 1969, at its fifth annual convention, FIGHT was at
the height of its powers. That night Minister Florence reported
to the membership on FIGHT's burgeoning program of economic development—the FIGHT housing project, the
FIGHTON Corporation, increased black employment, a
FIGHT-sponsored plan for redevelopment of the ghetto areas.
At the same meeting Florence lost the election for the FIGHT
presidency to a twenty-seven year old insurgent named Bernard J. Gifford. Florence was shocked and angry. The election
touched off a bitter internal battle between Florence and Gifford for control of the organization. FIGHT never recovered.

Gifford had been a staff director under Florence for a little over a year. He felt that he had been cut out of much of the action by Florence, so he formed a coalition of insurgents and won the election. Minister Florence, busy putting together the economic development program, ignored Gifford's bid for leadership until it was too late. In his zeal Florence had forgotten the basic rule of politics: "The first priority is always to get re-elected."

Even after the election furor receded, Gifford refused to allow Florence and his supporters any role in the organization. He could not move beyond his campaign oratory about severing all ties with Alinsky and Florence. His supporters were mostly younger blacks who were attracted to FIGHT by its economic successes but had played no part in its early struggles. After the election, Alinsky wrote a long friendly letter to Gifford in which he urged him to continue working with Florence. Even though Saul was upset by Gifford's attacks on him, the letter was respectful and conciliatory. He warned the young FIGHT president that he needed strong allies because many of his new supporters were, in Alinsky's words, "a species of political parasite who live off their people to even a more pernicious degree than slum landlords and other racist exploiters; they are the ones who use their color for personal capital gain and go to the white establishment to get high salaried jobs on the basis of their 'connections and influence' with a mass based organization such as FIGHT." Saul encouraged Gifford to initiate a "delousing period" to get rid of these parasites before the people of the community "turn away in disillusionment and despair from all the hopes which they had in the FIGHT Organization."[30]

But Gifford refused Alinsky's advice. He continued his war against Minister Florence and purged the organization instead of any lingering contacts with Alinsky or the urban ministry groups who sponsored FIGHT. In so doing, he lost much of the political capital Florence had built up. Gifford soon found himself saddled with the administration of the various FIGHT projects begun by Florence. The well-dressed, articulate Gifford had the makings of a good leader. Rochester liked him. "He's not like that loud-mouthed Florence," people said. But in dumping Florence, Gifford lost the best of the FIGHT leadership.

After two years, Gifford left FIGHT and Rochester for greener pastures. His successor as FIGHT's president was the Rev. Raymond Scott, once Minister Florence's assistant at the Reynold's Street Church of Christ. Without Gifford's leadership ability, Scott was soon left with only a handful of noisy young activists and the continuing vendetta against Florence. The once proud FIGHT organization had become another minuscule protest group. Its demise, when it came in the mid-1970's, was a blessing.

A few months before Alinsky died, one of the Rochester urban ministers asked him if he was ever discouraged when organizations like FIGHT failed to live up to their early promise. Saul gave his well-known scowl of exasperation and said, "Why is it you damn Christians never seem to have any faith?" Then he became serious, "Look, Father, what do you expect? FIGHT is alive. It can begin to grow again if the people want. There is a convention every year—if anyone wants to change leaders or policies or both. That's the way the democratic process works—a few steps forward, maybe only one back, if you're lucky." After a pause, he went on, "Look how Rochester has changed. Not as much as you'd like, sure, but what were the alternatives?"[31]

In the early 1970's Rochester, the former Smugtown—USA, was described in a Brookings Institution study as among the most organized cities in the nation.[32] In less than a decade over one hundred citizens' organizations and neighborhood associations had flowered. The study gave much of the credit for this surge of citizen participation to Alinsky and FIGHT. The researchers forgot the part played by the churches, but their point was correct. Another outgrowth of the Alinsky-Church-FIGHT era was the influence of grassroots organizing on the political picture of the city. Two young Republican city councilmen were the first politicians to understand what the new mood of citizen organization could mean for city government. Before they could convince their fellow Republicans, however, along came a group of young dissidents who took over the sleepy Democratic county organization. A couple of young hopefuls, who had cut their political teeth in Friends of FIGHT, gathered a few more restless Rochesterians and began reorganizing the local Democratic Party. Within four years they controlled not only the party, but City Hall as well.

Of course the city of Rochester still has many problems. Democracy doesn't solve all problems. Like most U.S. cities, metropolitan Rochester is torn by stupid city-suburban struggles over taxes and services, and a new generation of powerless blacks needs to organize a new FIGHT. But whatever its problems, the city is no longer the Smugtown of the 1950's slowly rocking itself to death in arteriosclerotic splendor. Rochesterians know how to get things done if and when they decide the struggle is worth the effort. Herb White, who has continued to organize cities, said later, "Rochester is different than it was in 1964 . . . because the whole damn place is organized on community levels."[33]

After Rochester, the turbulent 1960's were almost over. Changes were coming. Alinsky, sensitive to the signs of the times, was already making plans to refit the IAF and broaden its organizing focus for the 1970's.

7.

New Directions

IAF's Training Institute

After the IAF's project in Rochester was completed in late 1967, Alinsky called Ed Chambers back to Chicago. Saul had plans for a new IAF venture, and he wanted Chambers to direct it. Richard Harmon, his only other organizer in the field, was told to complete IAF's contract with the BUILD Organization in Buffalo and then return to Chicago. There would be no further organizing projects, Alinsky announced, until after IAF graduated the first class of organizers from the new IAF Training Institute.

Saul Alinsky, nearing his sixtieth birthday, was preparing a new metamorphosis. John Kifner described the professional organizer as he appeared at this period: "Like some wandering Jewish Robin Hood, Saul D. Alinsky ... has spent the last quarter century merrily goading politicians, businessmen, religious figures, well-meaning liberals and other agents of the 'Establishment' into paroxysms of wrath by his abrasive and successful methods of organizing the poor...."[1] Saul had no intention of retiring—his health was good, his bills were paid and his travel schedule was busier than ever. In the late 1960's Alinsky was delighted to find himself something of a national institution to a new generation of college students and young radicals. He loved every minute of it—especially the enthusiastic crowds of young people who flocked to hear him on the campuses. He would fly into the airport in Boston or San Francisco, where he would be met by a welcoming committee of students from Harvard or Berkeley who would drive him to the campus. The auditorium would be jammed for his lecture. Afterward he would remain as long as there were students with questions, often until midnight. After that, he would sit up over coffee with student leaders until the wee hours, catch a few hours sleep and fly off in the morning to the next campus. His schedule was exhausting, but Saul enjoyed every minute of it. The 1960's for Alinsky was a decade of long-overdue political ferment and action in the United States. The younger generation was leading the radical movement. Black and white collegians fought together in the civil rights' battles in the South and tried to organize in urban ghettos in the North; they organized and demonstrated successfully against the military draft and the continuing war in Vietnam; they forced a U.S. President out of office. It's true that Alinsky thought these young radicals had a lot to learn about political action and organizing, but he loved them for trying. That's why he was so willing to stay up nights, talking to them and sharing his thirty years of organizing experience. For Saul this generation of college kids was evidence that the United States had finally come through the fearful years of Joe McCarthy and the anti-Communist hysteria of the 1950's. After nearly two decades of apathy, homegrown radical activists were springing up all over the place. Alinsky wanted to gather up the cream of this new generation and train them to be effective professional organizers.

At the same time, the popularity Alinsky enjoyed was not an unmixed blessing. It brought with it an exacerbation of some old problems and a couple of new ones. As in the past, he suffered from a dearth of trained organizers at the very moment he was being besieged with offers to organize new communities. Chambers and Harmon were the only IAF organizers left of the dozen he had in the early 1960's. Von Hoffman was a successful Washington journalist; Cesar Chavez and Dolores Huerta were organizing the United Farm Workers. After a stint of organizing a Yaqui Indian community in Arizona and a short, unhappy teaching assignment at Syracuse University, Fred Ross had resigned from the IAF to work with Chavez and the farm workers' union. Tom Gaudette had refused to move to Kansas City and was now organizing a non-

IAF organization in Austin, on Chicago's West Side. Lester
Hunt had married and was teaching history at a college in
Chicago. Barry Menuez had left OSC to take a national job in
the urban affairs office of the Episcopal Church. Saul was
proud of all of them, but no one was coming forward to replace
them. As a last resort, Alinsky agreed to found a training
institute to turn out the needed organizers.

Part of the reason Alinsky couldn't hold on to his organizers was money. He had a true Depression mentality: "Don't
spend what you don't have." Saul paid low salaries and was
tight with expenses (a sign in his Chicago office said, "Low
Overhead = High Independence"). Even when IAF's financial
situation improved in the 1960's Alinsky remained committed
to a lean, highly mobile operation. Until the last few years of
his life, Saul received an annual salary of $20,000. The highest
salary he received was $30,000 (after his divorce from Jean in
1968 brought increased personal expenses). He had also an
endowment policy purchased by the foundation to assure him a
modest retirement. His organizers, however, were paid much
less. Young apprentice organizers received little more than
subsistence wages. More than once over the years Fred Ross'
wife complained that they had to dip into their small savings
just to survive.[2] It was true that no one came to work for
Alinsky for the money. They came because organizing was
exciting, the results were often dramatic, and it was fun. But
lack of money and the highly mobile nature of organizing
Alinsky-style insured that the IAF remained mainly a game for
young people with few responsibilities. (Alinsky's fiscal conservatism paid off at one point when the Internal Revenue Service
spent two years investigating IAF's financial affairs as a result
of charges made against him during the TWO-University of
Chicago feud. Despite a meticulous investigation, the IRS operatives could find nothing amiss.)

The idea of an IAF training school for organizers was not
new. For several years Jack Egan and some of the IAF trustees
had been urging Alinsky to set up a training program that
would assure IAF's future if anything should happen to Saul.
As early as 1965 a group of clergy and laymen in California
discussed with Alinsky the possibility of setting up an appren-

tice training program for organizers in the Bay Area. Saul told them to raise enough money for a school, and he would come to the West Coast as its director. However, when word leaked out that a group of churchmen were planning to invite Saul Alinsky to work in the Bay Area, a fierce "religious war" broke out within the churches.[3]

At first Alinsky resisted the idea of an IAF school for organizers. He was not at all sure that organizers could be produced from ordinary human clay, no matter who trained them. His own experience seemed to bear him out. For every von Hoffman or Chambers, there were six other hopefuls who fell by the way. At one point when Egan and others were arguing the point that the institute would help institutionalize IAF for the day when he would no longer be able to run it, Alinsky responded that the proposed venture sounded like a form of social security for IAF's staff. But as events in the late 1960's made him increasingly uncomfortable about IAF's future, Alinsky began serious discussion of the training program. The two new factors that worried Saul were the rising tide of black separatism in the cities and a drawing back of the churches from controversial direct action in the face of a real or imagined conservative backlash within their congregations.

For several years Alinsky had been trying to recruit black organizers to work in black communities. The problem arose as soon as the IAF began working in Chicago's Woodlawn. In his annual report to the IAF Board of Trustees, Alinsky talked about personnel: "Particularly with reference to the working in Negro communities, we are confronted with an inevitable and natural development of racial chauvinism so that it becomes particularly difficult for a white organizer working in a Negro community. . . . Mr. Edward Chambers, director of the Woodlawn Organization, is popularly described within the Foundation as 'the last white man out.' "[4] Subsequently in Woodlawn, Rochester, Kansas City and Buffalo, Alinsky's organizers were able to recruit young blacks as staff members, with the intention of training them to be organizers. A couple of these men showed promise but preferred to move on to more attractive positions.

In late 1966 the intrepid Monsignor John Egan began pressing Alinsky to organize the poverty-ridden, all-black community of Lawndale in Chicago. Egan had recently been appointed pastor of Lawndale's Presentation Church by Cardinal Meyer's successor as the head of the Chicago Archdiocese, Archbishop John Cody. The authoritarian Cody wanted nothing to do with community organization or civic controversy, so he moved Egan out of the Archdiocesan Office of Urban Affairs into a poor black parish (where his urban ministry talents would be appreciated, according to Cody's scenario). He figured that getting rid of Egan and the urban affairs post would also rid him of Alinsky.

Saul told Egan that he would gladly organize Lawndale, but the community needed a black organizer, and he didn't have one. A month later Egan returned with a promise of a sizable grant from Gordon Sherman of the Midas International Company. Through a mutual friend Egan met Sherman, the scion of the Chicago-based Midas Muffler empire. Over a dinner at Chicago's Standard Club, Sherman told Egan that he had made a promise to his wife that he would give $250,000 to a program that would promote justice in Chicago. He asked Egan for suggestions. Egan admits that he came to dinner groggy from a long day of meetings, but perked up as soon as he grasped what Sherman was saying. "Suddenly, I was fully awake," recalls Egan. "I've had a drink, and I'm thinking about what could be done with a quarter of a million dollars. So I said that I would like more than anything else to have Saul Alinsky develop a community organization in the Lawndale area comparable to TWO in Woodlawn. Bam!—just the right thing. The next thing I did was to take Sherman to meet Alinsky."[5]

As soon as Alinsky joined the conversations with Egan and Sherman, however, he shifted the focus to argue that the money would be better spent if it were to be used to open a training school for organizers in Chicago. Egan admits that he was nettled by Alinsky's fast-talking pitch to Sherman: "I thought it was really a rip off. Alinsky wanted that institute, and he saw Sherman's money as a chance to get it off the ground." To mollify Egan, Saul promised that Lawndale would get the first black organizer trained by the institute. Sherman agreed to Alinsky's plan. Egan still remembers his chagrin over Saul's theft of his angel: "I got nothing out of it, nothing except it was the best use of the money, and I never regretted it, really."[6]

By the time the Midas grant was available, Alinsky had recalled Chambers and plans for the institute were nearing completion. Despite his deal with Egan and Sherman, Saul delayed the announcement of the Chicago-based institute until he was certain that the Bay Area group could not come up with the money for a program on the West Coast. When they finally threw in the towel in 1968, Alinsky announced that the IAF Training Institute would open in Chicago in early 1969. The Midas grant was $200,000, considerably less than the $600,000 requested by Alinsky in his formal proposal. He received an additional grant of $200,000 from the Rockefeller Foundation to provide scholarships for trainees.

Another source of funds for the IAF Institute was a new national foundation set up by Saul's church allies to provide money for community organization. The Interreligious Foundation for Community Organization (IFCO) was actually an ecumenical front organization (Protestant, Catholic, Jewish) set up to shield the churches which were supporting community organizations from the growing anti-Alinsky, anti-black backlash within the churches. The Protestant church activists, in particular (especially in the wake of the Rochester and Oakland debates over Alinsky), were worried that these inter-church controversies would bring about a reaction against the national denominations and the National Council of Churches. George Todd, a staff member of the Presbyterian Board of National Missions, had all along warned the members of the urban ministry network (the "urban mafia") that one day "all the little old ladies in tennis shoes" are going to find out what we have been doing with their contributions to church mission funds.[7] In the meantime, however, the Protestant church agencies were receiving generous amounts of money to deal with the current racial unrest through programs like "Crisis in the Cities." Part of these "crisis funds" was being shunted into IFCO to provide needed support for Alinsky-style organizations in troubled cities.[8]

NEW DIRECTIONS   235

The idea for IFCO came out of Chicago (as did so many other ideas at this period) where a local foundation called the Interreligious Council on Urban Affairs had been set up by Egan, Doug Still of the Chicago Church Federation and Rabbi Robert Marx, originally as a way to bring Jewish religious support into local urban ministry programs. When Egan and Still brought up with Alinsky the idea of a church-sponsored foundation at the national level, Saul encouraged them to go ahead. At the time he envisioned the church foundation primarily as a means of supporting organizations already operating in minority communities in a number of cities.

When IFCO opened its office in New York in 1967, it consisted of Protestant, Jewish and Catholic organizations. (The only Catholic organization in IFCO was one put together on the spot by Egan and a half-dozen diocesan urban ministry directors to give Catholics a seat on the foundation until more representative support could be gathered. The arrangement was fragile indeed. It was two years before the new organization, called the Catholic Committee for Urban Ministry [CCUM] could raise enough money to pay its entrance fee and annual dues.) By now, the "black power" movement had reached into national Protestant church structures. Church leaders found themselves faced with increasing demands that funds for local black projects be turned over to groups of black churchmen and even to militant black groups outside church structures. As Alinsky feared, the IAF came under a lot of criticism from community black organizations who said they would accept only black organizers and wanted a "black Alinsky" who would train young black organizers to build community organizations with more of a "black perspective." Saul hoped to stave off a wasteful black-white confrontation over organizing. For many months he carried on conversations with the Rev. Martin Luther King, Jr., whose SCLC was preparing to open up a "second front" in Northern black communities. Alinsky and King were discussing a possible SCLC-IAF joint organizing effort, but nothing came of it.

IFCO's executive director was Lucius Walker, Jr., a black Baptist minister who had been directing a neighborhood settlement house in Milwaukee. Under his leadership the original

IFCO Board of Directors was soon broadened to include representatives from some "grass roots" black organizations. IFCO's allocation policy left room for non-minority organizing projects to receive funding. When the first year grants were announced, however, almost all went to black organizations. Walker issued a statement in which he said, "In accord with IFCO policy, set by the Board of Directors, most funded projects reflect a priority placed on the development of black community organization."[9] Alinsky had not been happy with the choice of Lucius Walker as IFCO's director. The first year's allocations did nothing to change his mind. To a white priest who was considering accepting the post of assistant director of IFCO Alinsky offered this advice, "You don't want to be the baloney in a black sandwich, do you?" In the early 1960's Chambers had tried to recruit Walker for the TWO staff. When Walker did not follow up on Chamber's invitation to meet with Alinsky, Saul evidently wrote him off. After that Alinsky was polite whenever he encountered Walker, but that was all. Saul often used first meetings to size up people—he did it with von Hoffman, Chavez, and Gaudette. Walker had not even shown up for the test. Whatever the reason, Saul did not trust Lucius Walker.

Shortly after Walker took over as IFCO's director, the Bay Area group came to him with a request for $500,000 to build Alinsky's training institute in San Francisco. The amount they requested was half of IFCO's first year's budget. Walker turned down the request. He figured that the Bay Area request was a probe by Alinsky to see how Walker would treat an IAF proposal. Now the stage was set for an angry confrontation when Alinsky got around to requesting funds from IFCO for the IAF Training Institute. The Rev. Douglas Still, one of the founders of IFCO, says now that he thinks that Walker and some of IFCO's board members misread the criticisms of Alinsky in certain church circles. There were always some in the churches (now joined by the "black supremacy" types) who wanted to encourage a model of community organizing that would minimize the controversial methods of Alinsky. Later, IFCO's Walker tried to set up a training center for minority and "third world" organizers in Washington, D.C. but it never got off the ground. When it came to organizing, then and later, Still agrees that Alinsky and the IAF-style organizers had the only game in town.[10]

Alinsky's IAF Training Institute finally opened its doors in February 1969. The open doors led into a modest suite of offices to the rear of an old office building on Chicago's North Michigan Avenue, near the Wrigley Building. The main room, which served as the classroom, was simply furnished: a dozen folding tables, metal folding chairs, chipped ashtrays, a blackboard, a water cooler and a battered coffee urn. The Institute's headquarters provided a place for trainees to gather for lectures and discussions, to write their weekly field reports, and to talk to their supervisor and receive their daily marching orders. There were no academic frills.

Instead of the nine member faculty, the distinguished visiting lecturers and the clerical staff of eleven envisioned in Alinsky's original proposal, the IAF Institute's staff was made up of Edward T. Chambers, director, Richard Harmon, assistant director, one secretary, the capable Karolyn Strassner, and occasional lecturer Saul Alinsky. Later Staughton Lynd, ex-Yale professor and anti-war activist, was added to the faculty to teach the IAF trainees something about the history of American radicalism. But Lynd and the IAF staff soon found themselves facing each other across a vast ideological chasm.[11] Lynd left after a year.

The day-to-day operation of the program Alinsky left to Chambers and Harmon. Of that first year or so, Chambers says, "There wasn't a lot of romance to it—at least on Harmon's and my part. It was an experiment—something the IAF had never done before, a major organizing effort, as important as any community we had ever organized.[12] They had no blueprint to follow, no curriculum, only Saul's two books and the "principles" of organizing that he and his little band of organizers had been developing, testing and reworking for thirty years. Chambers did not make it easy to enter the Institute. After the first announcement that the IAF Institute was open for business, further information was spread mostly by rumor. Individuals or organizations who inquired about the training program were sent a sheaf of mimeographed pages, containing basic information about the program and an application form to be filled out and returned. If the applicant was not frightened off by the cost of tuition ($15,000 for the fifteen-month course), the stern language of the information sheets ("Question: Where will you live? Answer: That's your business. Question: Will you have free time? Answer: Yes, about one day a week") and the ominous warning ("Our experience has indicated that the odds may be as high as fifty percent washout"), then he or she sent back the application and waited for an invitation to an interview. The process was an exercise in IAF-style "dragon slaying" ("If you want the hand of the princess, you must first slay the dragon") designed to screen out the weak and undesirables before they got to Chicago. At first it scared off legitimate recruits as well.[13]

All the early IAF trainees received tuition aid from outside sources: church organizations, local sponsoring groups looking for an organizer, professional organizations (The Student National Educational Association sent a number of its members) or from the Rockefeller Foundation's grant. Chambers' objective for the first couple of years was to recruit trainees with enough experience and maturity to survive the course, give himself time to develop IAF's approach into an educational curriculum and make the enterprise self-supporting and independent.[14] The IAF did not promise to hire any of the trainees. Graduates were encouraged to return to their home communities or to their sponsor's community to help build local organizations.

The Institute planned to train forty organizers in each fifteen-month class. To prevent the program from becoming a discussion group, Alinsky told Chambers and Harmon to build a new, large-scale organization in Chicago to be a training ground for the apprentice organizers. The organization, IAF's first attempt at a middle class, metropolitan-sized operation, became the CAP (Citizens Against Pollution, later changed to Citizens Action Program) and it proved to be a major test of the capacities of the IAF Training Institute, as well as the trainees.

Rules for Radicals

Once the IAF Training Institute was functioning, Alinsky felt free to return to his own agenda. In refusing to tie himself down, Saul said that he was willing to allow his organizing approach to be institutionalized, but that he did not want to be turned into some kind of wise, political rabbi ensconced in the Institute.[15] Nevertheless, during the first couple of years, Saul's frequent visits to lecture and discuss organizing with the trainees were the highlights of an otherwise pedestrian curriculum. Margery Tabankin (a former leader of the Students for a Democratic Society at the University of Wisconsin, who was recruited for the IAF Institute by Harmon and was one of the first women to attend, and who later was appointed the national director of VISTA during the Carter Administration) recalled one of Alinsky's visits: "The first day we were there, Saul came in and talked to us. He told us some anecdotes and talked about the philosophical question of ends and means. He was very different from what I expected from reading his books. Nowhere in his writings do you capture the spirit and magic of Alinsky. I came to love him as a human being. . . ."[16]

Most of the time, however, Alinsky was on the road, lecturing, consulting, and recruiting trainees. He was also writing for the first time in a long while: new material for the paperback editions of *Reveille for Radicals* and *John L. Lewis*.[17] The following year Saul completed a new book, entitled *Rules for Radicals*.[18] He had been working on it on and off for ten years.

Far more than the IAF Institute, *Rules for Radicals* was to be Alinsky's last will and testament. He wrote it for the new generation he was meeting on the nation's college campuses, the young radicals of the 1960's. He admired their courage and their idealism. He enjoyed their readiness to organize and demonstrate to make changes in the world. At the same time, Alinsky worried about them—their abysmal ignorance about history, their political artlessness, the problem they had in communicating beyond their own peer groups, their seeming inability to laugh, especially at themselves. Isolated from earlier American radicals by a decade or more, these young activists tended to grow impatient with the slow process of change. Some, like the Weatherman faction of SDS, were already turning to violence in an effort to hurry along the revolution. Saul criticized the student radicals for confusing revolution with revelation. They were looking for quick change, and so were unwilling to take the time necessary to organize and build the new coalitions with people over thirty. Broad coalitions of Americans were needed, said Alinsky, to bring about effective social and political change.

Alinsky hoped to convince some of these brilliant young radicals (Chicago was full of young radicals in the late 1960's— Tom Hayden, Paul and Heather Booth, Todd and Nanci Gitlin, Margery Tabankin—even Yippie leaders Abbie Hoffman and Jerry Rubin who, Saul said, couldn't organize a garden party) that they would have to start with the world as it was and organize new coalitions of people, especially the middle class—their own people. Saul worried that without a broader base these intelligent, creative young men and women would grow tired and drop out of the struggle to reorganize America. His *Rules for Radicals* was written, above all, for these young Americans, in "desperation," Saul wrote, "because it is what they do and will do that will give meaning to what I and the radicals of my generation have done with our lives."[19]

Many of Alinsky's readers were disappointed when the book finally appeared. It wasn't what they expected—a "follow-the-dots" manual on how to build a community organization in your spare time. *Rules for Radicals* was an update of the themes he wrote about in *Reveille for Radicals,* a quarter century ago. In the new book he shared his mature perspective on life and humanity, values and politics, explained his famed organizing principles and gave lots of practical advice for would-be-organizers. The book discussed all the ideas that bothered people about his approach to citizen organizing—the meaning of power, controversy, confrontation, compromise, communication, ends and means, self-interest, tactics. In case anyone was thinking of organizing as a spare-time hobby, he devoted a whole chapter to the difficult art of educating an organizer. All of this down-to-earth political philosophy Alinsky gathered together in a medley of heroic tales, funny anecdotes and memorable aphorisms. For $6.95 in hardcover edition, readers got all this with a taste of Alinsky's humor, his warmth and his colorful imagination.

The 1960's had convinced Alinsky that Americans were becoming more aware of the benefits of mass-based citizen organizations. The long struggle of FIGHT with Eastman Kodak made Alinsky aware of the crucial position of the American middle class. Three-quarters of the citizens of the United States in 1970 belonged to the middle class in terms of economy and self-perception. Rochester's organized black community could not have won its long struggle for jobs, Alinsky knew, without the help of middle class whites who belonged to the mainline churches and the other organizations involved in Friends of FIGHT. What Alinsky saw ahead for the 1970's and beyond was a renewal of democratic process which would mean greater citizen involvement, more effective local democracy and a greater degree of self-determination for individuals within their home and work communities. To accomplish this democratic renewal, new citizen coalitions would have to be organized, and they would include minorities and majorities, blacks and whites, "have-little-want-mores" and "have nots," blue, gray and white collar workers—all kinds of communities of self-interest banding together to deal with government and corporate institutions. Alinsky was seeing again the heady vision of American Populism, only this time he saw it bringing together Americans who live in cities and suburbs, in small towns and rural areas.[20] A lot had changed in seventy years. The American people of the 1970's were better educated than they were in the late 1800's. They were used to higher standards of living, the issues that demanded their attention were more widespread (e.g., pollution: Saul asked, "Will we be corpses buried in clean white shirts?"), and communications technology made information immediately available from coast to coast ("The feedback of the consequences of your acts is so immediate that the future is now").[21]

In the last chapter of *Rules for Radicals*, entitled "The Way

Ahead," Alinsky argued that the issues affecting the middle class majority were interconnected with the problems of the nation's poor and unemployed. He pointed to the spiraling inflation/recession phenomenon, to the increase of environmental pollution, and to what he called the "political pollution of the Pentagon." There was also a weakened Social Security system, increasing unemployment in a slumping economy, rising health care costs, higher and higher taxes on incomes, food, real estate, automobiles, and a "welfare industry" that was producing a whole class of dependent citizens. These problems were too serious to be left to the politicians. It was time, Alinsky said, to overcome the apathy of the black ghettos, the white ghettos, the "gilded ghettos of the middle class," and let bona fide community representatives meet with the accredited representatives of other communities to carry out the "pushing, hauling, dealing and temporary compromises" needed to make things work. Without this kind of citizen involvement, he saw the democratic process coming to a halt.[22]

At the end of *Rules for Radicals* Alinsky sent out a new call to the young activists who had cut their teeth on the issues of the 1960's to turn their attention to organizing middle class America. He urged them to return to the communities in which they were raised, to their own people, and to organize— to search out the leaders, help them identify the issues, develop the strategies, think up the tactics and move into action. This new generation of professional organizers could, if they wished, turn the American people on to the benefits of direct participation in the democratic enterprise.

Rules for Radicals was the veteran Saul Alinsky sharing his vision of democratic populism with another generation of American student organizers, local leaders, citizens. Tough times were ahead, predicted Alinsky, but there were also these encouraging signs that people were interested in doing something about their world. Alinsky, at sixty-two, sounded as hopeful as he had long ago in the Back of the Yards and in that brief moment of reveille at the end of World War II. "I salute the present generation," he wrote. . . . "Together we may find some of what we're looking for—laughter, beauty, love and the chance to create."[23]

The Asian Connection

During the time Alinsky was setting up the IAF Institute, his wife Jean divorced him. Today Jean says that at that time she was at the lowest point in her long battle with multiple sclerosis. She took out her frustration on the absent Saul, burned all his letters and sued him for divorce on the grounds of extreme cruelty. Saul did not fight back, but made a property settlement in which he agreed to provide her $1,000 a month alimony, pay a portion of her annual medical expenses and give her the Carmel house.[25] As long as he lived, Saul stopped to see Jean whenever he was in California, and she, on her part, continued to worry about him as he wandered around the country's trouble spots. A couple of years later Saul married for the third time. His new wife, Irene McGinnis, was a tall, attractive professor at Boston's Emerson College. Irene says that she and Saul enjoyed a delightful married life, even though it involved commuting between Chicago and Boston. She traveled with him as much as possible and took a keen interest in organizing. Irene was a good match for Saul—like him, an all-night, non-stop talker, and a woman who could give back as good as she got in wisecracks or arguments. Her interests in philosophy and communication influenced Saul's thinking in *Rules for Radicals.*[26]

In the spring of 1971 Saul and Irene went on an extended tour of Asia. It was a honeymoon of sorts. The trip was paid for by the United Presbyterian Church's Board of National Missions and was sponsored by the East Asian Christian Conference, a group of Asian Christian church leaders. There were a growing number of church-sponsored community organizations in Asian nations. The church officials wanted to talk to Alinsky about the possibilities for these organizations in Asia, but only after he had had an opportunity to see some of the problems of Far Eastern countries first-hand. It was Alinsky's first contact with Asia—in fact, his first contact with any of the developing nations. He was greatly impressed with the intensity of the drive for economic development in these countries.

Saul and Irene flew to Japan, the first stop on a grueling itinerary that took them to South Korea, Hong Kong, Singapore, Indonesia and the Philippines—all the places where community organizations were already operating. To Saul's disappointment, the People's Republic of China was not on the schedule. He was invited to visit India, but for some reason Saul refused to go there. He survived the rigorous schedule of talks and travel. As the journey continued, Saul's fascination with Asia increased. He was pleased to find how many people knew about his work in the United States. They had read *Reveille for Radicals* and dog-eared mimeographed copies of his articles and speeches that had been circulated by Asians who had been to the United States. Japanese, Korean, and Filipino audiences asked knowledgeable questions about the Back of the Yards, TWO and FIGHT. It was a whirlwind tour, not at all the usual tourist stuff. Thanks to the efforts of his hosts, Alinsky came away with a pretty good idea of the forces at work behind Asia's booming development and its attendant problems.

In Manila, before he and Irene flew back to the United States, Alinsky sat down for two days with key Asian church and local organization leaders to discuss his impressions and answer their questions about the organizing he had seen in their countries. In his opening remarks, he showed his audience that he understood and admired their national struggle for economic growth and independence. He saw also the interconnected problems of widespread poverty among large sectors of the populations and the growing tendency toward political repression of dissidents by a number of Asian governments. The weather was hot in Manila. Alinsky was suffering from diarrhea, too many cigarettes and sleepless nights. A couple of hundred people packed themselves into the hall. Others, unable to get in, crowded around the open doors and windows. Despite the stifling heat and his own discomfort, Alinsky, the "two-bit Socrates," came alive, as he always did, as the crowd warmed to him. Within five minutes he had them laughing. For the next two or three hours they engaged in a lively give-and-take discussion about the pros and cons of people organizing in Asia.

At one point in the meeting a local Manila organization leader brought up to Alinsky a serious organizing problem facing ZOTO (the *Zone One Tondo Organization*). ZOTO represented the 200,000 poor squatters living in the crowded shantytown along the edge of Manila's domestic harbor port. Homeless families in the Tondo district were facing relocation by the government to sites outside of Manila where there were no jobs. Organized by ZOTO, these squatters were trying to erect small houses on a large tract of vacant land owned by the government-owned Foreshore Development Authority. According to custom rooted in common law, if the squatters were able to get shelters erected on the vacant land, it would be most difficult for the government to drive them off. The development authority had stationed armed guards around the property to keep the squatters off. The people were stymied. The leader asked Saul, "Dr. Alinsky, how shall we handle these armed guards? Do we shoot them? How can we get around them?" The crowd grew still. By now Alinsky was in full stride—throwing out quips, striding up and down, his cigarette puffs keeping time with his remarks. The crowd was laughing, enjoying the show; everyone in the room was now involved in the man's problem. The meeting had turned into one of Alinsky's celebrated organizing sessions.

Earlier Saul had noted a shapely, young woman in red "hot pants" (the latest fashion rage in Manila) sitting in the front row. He beckoned her to come to the front of the room, asked her name, thanked her and told her she was free to return to her seat. After a careful pause to give her time to walk back to her front row seat, Alinsky turned and asked the men sitting at the front of the room, "What were you guys looking at just now?" They blushed; the crowd laughed. Then Saul said, "What would happen if next Sunday morning you sent Mrs. D . . . here and a couple of her friends, similarly attired, to bring hot coffee to those guards—say, about fifteen minutes before the squatters were ready to storm the property?" The crowd broke into applause. Later, when Alinsky was safely home, the "hot pants" tactic was used with great success.[27]

A few days later, Alinsky returned to the United States. For the next couple of months, he thought about what he had observed and wondered how much like Asia were the developing nations of Africa and South America. Should he set up an

IAF international consulting operation to help "third world" people get started training organizers and building people's organizations to deal with local problems? In most of the Asian countries he had visited it was evident that organizing people required a different approach than did organizing union workers and their families in the Back of the Yards or Chicanos in East Los Angeles. Only Japan and the Philippines had democratic governments which guaranteed civil rights like freedom of assembly and freedom of the press (this was one year before President Ferdinand Marcos placed the Philippines under martial law). In the other countries, where society was strictly controlled, whether Communist or anti-Communist, organizing people to take control of their own lives and communities would, of necessity, be a covert, underground operation. A totally different approach would be required, Alinsky knew, involving clandestine networks, secret meetings, hit-and-run tactics. Organizing would be a dangerous business, the organizations would be illegal, and penalties would be harsh—prison, torture, exile, even execution. Alinsky knew that these kinds of revolutionary organizations could be built—determined people have organized under the most repressive conditions—but it would be an entirely different matter than building even the most controversial organization in a free and open society like the United States. Any open organizing in national security states would bring harassment from the police and security forces. Open organizations would quickly become government controlled or allowed only to engage in social work by which the people could be kept dependent and politically inactive.

Even in the democratic countries, there were cultural and nationalistic factors to be considered. Asia was coming into its own in world economy and politics. Any organizing would have to be done by Filipinos, Japanese, and Indonesian organizers, trained in Asia. Before he left the Far East, Saul discouraged his hosts from sending organizer candidates to Chicago. He suggested that they set up a training center in Japan or in Hong Kong. Japan and the Philippines seemed to be the best places to begin organizing people on a large scale. Later, however, back in the United States, Saul wondered about the possibility of setting up an international IAF consulting service. But he never did it, nor did he return to Asia. One year, almost to the day, after the Manila meeting, Alinsky was dead.

The Asian trip stands, however, as a classic example of how Saul Alinsky operated. At the age of sixty-two he was almost resigned, with more than a touch of sadness, to a diminished role as IAF's elder statesman: an advisor to the staff and trainees of the Institute, a popular lecturer and author (*Rules for Radicals* was just reaching the bookstores). He was making notes for his autobiography. Nick von Hoffman and Saul had been talking about collaborating on this (they planned to call it *Saul D. Alinsky: An Unauthorized Autobiography*).[28]

When he was invited to go to Asia, Saul refused at first; then, after he agreed to go, he postponed the trip a couple of times. Finally he went only because he couldn't figure out a way to get out of it gracefully. Once he got there, however, and was faced, literally, with a whole new world of peoples and possibilities, Saul reacted as he always did. His batteries were recharged. In spite of his best efforts to remain the detached observer, he found himself thinking about what a few good organizers could do in some of these countries. When the discussion turned to working with people who were ready to take over their lives and communities, Alinsky, the professional, came alive and began organizing on the spot.

As it turned out, the Asian trip was the high point of Alinsky's last years. It was also the beginning of the end. He returned to the United States with an international perspective and new plans. The trip had exhausted him, however, more than he realized. For the first time since Helene's death, he found that he could not bounce back with his usual burst of energy. He didn't feel well physically. He had a respiratory infection all that winter and his chronic back trouble seemed to be worse. He was in pain much of the time.[29] The last straw came when his doctor insisted he had to give up smoking. For Alinsky his poor health was a harbinger of death. A couple of times, when he was depressed about his health, he talked about Ernest Hemingway's suicide. Saul was more a man of action then Hemingway. He did not fear death—he had lived with it too long to be afraid—but he was frightened by the prospect of becoming an invalid like Jean or John O'Grady. Illness to him was being held down, unable to move, surrounded by boredom. He never forgot those long months in his teens when he was strapped to his bed. Saul mentioned the possibility of one day taking his leave via the ".38 Special."

With the coming of spring, however, Saul seemed to improve. He still tired easily, but his spirits revived and his travel schedule expanded. In June he went to California and stopped to see Jean in Carmel. Afterward he drove into the town. He had a dinner appointment in Carmel with the lawyer who handled his financial arrangement with Jean. As Saul stepped onto the sidewalk, he fell to the ground. A physician lunching in a nearby restaurant was called to assist him. But he needed no help. On June 12, 1972, Saul David Alinsky met death, as he intended, head-on.[30]

One week later his friends gathered in Chicago for a memorial service and a celebration. The service was simple and short. It was held in the Hyde Park synagogue he had attended briefly after Helene's death. It might have been a bit stiff, but his old friends were all there to pay him heartfelt tributes, some spoken, some not. Joe Meegan was there from the Back of the Yards, as were Monsignor John Egan and George N. Shuster (he was president of the IAF Board of Trustees), who came up from the University of Notre Dame, Ralph Helstein, another IAF trustee, organizers Fred Ross, Nick von Hoffman, Ed Chambers, Dick Harmon, Tom Gaudette, lots of old friends like Mike Royko, the Rev. George Todd, Minister Franklyn D.R. Florence, and Daniel Patrick Moynihan. The tributes were just right, but the congregation seemed somehow to be waiting for Saul to break up the solemn proceedings with a funny remark and send everyone away laughing.

John Kifner caught the spirit of the occasion: "They said the Kaddish—the Hebrew prayer for the dead—for Saul David Alinsky, and then his friends went to the back room of a bar named the Boul' Mich and told stories and laughed, which was what he would have wanted."[31] Among those who came to the party to have a farewell drink and tell Saul stories were a variety of individuals who were living evidence of the many facets of this wonderfully controversial man: Roman Catholic priests, Protestant ministers, journalists, suburban housewives, black community leaders, young organizer recruits and old union guys from that first campaign in the Back of the Yards. All of them learned how to change things from this professional organizer who made a career of organizing because, he said, "I can't stand to see people pushed around."[32]

8.

The Professional Organizer

An American Radical

He was a controversial and complex character, this man Saul Alinsky. He would be hurt to hear himself being described today as a "1960's activist," as though he were the same kind of minor league radical as Yippie scoutmaster Abbie Hoffman or the Black Panther's Bobby Seale. It is true that Alinsky was an activist during the 1960's, but so was he during the 1930's, 1940's, 1950's and 1970's. But then all kinds of labels were applied to Alinsky during his career. He was called at various times—sometimes at the same time—a Communist, a conservative, a cynic, a crypto-Catholic, and, if that weren't enough, a fascist. None of them really stuck because he was too various a character, as Stephen Becker pointed out. No one really believed that this man who worked so closely with Catholic priests and Protestant ministers was a Communist, and as for being a conservative, they are not known for helping blacks and poor people, as he did, to get a larger share of the American pie.[1]

By far the most enduring charge made against Alinsky was that he was a cynic because he taught in the most straightforward manner that in the real world—as opposed to an angelic world we wish we lived in—the poor and powerless must organize themselves, not in terms of ethical abstractions, but to acquire self-interested power. According to his basic organizing principle, the greatest sin of all times was to refrain from acting when people around us were suffering from hunger, persecution, political powerlessness and poverty. "Do-Nothings" was what he called people who criticized his rough-and-tumble methods with wishy-washy statements like, "We agree with your ends, but not your means," or "This is not the time to act." In the gospel according to Alinsky, these "means and ends moralists . . . always wind up on their ends without any means."[2]

Herbert D. White, the minister who organized the churches to bring Alinsky to Rochester, remembers vividly his first visit to Saul's Chicago office. On the table were three photographs of the terrible ovens of Dachau. "The vividness of those pictures," he wrote later, "on that day in that setting returns when I hear Alinsky charged with cynicism for accepting 'life as it is' and for claiming that the social order is produced and maintained by self-interest. Cynicism may well be the mark of those who make such charges, for they are deaf to Alinsky's counterpoint: People . . . given the opportunity, will make the right decisions over the long haul—Dachau to the contrary."[3]

To those, like White, who knew him best, Alinsky was a happy phenomenon, "a once-a-generation comet flashing through our lives,"[4] a "rare and brilliant event that happened to America."[5] In our age of bigness, complexities, rapid change, instant communication—in a world where people live in the shadow of nuclear holocaust, environmental pollution, runaway economics, energy crisis, and third world revolutions —Saul Alinsky came along with a small traveling road show. His cast of characters was never more than a half-dozen, usually one or two. Unlike the traditional American heroes—inventors, soldiers, scientists, statesmen—Saul's genius was directed not toward epochal breakthroughs in technology, national power and global rearrangements. He came instead into typical American communities, populated by ordinary citizens—men and women, blacks and whites, white and blue collar workers, parents, teachers, merchants, members of the Chamber of Commerce, Elks and Kiwanis—and he showed them how to take up and use effectively the tools of democratic process to change whatever they thought needed changing in their lives, their neighborhoods and their cities.

It is impossible to separate Alinsky the educator from

Alinsky the organizer.[6] In his books and lectures, and in his famous late-night sessions with organizers, students or community leaders, Alinsky dealt with ideas as well as organizing tactics. He was an organizing genius (even conservative columnist William F. Buckley, Jr. nearly admitted that[7]) with a fascination for ideas. Lester Hunt, the Alinsky-organizer-turned-historian, says that Saul always dealt with ideas, wanted to talk about ideas, tested his ideas on friends. Because he was an activist and a popular educator more than he was a philosopher, however, Saul was not always as exacting about these ideas as he could have been. Hunt says that when Saul "talked about Hegelian dialectic, it sometimes sounded more like James Madison." Saul had read Madison; he probably hadn't read Hegel.[8]

   Therefore, more than once his ideas got him into trouble. His fascination with the contradictions in everyday life (how he got involved with Hegel in the first place) is a case in point. Alinsky's experiences as an organizer gave him a wealth of insights into the way people operate. The many contradictions, real and apparent, in life he used to teach his organizers how to look for positives within negative situations. He had a wonderful ability to break down situations into their components—to find a countermove in the way in which an opponent reacted under attack. Saul talked a lot about contradictions. In discussions he forced his listeners to go beyond the appearances of reality, to look beyond the myths that govern society and what passes for principles, dogmas, traditions, and somebody's sacred cows. The first step for people in breaking out of the prison of political passivity came, he said, when they started to question what was happening around them. In explaining these things in *Rules for Radicals,* Saul did a lot of philosophizing about contradiction, negatives and positives, duality, political relativity, even the implications for everyday life in quantum physics. Some of his readers were confused by this casual philosophizing; others were furious about what they took to be a statement of his ethical and theological beliefs. The kinds of ideas he played with in small groups, the creative examples he spun out in organizing sessions, did not stand up well in a book written for the general public.

Saul's friend Jacques Maritain saw the danger first. After Maritain read *Rules for Radicals,* he sent Alinsky a letter in which he praised the book ("a great book admirably free, absolutely fearless, radically revolutionary . . . the fruit of your experience as an incomparable creative organizer . . ."), but he also took a gentle swipe at Saul's philosophical meanderings. In particular he took issue with Alinsky's apparent praise of Hegel's concept of self-contradiction. "Seeking one's own intellectual liberation in an infinite proliferation of antinomies is madness on the level of philosophical thought," wrote Maritain. He understood what Saul, the educator-organizer, was trying to say. ". . . on the level of action a kind of boldness in practical self-contradiction is probably, as you suggest it, the sign of a healthy and fecund mind. Yet it makes me jumpy." What Maritain wanted his friend to do was to distinguish more carefully between a "philosophical truth"—essential to moral judgment—and a "truth of human experience"—what often passes for truth in everyday situations but is really nothing more than "moral justifications and moral pretexts . . . a mask used to hide merely egotistic motivations. . . ." The great philosopher (he calls himself in this letter a "pig-headed philosopher") was gently scolding Saul for his careless philosophizing, and thereby his running the risk of pushing the idea of truth in human affairs out of perspective. Maritain didn't want his old friend—whom he described here as "an incurable idealist, a living, I would say, heroic witness of Judaeo-Christian tradition and true democracy"—being dismissed as having an ignorant and cynical view of human affairs.[9] Alinsky accepted Maritain's criticism.

Not only did Alinsky love to discover and make use of the world's contradictions, but he was himself a man of many contradictions, real and apparent, which somehow came together to form in him a special kind of creativity and way of operating.

Saul Alinsky was a loner, an often strident one-man-band who made a career out of bringing people together and organizing them to make the democratic process work better. "The Lone Arranger" is what newspaper executive Christy C. Bulkeley calls him. He hated being tied down. He was a free man in a country that was invented and organized to ensure life, liberty and all the other things the Founding Fathers meant by the pursuit of happiness. When he decided to organize the residents who were getting pushed around by the meatpackers and the city politicians in Chicago's Back of the Yards, he did it—even though it cost him his job. When that community was working smoothly, he went to Kansas City because some people there asked him to help them get their neighborhood organized. Then, with the help of a couple of good friends, Saul set himself up in business as a professional community organizer. His objective was to spend his time making sure that Americans remained free citizens of a free nation. The Great Depression and the events leading to World War II convinced him that Jefferson, Madison and Tocqueville were right when they warned that life, liberty and all the rest could be taken away if citizens did not take an active part in their own governance.

At first he worked completely alone, traveling back and forth across the country from one city to another. He loved every minute of it, even the weekend jail in Kansas City. Later, after Helene died, he decided that he could use a couple of good organizers to help him get to more places. With Fred Ross, Nick von Hoffman and a couple of others he was then able to leave an organizer in a community for a couple of months or years to get people started. This arrangement left him free to keep moving, looking for likely places to build other organizations.

Alinsky never had any intention of building a big organization to expedite the reorganization of America. It was enough for him to train a few good prospects along the way to keep the operation going. The IAF was a kind of a franchise operation, but small, spare, easily deployed, decentralized, with little management required. Alinsky wasn't going to be tied down to a desk somewhere, managing a far-flung operation. The IAF Board of Trustees met once a year in a hotel room in New York City. His best organizing sessions were held in his living room or over dinner at a good restaurant. His motto remained: "Low Overhead, High Independence." Life was too short, he thought, to spend it building things that had to be watched and worried about.

Over the years, other radicals criticized Alinsky for his lack of a well-worked out vision of what he wanted the world to look like as a result of his organizing. Saul laughed at them, for the truth was that he didn't have any clear idea what the world should look like. He said he would leave that to the people he organized. He hoped they would build many different kinds of communities within the democratic enterprise that was America. His faith in a free people was immense. One of his rules for his organizers was that they have a somewhat blurred vision of a better world. He wanted them to have ideas and suggestions, but he didn't want them to start pushing people around to make their personal vision come true.

Another facet of Alinsky's loneness was the non-ideological nature of his brand of organizing. Organizer Jessica Fernandez-White says that Saul made would-be-organizers understand that ideology was one of the many thresholds that must be crossed—"that to be with and for the people . . . is to fight any system which oppresses them."[10] Alinsky, like the great mystics, believed that life meant being on the way—the promised land was not yet.

As we have seen, this lone-hand mode of operation entailed some persistent weaknesses. Often Alinsky and his organizers had to move on before a fledgling organization was ready to be on its own. His minimal organization of the IAF hampered a systematic follow-through with the organizations he built. IAF's recruitment-training program for new organizers before he founded the Institute was haphazard at best. Everything hinged on him; it was difficult to delegate and share leadership in a one-man-band.

Whenever critics mention Alinsky today they remember his famous dictum about "rubbing raw the sores of discontent." It's not exactly what he said, but no matter. He taught his organizers that it was often necessary to encourage community conflict to activate organized citizen participation. His critics, especially the academics, pilloried him for saying that consensus is usually arrived at through conflict in an imperfect world. But he went on saying it, probably most clearly in a speech he gave to a meeting of social workers in 1963. The organizer, Alinsky said, must be an agitator who is able to force people to move, to participate, to develop and harness the power to attack prevailing patterns and change them. He must be an "abrasive agent to rub raw the resentments of the people of the community; to fan the latent hostilities of many of the people to a point of overt expression; to search out the controversial issues, rather than avoid them, for unless an issue is controversial it means that people are not sufficiently concerned about it to feel deeply and to act; to stir up dissatisfaction and discontent; to provide a channel into which they can angrily pour their frustrations of the past, to create a mechanism which can drain off underlying guilts for having accepted the previous situation for so long a time."[11]

That's why he gloried in being called an agitator, a troublemaker, a radical. He wasn't just a troublemaker, however, despite what his critics said. Alinsky didn't get people aroused and then walk away. He stayed around and taught them how to channel their anger and new-found collective power into active participation in the commonweal. It's in these terms that Douglas Still, who worked with Alinsky in Chicago, describes him as a truly compassionate man who went beyond good will and good intentions and gave ordinary people a practical means of solving their own problems. Still explains that Alinsky demonstrated over many years that "his conflict method of organizing was really oriented to the reconciling of differences. . . ." Saul defined the issues in a community so that on the surface it seemed to exacerbate the problems. In practice, however, he brought people together to equalize the forces on both sides of the issue and made possible a reconciling process on the basis of compromise and so the first steps toward a long-range solution of the community's problems.[12] For Saul, this early use of conflict in a community was a little like lancing a boil to get rid of infection. It hurt like hell at first, but eventually brought relief.

Critic at Large

In terms of other organizations which Alinsky recognized as his allies in the struggle for the empowerment of people, he served as the loyal, often vociferous opposition. Nowhere was this more evident than in his harsh treatment of organized labor in the United States. He learned his organizer's craft from John L. Lewis and the CIO organizers of the 1930's. In his early organizations Alinsky worked closely with local unions. In the Depression years he said that unions not only represented the vocational interests of the working people, but served as a "medium through which these people express their secular hopes and desires for economic security."[13] For Alinsky free labor unions were a crucial institution within democratic society. For that reason, however, he later belabored the union leaders at every turn for not living up to their potential. In *Reveille for Radicals* Alinsky attacked the labor movement in the United States for being overcentralized, conservative and unimaginative. He had just come from visiting war plants during World War II. He also criticized the labor leaders for not directly combating racial discrimination in American factories and businesses. What really angered Alinsky about the American labor movement, however, was that it was no longer radical. He wanted organized labor to move beyond strictly vocational and workplace issues to involve its members in all the issues that touched them, their families and their neighbors. He wanted the unions to help him organize American workers so that they could apply the principles and practices of collective bargaining at all levels of American society.

In reality, however, Alinsky was no harder on the American labor movement than he was on the Back of the Yards Council which he had built thirty years before. His criticism of both organizations—first cousins in the people-organizing business—boiled down to the fact that they had both become institutionalized and thus less radical, more prosperous, and less adventurous since the days of the Great Depression. But God help labor's real enemies if they tried to use Saul's scolding of the unions or citizen's organizations as though he were on the side of those who wanted to do away with these basic democratic voluntary organizations. He did not. Instead, he wished both kinds of people's organizations to have a revolution within their ranks, a new generation of pesky activist members, a crisis big enough to cause a new call to arms, and, best of all, a situation that would push the two organizations into new home-workplace coalitions, what he called organized "communities of interest."

Nick von Hoffman said that Alinsky was a genuine American revolutionary: "He saw our history as a series of revolutionary upheavals. His favorite Jefferson quote was about America needing a revolution every twenty years. Nothing, he believed, should be allowed to stand longer than that without a screamingly painful kick in the fanny."[14]

No one who considered himself an agnostic in religious matters, as did Alinsky, was ever more involved with churches. From Chicago's Back of the Yards to Rochester's FIGHT, Alinsky found the chief support for his people's organizations among the Christian churches. Two generations of priests, sisters, ministers and laity learned from him a practical method of loving their neighbors and of doing something effective to help the poor, the hungry, the imprisoned, the powerless. Tom Gaudette explains the attraction that church people felt toward Alinsky: "I always said that the Church confused us by saying that we should do something for people. I'll do anything. But they never told me what to do. . . . The Church says 'Give your wealth and follow me.' Come on—that doesn't make sense. Tell me what I can do with my power, my talents and my abilities. . . . Then Saul came along and said, 'Gaudette, you son of a bitch, if you want to organize Northwest Chicago, then quit your job, and I'll help you do it.' "[15]

But not all church people were so enamored of Alinsky. While Cardinal Stritch hired him to train the Chicago priests, Cardinal Cody fired Monsignor Egan to get rid of him and Alinsky; Pope Paul VI and theologian Reinhold Niebuhr respected him, but *The Christian Century* of the early 1960's called him a Marxist and fought a holy war against him; whole congregations and denominations split over backing Alinsky projects. The good Pope John XXIII, whom Alinsky loved but never met, sounded as though he had Alinsky's work in mind when he wrote in his encyclical *Mater et Magistra* (1961) of "that human and natural inclination, scarcely resistible, whereby men are impelled voluntarily to enter into association in order to attain objectives which each one desires, but which exceed the capacity of single individuals."

For Alinsky the internal church debate over organizing was part of the ongoing split between ritual Christians and religious ones. In the first address he made to Monsignor John O'Grady's National Conference of Catholic Charities in 1942, Saul applied this distinction to Catholics, but he said that it applied as well to Protestants and Jews. For Alinsky, "ritual" Catholics were those for whom the "teachings of the Church are simply a set of ceremonials . . . Baptism, Mass on Sunday, Communion, Confirmation, fast days or dispensations, an occasional retreat and Extreme Unction." He thought that these ritualists formed the majority in the Church. On the other hand, the "religious" Christians were those who carried with them, deep in their hearts and minds, "those precepts, teachings, morals and the faith, which in themselves constitute the Catholic Church. These were the church people who lived their faith in everyday life. One rarely hears," Saul noted, "the cry of prejudice arising from religious Catholics."[16] Needless to say, Saul considered the latter types, the church people who followed the sound teachings of the churches and joined him on the urban barricades, the religious ones; the rest, he said, were stuck in the "old ritualistic rut" and were no help to anyone.[17] Obviously Saul did not believe in waiting for the Last Judgment to separate the sheep from the goats.

Monsignor Egan explains his long-time relationship to Alinsky in terms of his own priesthood: "I was attracted to Saul because he wanted to do for people what I believed God wanted done—to give them freedom and some say over the things that affected them the wrong way. I used to kid him about it. I never said he was a good Christian—he would have attacked me if I had—but Saul was a great human being because he recognized the dignity of the human person as God had created him—that every man and woman should have something to say about how his or her life should be lived."[18]

But it was not always easy to agree with Alinsky. Even his greatest supporters found him hard to take at times. This was especially true in the 1960's when he became something of a media darling. He enjoyed saying the most outrageous things whenever a television camera or microphone was pointed in his direction. More importantly, when Saul was masterminding a crucial battle between one of his people's organizations and some particular "Establishment," he demanded disciplined support from his allies. There was time enough, he said, to discuss the pros and cons of certain tactics after the battle. Clergy, especially, who tended to be only reluctant activists sometimes became frightened and went into a state of temporary ethical paralysis under fire. In a fight, Alinsky had no patience with such timid souls.

Along this line, IAF President George N. Shuster gave this reply to a young seminarian who was worried about Alinsky's tough tactics: "This is a pretty hard-hitting movement and sometimes people who initially approve get cold feet as the situation develops. . . . Cardinal Meyer . . . began to worry a bit. Still, I am sure that Mr. (Charles E.) Silberman was right. Alinsky's method is the only one which has really worked."[19]

Despite his tough tactics and his elevation of impoliteness to the policy level, his friends and supporters agreed that they had never known Alinsky to violate the law or advocate the violation of it.[20] The difference between Alinsky and the accepted model of Christian benevolence was that Saul was a flat-out fighter on the side of the poor and the powerless, and it was a hard, noisy, sometimes bloody crusade. Nevertheless, Jacques Maritain, who knew and loved Saul as much as anyone, described him to Robert Maynard Hutchins as a "great soul, a man of profound moral purity and burning energy . . . his natural generosity is quickened, though he would not admit it, by genuine evangelical brotherly love."[21]

When it came to the government, Alinsky was wonderfully inconsistent. Nowhere else did he reveal his homegrown American radicalism as clearly as he did in dealing with government leaders and bureaucrats. Above all, it was in this arena, says his friend von Hoffman, that Saul himself was as "one of the descendants of obnoxious characters like Tom Paine and Sam Adams."[22] Never did he advocate the overthrow of the American government. His respect for the form of government laid out by the Founding Fathers in the Constitution was as close as he ever came to an absolute. His patriotism laid its emphasis, however, on the necessity of preserving and enhancing the sovereignty of the people, "We, the People," who did "ordain and establish this Constitution for the United States of America."

To a great extent Alinsky's attitude toward the government was colored by his experience of the Great Depression. He had no great love for political leaders. To him they were servants of the people, and they came and went with every election. The crucial point in a democracy was that politicians must have a strong constituency behind them who can keep them responsive to the needs and interests of that constituency. In his biography of John L. Lewis, Alinsky enjoyed telling about the labor leader's penchant for standing up to the President and Congress and telling them what he wanted them to do. In his prime Lewis had the power to make himself heard by these servants of the people. His open rebellion helped his contemporaries overcome the attitude of supine obedience that Americans have toward duly constituted authorities. Part of Alinsky's great respect for Lewis was his readiness to take on the whole Washington establishment when necessary.[23]

At the same time, Saul had great respect for President Franklin D. Roosevelt whose New Deal had helped roll back the Depression. FDR took command of the nation at its lowest ebb and rebuilt the country and the people's pride in themselves. Saul always remained suspicious of centralized government. He believed that democracy works best when its strength is built up from a freely organized, active citizenry. Alinsky was never, however, the kind of reactionary conservative heard from today. For Alinsky, the problem was not so much getting the government off our backs as getting it off its rear end.

So, while Alinsky was spending a third of a century building up American government from the bottom and providing alternatives to citizen apathy and ineffective revolts, he was always ready and happy to excoriate politicians when he thought they were not doing their job. In Chicago he and his organizations regularly took on City Hall, and even the famous

Mayor Richard J. Daley learned to treat Alinsky's organizations with respect. During the 1960's Alinsky attacked the federal government for its poorly designed urban renewal and anti-poverty programs. In each instance he accused these "liberal" social programs of doing things for people without giving them any real opportunities to participate in planning and running them. His sharpest scorn was leveled at the vaunted "War on Poverty" of the Johnson administration directed by Kennedy brother-in-law Sargent Shriver. Alinsky angered liberal Washington when he labeled the new program as a "prize piece of political pornography ... a huge political pork barrel, a feeding trough for the welfare industry and ... those new professional parasites called 'coordinators and consultants.' " He charged that the new top-down bureaucracy ignored the poor and gave the money to city halls and social welfare agencies.[24]

The anti-poverty program, Alinsky charged, was set up to fail. It was worse than waste. Basing his argument on the political principle that power to bring about change cannot be given to people, only taken, Alinsky went on to flay the poverty program architects for raising people's hopes through the formation of local community action councils. These councils promised power to the poor through what looked like Alinsky-style community organization. He warned that these federally subsidized councils would be cut off without a cent as soon as nervous Congressional leaders realized that these poor people's organizations were becoming effective. All over the country liberal leaders attacked Alinsky for "cynicism," "sour grapes" and "sick humor."

What was overlooked, however, in the hullabaloo over the war on poverty was Alinsky's positive suggestion that Congress and the President put forward a true poverty program that would replace the totally inadequate welfare program with some form of guaranteed annual income for those unable to work and join to it massive public works projects like the TVA to develop the country's poorer regions and provide real jobs for the unemployed and underemployed. In the meantime, Alinsky continued to urge poor people to organize themselves into independent power blocs to assure themselves representation at the federal, state and local level.

Only a handful of government officials understood what Alinsky was trying to say in his harsh critique of the antipoverty program. One was Senator Robert F. Kennedy of New York. Kennedy understood what Saul meant about poor people needing to have a hand in planning and running programs for their communities. Unlike many legislators, Bobby Kennedy was not afraid to go into the fields of California and the shacks of rural New York State to talk to poor people. He also had the ear of the "Have-Little-Want-Mores," the white middle class workers and their families.[25] More politicians like Kennedy would be needed to bring together the new coalitions of poor, minority and middle class Americans if anything was to change for the better.

Another politician who listened to Alinsky was Daniel Patrick Moynihan of Harvard and Washington. Later Moynihan wrote his own critique of the poverty program in which he used much of Alinsky's original insights.[26] During the first Nixon Administration, Moynihan, the President's assistant for urban affairs, developed a far-reaching welfare reform program which was shot down in the Senate. Some of the reason for the failure of Moynihan's plan was precisely the growing backlash among middle class Americans against the poor which Alinsky had warned about in his criticism of the ill-conceived poverty program.

The stock proxy used by Rochester's FIGHT organization to win a jobs training program with Eastman Kodak Company in Rochester was an eye-opener for Alinsky. Over the next couple of years he thought a lot about how he might develop a national "Proxies for People" program. That research gave him new insights into the corporate sector of American business. Here, as always, Alinsky was a flexible radical, more interested in effective reform than in socialist daydreams. He didn't want corporations to fail, but to take a greater responsibility for the commonweal—to work together effectively for full employment, meaningful jobs, better products, protection of the environment, vital local communities and healthy citizens. In the battles he led, with citizen organizations pitted against corporations, his objective was to bring both sides to the bargaining table where they would hammer out a settlement with something in it for everybody. Saul thought ongoing labor-management war was stupid. The day after the Kodak-FIGHT agreement was repaired, Alinsky was met at the Rochester airport by a swarm of reporters who wanted to know what he thought now about Eastman Kodak. Alinsky seemed to brush off the question, but a moment later he stopped a news photographer about to take his picture. "Is that Kodak film you're using? Good! I insist that anyone taking my picture use Kodak film." For Alinsky there were no permanent enemies, only a variety of organizations and interests coming together to work out their self-interests in a free society.

The stock proxy tactic gave him a handle to organize the middle class citizens who were the American masses, and, at the same time, bring the corporations to accept a greater share of responsibility for the well-being of the people. He disagreed with business leaders who said that profits and good management were the only real responsibilities of the corporate sector—the original "trickle down" theory of economics. For Alinsky there was no such thing as a totally private sector; government, business and citizens were bound together in a common enterprise, with each group dependent to some degree on the others. A good example, Alinsky said, was the interrelationship between government contracts, taxes on individuals and jobs and community welfare.

Alinsky painted a picture of thousands of individual shareholders meeting together in Yankee Stadium or the Astrodome to hear reports from their company's officers and to cast their votes for or against management.[27] Saul wanted to organize these individual stockholders into mass shareholder organizations so they could make their interests known to corporation managers. Shareholders in a company were also workers, consumers, residents of the communities in which companies were located. In Alinsky's plan these shareholders would pool their interests and their votes, not to attempt a take-over of any company, but to demand that corporations take a fair share of responsibility for local communities, the environment, the health and welfare of their employees and neighbors, the products they advertised and sold, company mergers, corporate political contributions, overseas markets and the total effect of relocating or expanding their businesses.

Once the door was opened to a more democratic management of corporations, Alinsky believed that millions of educated, thoughtful middle class Americans would take a greater interest in corporate policies, practices and budgets. Through the corporations citizen-stockholders would be able to exercise greater control over the Pentagon and the growth of the nation's military budget. That was Alinsky's dream all along: finding ways to organize Americans at every level so that they share in the power to look after their own interests. The spread of higher education and new communications technologies meant to Alinsky that Americans could now gain a better understanding of how each group's interests depended on the interests of other groups. Once that began to happen, Alinsky said that he could see them joining together and advancing from issue to issue, forming coalitions, negotiating compromises, making trade-offs until, in time, their interests became truly shared, and became "enlightened self-interests" in ethical terms.

A realistic idealist, however, Alinsky admitted that history and experience did not augur well for the growth of enlightened self-interest. Alinsky's answer to the doubters was to repeat his credo in people and the democratic process. In his thirty-five years of organizing all kinds of people, he had found nothing to shake that democratic faith. "We must believe," he said, "in man's struggle for an ever better world, that man is moving toward a world of more beauty, love, laughter and creation. That is the vision of man."[28]

Something of a Man

His friends and comrades-in-arms all agree that Saul Alinsky was an original. He resisted categories the way he resisted the status quo. Asked to sum up what made Saul special, Herb White said that there was something "gypsy" about him, a mixture of magic, insight, free-spiritedness, independence, earthiness, humor, passion and fierce loyalty.[29] Alinsky was willing to live with an incomplete vision of the world, take half a loaf, organize people and leave them to work things out for themselves.

There were things about him that we like to think of as quintessentially American: the tough individualist with few illusions, the nomadic lawman of the Old West (he had a business card that said, "Have Trouble, Will Travel"), the romantic loner like Humphrey Bogart's Rick in the movie "Casablanca"—"a pushover for a real dame or someone in trouble," even a Franciscan troubador (Saul's prayer for radicals was the one by St. Francis which begins, "Lord, make me an instrument of your peace . . .").

In his sworn enmity toward the deadly institutionalization and routinization that afflicted social structures, Alinsky was something of a grown-up Huck Finn—the gaudy outcast lighting out for a new territory before anyone could civilize him. Alinsky's mobility was crucial; was it that particularly American freedom or was it personal restlessness, or both? Was there something uniquely Jewish in his always having his bag packed, ready to go at a moment's notice? (He often said that an organizer shouldn't stay in one town more than three years because of the danger of being crucified.) In a wonderful letter to a fellow wanderer, the international journalist Georgie Ann Geyer, Alinsky told her about his packed suitcase. "I have a very good and expensive suitcase which is packed with a toilet kit, suit, sport jacket, trousers, five shirts, underwear and about $1,500 in traveler's checks which is all locked up in my closet —all ready to go . . . every so often I look at it and get a feeling of warm security."[30]

Despite the encomiums of his friends, however, Alinsky was not always nice. There was, as might be expected, another, less attractive side to the radical organizer. He was hard-nosed, outspoken, and profane; when he wanted to be, he could be loud, bullying, impatient, and scornful of questions he thought stupid or elementary. Saul was not a model family man; an erratic parent, for the most part his work came ahead of his wife and kids. In his portrait of the good organizer he made a big point about explaining that most organizers had disastrous marriages. People who were subjected to his prodding, testing, elbowing approach to character analysis often came away angry and psychologically black and blue. Some people hated him with an apoplectic fury. To this day you have only to mention Alinsky in some circles to start a row.

Not even his most loyal friends, therefore, ever dared to claim sainthood for Saul. His soul, like his genius for organizing, was rough, profane, pushy and funny—whether he was slugging it out toe to toe with university presidents, corporation executives, big-city mayors, or arrogant church leaders (he once called Cardinal James McIntyre of Los Angeles an "un-Christian, pre-historic muttonhead") or when he stood all alone in an airport in the Deep South, surrounded by Ku Klux Klan hoodlums. He saw his own life in existential terms, a modern-day Sisyphus moving his stone to the top of the hill. More than once he slipped and found himself and the stone at the bottom of the hill. But each time he brushed himself off and started up again.

When Saul Alinsky's career was finished, there on the streets of Carmel, he had organized, in one way or another, a couple of million men and women to take control of their lives. He made many more Americans aware of the power of organized citizen participation in a democracy to make needed changes in social institutions and government regulations. Alinsky taught people the varied use of planned demonstrations to gain a hearing or draw attention to community problems. The large-scale citizen mobilizations of our time—women, anti-war and nuclear activists, consumers, environmentalists—whether they know it or not, owe most of their bottom-up organizational strategy and hard-hitting, non-violent tactics to Saul Alinsky. Along with the Rev. Martin Luther King, Jr., Alinsky deserves credit also for freeing American churches from suburban captivity and ghetto sanctuaries and bringing church people into the city streets and village roads where people were struggling with the problems and possibilities of everyday life.

Like all great men, Saul had a generous share of successes

and failures. He remained, however, an American radical to
the end and died happy, said Nick von Hoffman, "in the
knowledge that he had not accomplished what he started out to
do, that his life's work was not complete, the job was not over.
Saul Alinsky knew that when it was over, America would be
over too."[31]

An Alinsky in Your Future

Ten years after Alinsky died, Americans were busily reading a best-selling book entitled *Megatrends* by John Naisbitt, a
down-to-earth futurist. Naisbitt's thesis is that America is en-
tering a new era of growth. Underneath the nation's current
problems of economic recession and stagnation, long-range
changes are taking place that are deeply affecting the way
Americans live, work, think and relate to their government.
The author goes on to outline ten critical areas in what he sees
as a major restructuring of the country. It is still impossible to
predict, he admits, the form that American society will assume
in the years ahead, but it is possible to detect and study the
broad outlines, the "megatrends," of major structural and oper-
ational changes already in gear.

The research data for Naisbitt's book has been gathered by
him and his associates over twelve years from "content analysis" of local events taking place in U.S. cities and states and
reported in local newspapers. The method of content analysis
was developed by social scientists during World War II and
was used by American intelligence to study what was going on
inside wartime Germany. Major social trends are discernible
over a period of time, according to this method, because newspapers operate with a limited "news hole"—the amount of
space devoted to news in the daily paper. As new events arise
and are reported, they tend to push out of the news columns
less current matters. The example is given of the gradual
replacement of civil rights stories in the 1970's by stories about
environmental concerns. Because the data Naisbitt used for his
book came from local communities and local newspapers across
the United States, the major trends he discerned are bottom-up

or grass roots movements rather than the "Boys on the Bus" bias of national news reporting that comes out of New York and Washington, D.C. Naisbitt's research tells him that nothing of importance is created or generated in New York or Washington.

Among the ten megatrends the author outlines, he discerns a growing tendency toward decentralization in the political and economic patterns of the United States. Underneath the recessionary struggles Americans are busy restructuring the country by building new, smaller, localized voluntary structures—community-based, economic, social, governmental units, to help them deal with issues they believe are crucial to their families, work, churches and neighborhoods. It is Naisbitt's hypothesis that we are witnessing the passing of a centralizing trend in American life that began in the days of its early industrial development and became dominant in the national struggles to end the Great Depression and to defeat the world fascist powers in World War II. With those problems no longer crucial, Americans are once more moving toward diversity and local control. President Reagan and his administration cohorts are attempting to ride with the trend, not leading it, as they would have us think.

If his research data is correct, Naisbitt believes that the citizen organizing of Alinsky and his heirs is an important element in this decentralizing trend. All over the country citizens are joining together at the local level to reorganize and restructure the nation from the bottom-up. Naisbitt says there are twenty million Americans organized in these local units, and they are moving toward larger coalitions and networks at metropolitan, state and regional levels.

This citizen restructuring is already influencing our politics, business and culture. Examples are cited. City planners are moving away from top-down master plans in favor of dealing with citizen groups to develop planning alternatives. Citizen organizations are pressing state governments for greater citizen participation in state regulatory agencies, especially as regards energy, environmental protection and consumer issues. In some places, nervous local politicians are trying to head off the trend toward citizen participation by appointing citizen advisory groups. Other citizen groups are demanding an end to at-large city council representation in favor of ward or district representatives.[32]

If Saul Alinsky were to see the book, he would be saying, "I told you so." Shortly before he died, Saul told an old friend that there would be a great surge in citizen organizing. "You know," Alinsky said with a chuckle, "someday soon this whole business is going to turn into national industry."[33] For the most part his organizing heirs are hard at work. They have not attempted to freeze his organizing legacy into a jealously guarded body of doctrine. They know that Saul promised to come back to haunt them if they tried it.

Besides the work being done by Alinsky's own organization, now called the IAF Alinsky Institute, another veteran Alinsky organizer, Tom Gaudette, is helping to train organizers and assist organizations in an informal network of citizen groups across the country. Other organizers whose roots lie in the Alinsky tradition, Shel Trapp, Gale Cincotta, Herb and Jessica White, John Baumann, Heather Booth, Mike Miller, Scott Reed, and dozens more are organizing, training leaders, and building coalitions around a wide variety of local and regional issues. All of these organizers are freely making changes in Alinsky's approach, breaking his "rules" when necessary, devising new tactics, even as they continue to pursue his objective—to help people get the power they need to run their own lives and communities.

The issues around which this local organizing is taking place run the gamut of contemporary concerns: energy, jobs, government priorities, environmental damage, housing, banks and mortgage policies, consumer interests, community development and many more. A few of the organizers like Heather Booth, president of the Midwest Academy, a training center for citizen groups, are attempting to push citizen organizations in the direction of electoral politics—recruiting and running candidates for office, developing new alliances between citizen groups and labor unions, building new electoral forces for local, state and national elections.[34] The majority of Alinsky-style organizers and local organizations, however, remain outside of electoral politics, preferring to build local democratic structures and networks that will give citizens greater participation in and control over government and the corporate business sector. For the most part Alinsky would be pleased by the way his one-man-band is growing into a national populist movement.

In accordance with Alinsky's dictum, "Low Overhead —High Independence," local organizations continue to "live off the land" as much as possible. They do not depend for their day-to-day operation on government or foundation funds that can easily be withdrawn under pressure. Organization leaders are better fund raisers today than in Alinsky's heyday. The churches are still the key institutional supporters of local citizen organizations. Local parishes and congregations pay annual dues that go toward the basic operating budget. Some funding comes from metropolitan and denominational church sources—from domestic church mission funds, for instance. The largest single contributor to these citizen organizations over the last decade has been the Campaign for Human Development, an annual Thanksgiving collection authorized by the National Conference of Catholic Bishops and taken up in parish churches across the nation. With an admirable "bare-bones" national staff, CHD has provided start-up and training funds for local organizations, especially in distressed communities. Still, the outside funding remains minimal; today's citizen organizations raise their own frugal budgets from local community sources, some from businesses and small local foundations, the rest from their own constituencies through raffles, bake sales, bingo, neighborhood festivals, walk-a-thons and marathons. They understand that fund raising is also organizing.

The IAF Alinsky Institute remains the most advanced of these new organizing networks of local citizen organizations. Its headquarters are in Huntington, N.Y., outside New York City. The IAF's director is Edward T. Chambers, a twenty-five-year veteran of the organizing wars. Chambers has been the main architect of the gradual professionalization of Alinsky's art of organizing. Gone is Saul's serendipitous approach to the recruitment and training of organizers. Today's recruits are carefully screened, trained under Chambers' watchful eye, apprenticed to senior organizers in the field and supported within IAF's close, warm network of organizers and local leaders. Continuity is the watchword of today's IAF. Chambers is still the "nuts and bolts man" praised by Fr. "Doc" Farrell twenty years ago in Woodlawn.

Working conditions for organizers have improved in most of today's organizing networks. According to Chambers, the "movement days" of minimum wages and marginal living conditions are past. In this area too IAF has led the way with professional-level salaries for its organizers, fringe benefits, retirement provisions and vacations. No one will get rich being an organizer, but the men and women who are the necessary catalysts of the citizen organization movement are now able to maintain a normal family life and pass up, if they wish, other job offers in favor of remaining professional organizers.

The success enjoyed by the IAF organizers in working with parish churches and neighborhood congregations has encouraged other organizers to take another look at involving local churches. In the 1960's local church involvement, at least outside of Chicago, often meant a few of the younger clergy and a minority of lay members. Moreover, the young middle class radicals who worked in civil rights, anti-poverty and anti-war organizing usually looked down upon the churches as havens for middle class racists, hardhats—certainly not allies —part of the problem, not of the solution. These radicals were willing to accept church funds, "ripping off the churches" in the radical parlance of the day, but they could care less about the churches and church people. Some of these organizers who cut their radical teeth in the movement stuff of the 1960's carried over this anti-church attitude to their later local organizing.

The IAF network inherited Alinsky's regard for local churches, however, and began to build upon it again during the past ten years. The growth of the ecumenical movement bringing closer cooperation between the various Christian churches and Jewish and other congregations has removed much of the inter-church suspicions and prejudices that plagued Alinsky's early years. In the 1970's the IAF organizers depended upon local churches as the backbone of the local organizations they put together. Today's organizers spend more time recruiting, educating and involving pastors and congregations in citizen organizations. In the beginning of a new project the organizer and local leaders meet individually with the pastors and lay leaders to discuss with them the local issues, recruit them for the organization and request an annual contribution from the church. Whenever possible, meetings are held in church meeting rooms and parish halls.

From an organizer's point of view, churches are a collection of families, often living in the same geographical area. Clergy and parish properties share the problems of their flocks —declining neighborhoods, joblessness, lack of decent, affordable housing, sky-high mortgages, lack of transportation, bad schools, cutbacks in police and fire protection. Today's clergy and lay leaders of local churches see part of the church's social mission in helping their people organize themselves to provide safe, clean neighborhoods, good schools, more responsive government and improved relationships with neighboring communities. One pastor said simply, "The parish will die if this community dies." Church people today seem to understand better than their parents that a little community controversy is often a necessary price in the beginning to bring about neighborhood health and stability.

When times are bad for a lot of people, as in the Great Depression or in the severe economic struggles of the early 1980's, pastors and people in affected areas draw together to fight for survival and care for the poor, the hungry, and the homeless among them. Hundreds of local organizations across the country are now reaching out to organize the millions of middle class and poorer people who are angry and frustrated by the ailing economy, government paralysis and anti-community corporate policies. Local clergy become more outspoken as they see the anguish of their people. A pastor in a middle class Polish neighborhood in snowy Buffalo—hardly a radical area —spoke out recently about the rising natural gas prices that are hurting his flock and the parish budget. "My people are being forced to choose between food and heat," the priest said. "I told them to start writing letters. I told them to start screaming that Congress is letting us bleed."[35] Situations like that in Buffalo are making church and community leaders turn to organizing themselves to fight for their rights against unresponsive government and irresponsible companies.

Saul Alinsky left behind a rich legacy of local, broad-based, community organizations. It was his belief, bolstered by his long experience, that the survival of the American democratic system depended on an activist citizenry. A few months before his death, he was talking to a group of college students. He told them what Tocqueville said nearly one hundred and fifty years before—that if the American people ever came to feel that they no longer had any say about the decisions of their life except to vote every four years, then America would be finished as a democratic nation. "You see, in a free and open society like ours," Saul explained, "its power, its heart, its soul, its everything is in terms of its people; popular participation—that's the real meaning of that slogan, 'Power to the People.' . . . The only way people can have power is through organization. You can't do it as an individual. . . . That free and open system carries within itself the ax of its own destruction. If the populace lacks power to actively participate in the process, the whole thing will be destroyed. . . ."[36]

That was Alinsky's reveille for radicals. He believed that it had to be sounded for each new generation of Americans descended from Thomas Jefferson and the other Founding Fathers. Saul kept blowing that American radical reveille on his slightly off-key bugle until his breath was gone. It really was his whole act, and it came complete with directions for assembling an organization in every U.S. neighborhood or barrio. For thirty-five years Alinsky gave out the same message as he tramped around the city neighborhoods, paced up and down in parish halls, roared along on trains, flew on jets, and slept in ten thousand look-alike motels. When he died, he left behind a half-dozen good organizers, three books, a lifetime supply of funny stories, helpful anecdotes and a collection of Alinsky's aphorisms about the art of organizing free people to make America work.

Ten years later, his legacy has grown to hundreds of organizers and millions of Americans working together in local organizations. Alinsky's part is done. What "We the People of the United States" do with our power and freedom to act as citizens is in our hands.

NOTES

INTRODUCTION

1. Eric Norden, "Saul Alinsky Interview," *Playboy*, March 1972, p. 60.

2. Saul D. Alinsky, *John L. Lewis: An Unauthorized Biography* (New York: Random House, Vintage Edition, 1970), pp. x–xiv.

3. Harry C. Boyte, *The Backyard Revolution: Understanding the New Citizen Movement* (Philadelphia: Temple University Press, 1980), pp. xii–xiii.

4. Saul D. Alinsky, *Reveille for Radicals* (New York: Random House, Vintage Edition, 1969), pp. 62–63.

5. P. David Finks, "Crisis in Smugtown: A Study of Conflict, Churches and Citizen Organizations in Rochester, New York—1964–1969," (Ph.D. diss., Union Graduate School, 1975), p. 290.

6. Saul D. Alinsky, *Rules for Radicals: A Practical Primer for Realistic Radicals* (New York: Random House, 1971), p. xxvi.

CHAPTER 1

1. Much of the material in this chapter comes from conversations with Saul Alinsky and later with Jean Graham Alinsky, Irene McGinnis Alinsky and his friend Nicholas von Hoffman, in addition to written sources.

2. Jane Addams, *Twenty Years at Hull House* (New York: New American Library, Signet Classic, 1961), p. 81.

3. Norden, "Alinsky Interview," p. 62.

4. Robert E.L. Faris, *Chicago Sociology, 1920–1932* (Chicago: University of Chicago Press, 1967), p. 29.

5. Saul D. Alinsky, "Report on Dreamland Ballroom," class report for Sociology 268 (Professor Ernest K. Burgess), University of Chicago, 1929, Mike Miller, San Francisco.

6. The Capone anecdotes are contained in at least three published interviews with Alinsky: Marion K. Sanders, *The Professional Radical: Conversations with Saul Alinsky* (New York: Harper and Row, Perennial Library, 1970), pp. 19–20; Studs Terkel, *Hard Times: An Oral History of the Great Depression* (New York: Pantheon, 1970), p. 311; Norden, "Alinsky Interview," p. 66.

7. Anthony Sorrentino, *Organizing Against Crime: Redeveloping the Neighborhood* (New York: Human Sciences Press, 1977), p. 59.

8. Frederic M. Thrasher, *The Gang: A Study of 1,313 Gangs in Chicago* (Chicago: University of Chicago Press, Phoenix Books, 1927, 1963), p. 13.

9. Arthur M. Schlesinger, Jr., *Robert Kennedy and His Times* (Boston: Houghton Mifflin Company, 1978), p. 164.

10. Norden, "Alinsky Interview," p. 68.

11. Saul D. Alinsky, "A Sociological Technique in Clinical Criminology," *Proceedings of the American Prison Association* 1934.

12. James B. Jacobs, *Stateville: The Penitentiary in Mass Society* (Chicago: University of Chicago Press, 1977), p. 18.

13. Sanders, *Professional Radical*, p. 25.

14. Clifford R. Shaw to Judge Theodore Rosen, June 11, 1935, Clifford Shaw Papers, Chicago Historical Society.

15. Sanders, *Professional Radical*, pp. 29–30.

16. Sorrentino, *Organizing Against Crime, passim.*

17. Upton Sinclair, *The Jungle* (Cambridge: Robert Bentley, Inc., 1905, 1972).

18. Saul D. Alinsky, "Community Analysis and Organization," *American Journal of Sociology*, Vol. 46, No. 6 (May 1941), p. 798.

19. Carl Sandburg, "Chicago," *Harvest Poems: 1910–1960* (New York: Harcourt Brace Jovanovich, 1960), pp. 35–40.

20. Alinsky, *Rules for Radicals*, p. 67.

21. Agnes E. Meyer, "Orderly Revolution," *Washington Post*, June 7, 1945.

22. "Meat and a Bishop," *Time*, July 24, 1939, p. 12.

CHAPTER 2

1. Alinsky to Jon D. Snodgrass, May 4, 1971, Alinsky Papers, IAF Institute, Huntington, New York.

2. Michael P. Connolly, "An Historical Study of Change in Saul D. Alinsky's Community Organization Practice and Theory, 1939–1972" (Ph.D. diss., University of Minnesota, 1976), p. 32.

3. Alinsky to Snodgrass, May 4, 1971, Alinsky Papers, IAF Institute.

4. Jon D. Snodgrass, "The American Criminological Tradition: Portraits of the Men and Ideology in a Discipline," (Ph.D. diss., University of Pennsylvania, 1972), p. 213.

5. Jon D. Snodgrass, "Clifford R. Shaw and Henry D. McKay: Chicago Criminologists," *British Journal of Criminology*, Vol. 16, No. 1 (January 1976).

6. Interview with Joseph Meegan, Chicago, February 22, 1977.

7. Meyer, *Washington Post*, June 9, 1945.

8. Stephen Becker, *Marshall Field III: A Biography* (New York: Simon and Schuster, 1964), p. 11.

9. *Ibid.*, p. 187.

10. Industrial Areas Foundation Brochure, Chicago, c. 1940, Alinsky Papers, IAF Institute.

11. *Ibid.*

12. Connolly, "Community Organization," p. 114.

13. Alinsky, "Community Analysis," p. 807.

14. Norden, "Alinsky Interview," p. 150.

15. Dean Acheson, *Present at the Creation* (New York: New American Library, Signet Book, 1969, 1970), p. 35.

16. Interview with Jean Graham Alinsky, Monterey, Calif., September 13, 1978.

17. Alistair Cooke, *Six Men* (New York: Berkley, 1977), p. 233.

18. Alinsky, *Reveille for Radicals*.

19. Ralph Bates, *The Nation*, April 20, 1946.

20. Jacques Maritain to Alinsky, August 18, 1945, Alinsky Papers, University of Illinois, Chicago.

21. Alinsky, *Reveille for Radicals*, p. 5.

22. *Ibid.*, pp. 13–15.

23. *Ibid.*, p. 34.

24. *Ibid.*, p. 56.

25. Adrienne Koch, *Jefferson and Madison: The Great Collaboration* (New York: Oxford University Press, Galaxy Book, 1950, 1977), p. 45.

26. James Madison, "Federalist No. 51," *The Federalist* (New York: Modern Library, 1937), p. 337.

27. Alexis de Tocqueville, *Democracy in America II* (New York: Schocken, 1961, 1974), p. 384.

28. Sam Bass Warner, Jr., *The Urban Wilderness* (New York: Harper and Row, 1972), p. 134.

29. Charles T. Leber, Jr., to *Saturday Evening Post*, May 7, 1961.

30. Alinsky to Valentine E. and Harriet Macy, July 25, 1944, Alinsky Papers, University of Illinois, Chicago.

31. Interview with Fred Ross, Sr., Boston, Mass., June 28, 1977.

32. *Ibid.*

33. *Ibid.*

34. *Ibid.*

35. *Ibid.*

36. *Ibid.*

37. *Ibid.*

38. *Ibid.*

39. *Ibid.*

40. *Ibid.*

41. *Ibid.*

42. Carey McWilliams, *The Education of Carey McWilliams* (New York: Simon and Schuster, 1978, 1979), pp. 110–111.

43. Ross, Interview, June 28, 1977.

44. *Ibid.*

45. *Ibid.*

46. Interview with Ralph Helstein, Chicago, April 11, 1977.

47. Alinsky, *John L. Lewis*, p. 388.

48. *Ibid.*, p. 387.

49. *Ibid.*, pp. 176–191.

50. *Ibid.*, p. xiv.

51. Emmett Dedmon, *Chicago Sun*, November 3, 1949.

52. Edward S. Skillin, *Commonweal*, November 25, 1949.

53. Interview with Nicholas von Hoffman, Washington, D.C., December 15, 1978.

54. It is of some interest that the authors of a recent biography of John L. Lewis have attempted to dismiss Alinsky's book in an arrogant and offhand manner (Melvyn Dubofsky and Warren Van Tine, *John L. Lewis: A Biography* [New York: Quadrangle/New York Times, 1977]). Unable to find written records of the meetings between Lewis and Alinsky, the authors proceed to question whether a close relationship ever existed between the two men. Dubovsky and Van Tine suffer from an advanced case of academicism. Alinsky admitted that he intended to write a personal tribute, based on his friendship and deep respect for Lewis. His book was more an exercise in oral history than formal historiography. But even his sternest critics never questioned Alinsky's veracity. Even those dissenters whom the *Saturday Review* called the "hate Lewis coterie" among the top leadership of the CIO questioned only Alinsky's interpretations, not his facts (Wel-

lington Roe, *Saturday Review,* February 11, 1950).

The disappearance of Alinsky's notes for the book are certainly a loss to historians and biographers. That they have disappeared, however, is no proof that they never were. From the time of Helene's death in 1947 to 1951 when Alinsky went back to work, few written records of any kind survive. He had no regular secretary. His friends, like Helstein, say that he neglected his work. He seems to have had little interest in preserving anything during those moody days.

55. Alinsky, *John L. Lewis,* p. 369.

56. Arthur M. Schlesinger, Jr., *The Age of Roosevelt: The Coming of the New Deal* (Boston: Houghton Mifflin Co., 1959), pp. 418–419.

57. Alinsky, *John L. Lewis,* p. 360.

58. *Ibid.,* p. xvii.

59. Helstein, Interview, April 11, 1977.

60. Ross, Interview, June 28, 1977.

61. Josephine Whitney Duveneck, *Life on Two Levels* (Los Altos, Calif.: William Kaufman, 1978), p. 254.

62. Jacques Maritain to *Harper's* Magazine, August 1965.

63. Sanders, *Professional Radical,* p. 36.

64. Alinsky to Maritain, October 21, 1963, Alinsky Papers, IAF Institute.

CHAPTER 3

1. Jean Graham Alinsky, Interview, September 13, 1978.

2. Alinsky to Milton Mayer, May 1, 1953, Alinsky Papers, IAF Institute.

3. *Ibid.*

4. Alinsky, "Fights of Bishop Sheil," *Catholic Digest,* August 1951, pp. 75–80.

5. Alinsky to Harriet Macy, March 31, 1945, Alinsky Papers, University of Illinois, Chicago.

6. Meyer, *Washington Post,* June 4–9, 1945.

7. Chalmers Roberts, *The Washington Post: The First 100 Years* (Boston: Houghton Mifflin Co., 1977), p. 265.

8. *Ibid.,* p. 265.

9. Alinsky to Maritain, September 27, 1951, Alinsky Papers, University of Illinois, Chicago.

10. Alinsky to Henry Siegbert (Hofheimer Foundation) October 5, 1951, Alinsky Papers, IAF Institute.

11. Norden, "Alinsky Interview," p. 169.

12. Sanders, *Professional Radical*, pp. 27–28.

13. Alinsky to Maritain, September 27, 1951, Alinsky Papers, University of Illinois, Chicago.

14. Alinsky to Macys, August 27, 1945, Alinsky Papers, University of Illinois, Chicago.

15. Carl Tjerandsen, *Education for Citizenship: A Foundation's Experience* (Santa Cruz, Calif.: Emil Schwartzhaupt Foundation, 1980), p. xiv.

16. Ross, Interview, June 28, 1977.

17. Jacques Levy, *Cesar Chavez: Autobiography of La Causa* (New York: W.W. Norton, 1975), p. 102.

18. Duveneck, *Two Levels*, p. 256.

19. Interview with Cesar Chavez, May 3, 1977, La Paz, Keene, Calif.

20. *Ibid.*

21. Ross, Interview, June 28, 1977.

22. Tjerandsen, *Education for Citizenship*, pp. 84–85.

23. *Ibid.*, p. 84.

24. *Ibid.*, p. 135.

25. Ross, Interview, June 28, 1977.

26. Tjerandsen to Alinsky, January 2, 1953, Alinsky Papers, IAF Institute.

27. Alinsky, *Reveille for Radicals*, p. 155.

28. Tjerandsen to Alinsky, January 2, 1953.

29. Alinsky to Paul McGhee, August 17, 1955, Alinsky Papers, IAF Institute.

30. Jean Graham Alinsky, Interview, September 13, 1978.

31. Ross, Interview, June 28, 1977.

32. *Ibid.*

33. *Ibid.*

34. Tjerandsen, *Education for Citizenship*, p. 106.

35. Alinsky to Tjerandsen, July 16, 1962, Alinsky Papers, IAF Institute.

36. Alinsky, "IAF Annual Report," December 1964.

37. Alinsky, "Community Analysis," p. 799.

38. Norden, "Alinsky Interview," p. 76.

39. Editors of *Fortune, USA: The Permanent Revolution*, New York, 1951.

40. Douglas T. Miller and Marion Nowak, *The Fifties: The Way We Really Were* (Garden City: Doubleday, 1977), p. 110.

282   THE RADICAL VISION OF SAUL ALINSKY

41. Alice Padgett, "Monsignor John O'Grady: Lover of People," *Catholic Charities Review*, March 1960.

42. John O'Grady, "Memoirs," unpublished, O'Grady Papers, National Conference of Catholic Charities (NCCC) and Catholic University, Washington, D.C.

43. G. Howland Shaw, *Proceedings of the National Conference of Catholic Charities*, November 17–22, 1949.

44. Cardinal Samuel Stritch, "Speech to Chicago Pastors," November 26, 1952, O'Grady Papers.

45. *Ibid.*

46. Father Adrian Fisher, O.F.M., "Speech to Chicago Pastors," November 26, 1953, O'Grady Papers.

47. Alinsky, "Speech at NCCC Annual Meeting, September 29, 1953, Alinsky Papers, University of Illinois, Chicago.

48. Von Hoffman, Interview, December 15, 1978.

49. Alinsky, "Speech to NCCC Annual Meeting," September 29, 1953, Alinsky Papers, University of Illinois, Chicago.

50. Interview with Carl Tjerandsen, Santa Cruz, Calif., April 30, 1977.

51. Alinsky to Jane Gallagher, March 2, 1956, O'Grady Papers.

52. Von Hoffman, Interview, December 15, 1978.

53. *Ibid.*

54. *Ibid.*

55. O'Grady, "Interim Report on the Lackawanna Project," November 5, 1957, O'Grady Papers, p. 5.

56. *Ibid.*, p. 9.

57. Tjerandsen, *Education for Citizenship*, p. 271.

58. *Ibid.*, p. 273.

59. Tjerandsen, Interview, April 30, 1977.

60. Alinsky to Tjerandsen, June 26, 1959, Alinsky Papers, IAF Institute.

61. Interview with Lester Hunt, Chicago, May 16, 1977.

62. Tjerandsen, Interview, April 30, 1977.

63. Field Foundation "Minutes," copy, January 15, 1953, Alinsky Papers, IAF Institute.

64. *New York Times*, February 18, 1953.

65. Alinsky to Dr. Leona Baumgartner, New York City, December 2, 1953, Alinsky Papers, IAF Institute.

66. Alinsky to Macys, December 11, 1953, Alinsky Papers, IAF Institute.

67. Alinsky, "Report to New York Foundation, June 1955, Alinsky Papers, IAF Institute.

68. Alinsky to McGhee, August 17, 1955, Alinsky Papers, IAF Institute.

69. Meyer, *Washington Post,* June 8, 1945.

70. Alinsky, *Reveille for Radicals,* p. 67.

71. O'Grady, *Catholic Charities Review,* January 1957.

72. McGhee to Alinsky, February 11, 1956, Alinsky Papers, IAF Institute.

73. *Ibid.*

74. Interview with Julius Edelstein, New York City, March 4, 1977.

75. H. Daniel Carpenter, "A Citizen Participation Project . . ." prepared c. February 1956, Alinsky Papers, IAF Institute.

76. Alinsky to Carpenter, March 14, 1956, Alinsky Papers, IAF Institute.

77. Leo Gerngross (Schwartzhaupt Foundation) to H. Daniel Carpenter, June 11, 1956; D. John Heyman (New York Foundation) to Carpenter, June 18, 1956, Alinsky Papers, IAF Institute.

78. Alinsky to McGhee, March 30, 1956, Alinsky Papers, IAF Institute.

79. Tjerandsen, Interview, April 30, 1977.

80. Hunt, Interview, May 16, 1977.

81. *New York Times,* September 10, 1956.

82. Bruce K. Irvine, "Saul Alinsky in Chelsea: A History of the Chelsea Community Council, 1956–1960" (M.A. diss., Columbia University, 1967), p. 47.

83. Alinsky to Carpenter, November 21, 1956, Alinsky Papers, IAF Institute.

84. Everett C. Parker, "How Chelsea Was Torn Apart," *Christian Century,* January 3, 1960, p. 131; Alinsky to Leonard Rieser, November 17, 1958, Alinsky Papers, IAF Institute.

85. Interview with Father Robert T. Dunn, Briarcliff Manor, New York, June 2, 1977.

86. Irvine, "Alinsky in Chelsea."

87. Parker, "How Chelsea Was Torn Apart."

88. Alinsky, "Memorandum to Father Robert T. Dunn," February 10, 1960, Alinsky Papers, IAF Institute, p. 10.

89. Hunt, Interview, May 16, 1977.

90. Alinsky, "Memorandum to Dunn," February 10, 1960.

91. Dunn, Interview, June 2, 1977.

92. Alinsky to Dunn, December 16, 1963, Alinsky Papers, IAF Institute.

CHAPTER 4

1. Alinsky to Rieser, April 11, 1957, Alinsky Papers, IAF Institute.
2. Alinsky "Memorandum to Cardinal Samuel Stritch," November 14, 1957, Alinsky Papers, University of Illinois, Chicago.
3. *Ibid.*
4. Von Hoffman, Interview, December 15, 1978.
5. *Ibid.*
6. Alinsky, "IAF Annual Report," December 22, 1957.
7. Sanders, *Professional Radical,* p. 9.
8. Alinsky to Gordon Clapp, August 5, 1958, Alinsky Papers, IAF Institute.
9. Alinsky to George N. Shuster, October 23, 1958, Alinsky Papers, IAF Institute.
10. Alinsky to Rieser, November 10, 1958, Alinsky Papers, IAF Institute.
11. *Ibid.*
12. O'Grady to Cardinal Domenico Tardini, August 21, 1959, O'Grady Papers.
13. Alinsky to O'Grady, August 27, 1959, O'Grady Papers.
14. Monsignor Angelo Dell' Acqua to O'Grady, November 10, 1959, O'Grady Papers.
15. Dell' Acqua to Alinsky, March 24, 1960, O'Grady Papers.
16. Alinsky to Jean Graham Alinsky, April 19, 1960.
17. *Ibid.,* n.d.
18. *Ibid.,* April 21, 1960.
19. *Ibid.,* n.d.
20. *Ibid.,* n.d.
21. *Ibid.,* n.d.
22. Alinsky to O'Grady, June 9, 1960, O'Grady Papers.
23. Alinsky to Tjerandsen, June 26, 1959, Alinsky Papers, IAF Institute.
24. Von Hoffman, Interview, December 15, 1978.
25. Interview with Monsignor John J. Egan, Notre Dame, Ind., November 14, 1976.
26. *Ibid.*
27. "Minutes of Southwest Pastors' Meeting," Chicago, January 6, 1959, Alinsky Papers, IAF Institute.
28. Robert Christ, "Local Church in Community Organization, January 1959–October 1961," Alinsky Papers, IAF Institute.
29. Alinsky, "IAF Annual Report," December 1961.

30. Egan, Interview, November 14, 1976.

31. Alinsky, "Testimony before Civil Rights Housing Hearing," U.S. Commission on Civil Rights, May 5, 1959, Chicago.

32. Stanley A. Koven, "The Day the Chicago Racists Lost," *The Catholic World*, August 1960.

33. Interview with D. Barry Menuez, New York City, March 3, 1977.

34. *Christian Century*, October 21, 1959.

35. Christ, "Local Church," Alinsky Papers, IAF Institute.

36. Koven, *Catholic World*, August 1960.

37. Interview with Edward T. Chambers, Chicago, September 15, 1977.

38. *Ibid.*

39. John Fish et al., *Edge of the Ghetto* (Chicago: Divinity School, University of Chicago, 1966), pp. 21–22.

40. Alinsky to Rieser, February 13, 1959, Alinsky Papers, IAF Institute.

41. Interview, Chambers, September 15, 1977.

42. Monsignor John McMahon, *Priests–USA*, National Federation of Priests' Councils, Chicago, July 1972, p. 5.

CHAPTER 5

1. Milton Viorst, *Fire in the Streets: America in the 1960s* (New York: Simon and Schuster, 1979), p. 169.

2. Theodore H. White, *The Making of the President, 1960* (New York: Atheneum, 1961), p. 257.

3. *Ibid.*, p. 377.

4. C. Wright Mills, "The New Left," 1960, contained in *Power, Politics and People*, Irving L. Horowitz, ed. (New York: Ballantine), p. 259.

5. Von Hoffman, Interview, December 15, 1978.

6. *Ibid.*

7. Charles E. Silberman, *Crisis in Black and White* (New York: Random House, Vintage, 1964), p. 328.

8. Interview with Father Martin Farrell, Chicago, February 22, 1977.

9. Farrell to Alinsky, February 22, 1958, Alinsky Papers, IAF Institute.

10. Ulysses B. Blakely and Charles T. Leber, Jr., "The Great Debate in Chicago," *Presbyterian Life*, June 15, 1961, pp. 36–38.

11. Alinsky, "Memorandum," March 16, 1959, Alinsky Papers, IAF Institute.

12. Interview with Bryant George, New York City, June 3, 1977.

13. Interview with Charles T. Leber, Jr., Newark, New Jersey, May 31, 1977.

14. *Ibid.*

15. *The Christian Century,* April 3, 1963.

16. Leber, Interview, May 31, 1977.

17. George, Interview, June 3, 1977.

18. Leber, Interview, May 31, 1977.

19. Alinsky, "Down Here," Speech given to the American Crisis Forum, Adult Education Council of Greater Chicago, November 14, 1960, Alinsky Papers, IAF Institute.

20. John H. Fish, *Black Power/White Control* (Princeton, N.J.: Princeton University Press, 1973), p. 30.

21. Cardinal Albert Meyer to Alinsky, September 23, 1960, Alinsky Papers, IAF Institute.

22. Egan, Interview, November 14, 1976.

23. Fish, *Black Power,* p. 32.

24. Arthur M. Brazier, *Black Self Determination: The Story of The Woodlawn Organization* (Grand Rapids: Eerdmans, 1969), pp. 38–41.

25. Nicholas von Hoffman, "Finding and Making Leaders," mimeographed, n.d., Alinsky Papers, IAF Institute, p. 12.

26. *Ibid.,* p. 2.

27. *Ibid.,* p. 4.

28. Silberman, *Crisis in Black and White,* p. 346.

29. *Woodlawn Banner,* Chicago, November 11, 1961.

30. Interview, Farrell, February 22, 1977.

31. Silberman, *Crisis in Black and White,* p. 343.

32. Jane Jacobs, "Chicago's Woodlawn," *Architectural Forum,* May 1962, pp. 122–124.

33. Silberman, *Crisis in Black and White,* p. 344.

34. See Alinsky, "Citizen Participation and Community Organization in Planning and Urban Renewal" (Chicago: Industrial Areas Foundation, 1962).

35. Elinor Richey, "The Slum That Saved Itself," *The Progressive,* October 1963.

36. Farrell, Interview, February 22, 1977.

37. *Ibid.*

38. Von Hoffman, "Finding and Making Leaders," pp. 2–3.

39. Silberman, *Crisis in Black and White,* p. 318.

40. Interview with Saul D. Alinsky, West Chester, Pa., March 1971.

41. Egan, Interview, November 14, 1976.

42. Craig Heverly, "Report on the Near Northwest–East Humboldt Area of Chicago," mimeographed, March 1963, Alinsky Papers, IAF Institute.

43. Egan, Interview, November 14, 1976.

44. Interview with Tom Gaudette, Chicago, June 28, 1976.

45. *Ibid.*

46. Egan, Interview, November 14, 1976.

47. Heverly, "Report," May 24, 1962.

48. *Ibid.*

49. Hillel Black, "This Is War," *Saturday Evening Post,* January 25, 1964.

50. *Ibid.*

51. Alinsky, "IAF Annual Report," December 1960.

52. Rev. Douglas Still, "The Local Church and Community Organization," mimeographed, Church Federation of Greater Chicago, 1962, Alinsky Papers, IAF Institute.

53. Don Benedict to Rev. Lloyd A. Peterson, January 13, 1965, Rochester Board for Urban Ministry Papers, Institute on the Church in Urban-Industrial Society, Chicago.

54. Cardinal Albert Meyer, "Remarks to the Second NCO Congress," mimeographed, Chicago, May 17, 1964, Alinsky Papers, IAF Institute.

55. Interview, Egan, March 14, 1977.

56. *Ibid.*

57. Tjerandsen, *Education for Citizenship*, p. 113.

58. Interview, Ross, June 28, 1977.

59. Alinsky to Tjerandsen, July 16, 1962, Alinsky Papers, IAF Institute.

60. *Ibid.*

61. Levy, *Cesar Chavez*, p. 147.

62. Ross to Alinsky, May 20, 1962, Alinsky Papers, IAF Institute.

63. Levy, *Cesar Chavez*, p. 149.

64. Silberman, *Crisis in Black and White.*

65. Hunt, Interview, May 16, 1977.

CHAPTER 6

1. *Rochester Times-Union,* July 25, 1964.

2. Jimmy Breslin, *The World of Jimmy Breslin* (New York: Ballantine, 1967), p. 84.

3. This account of Alinsky's project in Rochester is taken from

a fuller treatment written by the author as a doctoral dissertation: "Crisis in Smugtown: A Study of Conflict, Churches and Citizen Organizations . . ." (Ph.D. diss., Union Graduate School, 1975).

4. Rochester Board for Urban Ministry "Minutes," October 20, 1964, Institute on the Church in Urban-Industrial Society.

5. Rochester Board for Urban Ministry, "The Development of Powerful Community Organization in Rochester's Negro Ghetto," 1964, reprinted in Finks, "Crisis in Smugtown," pp. 318–321.

6. Herbert D. White, Personal Communication, November 11, 1964, Board for Urban Ministry Papers.

7. Alinsky to White, February 5, 1965, Board for Urban Ministry Papers.

8. *Chicago Sun-Times*, December 13, 1964.

9. *Catholic Courier Journal*, Rochester, February 25, 1965.

10. Board for Urban Ministry, "Minutes," February 1, 1965.

11. Finks, "Crisis in Smugtown," p. 49.

12. Stephen C. Rose, "Saul Alinsky and His Critics," *Christianity and Crisis*, July 20, 1964; Dan W. Dodson, "Does Community Organization Process Preserve and Enhance the Dignity and Worth of the Individual?" mimeographed, National Council of Churches, December 1964.

13. *Rochester Times-Union*, February 5, 1965.

14. White to Alinsky, March 19, 1965, Alinsky Papers, IAF Institute.

15. Board for Urban Ministry, "Minutes," April 5, 1965.

16. James Q. Wilson, *Political Organizations* (New York: Basic Books, 1973), p. 195.

17. Curt Gerling, *Smugtown–USA* (Webster, N.Y.: Plaza Publishers, 1957).

18. Patrick Anderson, "Making Trouble Is Alinsky's Business," *New York Times Magazine*, October 9, 1966, p. 82.

19. Gerling, *Smugtown-USA*, pp. 1–5.

20. Alexander Hawryluk, "Friends of FIGHT: A Study of a Militant Civil Rights Organization (Ph.D., diss., Cornell University, 1967).

21. Blake McKelvey, "The Changing Face of Rochester," *Rochester History*, April 1964.

22. Loftus C. Carson, "Areas Where Rioting Occurred, Rochester, New York—July 1964" (Rochester: Monroe County Human Relations Commission, July 15, 1965).

23. Marvin Chandler, "Report to the FIGHT Organization," May 12, 1967, Board for Urban Ministry Papers.

24. *Ibid.*
25. *Ibid.*
26. Eastman Kodak Company, News Release, December 22, 1966.
27. Bishop Fulton J. Sheen to P. David Finks, January 3, 1967, personal papers of author.
28. White, Personal Communication, December 1970.
29. Dan Lovely, "Decade of Decision," *Rochester Democrat and Chronicle,* July 7, 1974.
30. Alinsky to Bernard Gifford, June 9, 1969, Alinsky Papers, IAF Institute.
31. Finks, "Crisis in Smugtown," p. 290.
32. *Rochester Democrat and Chronicle,* December 24, 1972.
33. White, Personal Communication, December 1970.

CHAPTER 7

1. *New York Times,* January 15, 1967.
2. Interview, Ross, June 28, 1977.
3. Robert Lee and Russell Galloway, *The Schizophrenic Church: Conflict Over Community Organization* (Philadelphia: The Westminster Press, 1969).
4. Alinsky, "IAF Annual Report," 1963.
5. Egan, Interview, November 14, 1976.
6. *Ibid.*
7. Finks, "Crisis in Smugtown," p. 297.
8. Menuez, Interview, June 3, 1977.
9. *I.F.C.O. News,* November 1968.
10. Interview with the Rev. Douglas Still, Cottage Grove, Or., May 6, 1977.
11. Interview with Margery Tabankin, Washington, D.C., May 27, 1977.
12. Chambers, Interview, September 15, 1977.
13. IAF Training Institute Preliminary Application Form, 1969, Alinsky Papers, IAF Institute.
14. Chambers, Interview, September 15, 1977.
15. Interview with Richard Harmon, New York City, March 4, 1977.
16. Tabankin, Interview, May 27, 1977.
17. Alinsky, *Reveille for Radicals* (Random House, Vintage Edi-

tion, 1969); *John L. Lewis: An Unauthorized Biography* (New York: Random House, Vintage Edition, 1970).

18. Alinsky, *Rules for Radicals*, (New York: Random House, 1971).

19. *Ibid.*, p. xiii.

20. An excellent study of the Populist Movement is Lawrence Goodwyn's *Democratic Promise: The Populist Movement in America* (New York: Oxford University Press, 1976).

21. Alinsky, "The Double Revolution," paper given at the Smithsonian Institution, November 19, 1970, included in *The Cultural Drama: Modern Identities and Social Ferment*, Wilton S. Dillon, ed. (Washington, D.C.: Smithsonian Institution Press, 1974), pp. 288–303.

22. Alinsky, "Grant Application to the Rockefeller Foundation," 1968, Alinsky Papers, IAF Institute.

23. Alinsky, *Rules for Radicals*, p. xxvi.

24. Jean Graham Alinsky, Interview, September 13, 1978.

25. Edward G. Bernstein, Attorney, to Saul D. Alinsky, August 14, 1968, Alinsky Papers, IAF Institute.

26. *Chicago Tribune*, December 26, 1972; Interview with Irene McGinnis Alinsky, Boston, November 16, 1976.

27. Interview with Herbert D. White, New York City, April 30, 1979.

28. Von Hoffman, Interview, December 15, 1978.

29. Chambers, Interview, September 15, 1977.

30. *Rochester Democrat and Chronicle*, June 13, 1972.

31. *New York Times*, June 26, 1972.

32. Egan, "Saul David Alinsky, 1909–1972—A Memorial," *Community Organization Bibliography* (Chicago: Institute on the Church in Urban-Industrial Society, 1974), pp. 5–6.

CHAPTER 8

1. Becker, *Marshall Field III*, pp. 362–363.

2. Alinsky, "Of Means and Ends," *Union Seminary Quarterly*, Vol. 22, No. 2, January 1967, p. 108.

3. White, "Saul Alinsky and the Ethics of Social Change," *ibid.*, p. 129.

4. White, Interview, April 30, 1979.

5. Tabankin, Interview, May 27, 1977.

6. Von Hoffman, Interview, December 15, 1978.

7. William F. Buckley, Jr., "Is There an Alinsky in Your Future?" *Steubenville Register*, November 10, 1966.

8. Hunt, Interview, May 16, 1977.

9. Maritain to Alinsky, September 19, 1971, Alinsky Papers, IAF Institute.

10. Jessica C. Fernandez, "Review of *Rules for Radicals* and *Reveille for Radicals*," *Notes on Urban-Industrial Mission*, Chicago: Institute on the Church in Urban-Industrial Society, November 1972, p. 3.

11. Alinsky, "Principles of Social Action," mimeographed, State Conference of the Washington Association for Social Welfare, Tacoma, Wash., May 27, 1963, Alinsky Papers, IAF Institute.

12. Still, Interview, May 6, 1977.

13. Alinsky, "Community Analysis," p. 799.

14. Von Hoffman, *Washington Post*, June 16, 1972.

15. Gaudette, Interview, June 28, 1976.

16. Alinsky, "Catholic Leadership," Speech to the Annual Meeting of the National Conference of Catholic Charities, Kansas City, Mo., September 28, 1942, Alinsky Papers, University of Illinois, Chicago.

17. Alinsky, *Reveille for Radicals*, p. 222.

18. Egan, Interview, November 14, 1976.

19. Shuster to seminarian, April 9, 1965, Alinsky Papers, IAF Institute.

20. Rose, *Christianity and Crisis*, July 20, 1964.

21. Maritain to Robert Maynard Hutchins, May 27, 1951, Alinsky Papers, University of Illinois, Chicago.

22. Von Hoffman, *Washington Post*, June 16, 1972.

23. Alinsky, *John L. Lewis*, p. 360.

24. Alinsky, "War on Poverty: Political Pornography," *Journal of Social Issues*, January 1965, pp. 41–47.

25. Jack Newfield, *Robert Kennedy: A Memoir* (New York: E.P. Dutton and Co., 1969).

26. Daniel P. Moynihan, *Maximum Feasible Misunderstanding: Community Action in the War on Poverty* (New York: Free Press, 1969).

27. Alinsky, *Rules for Radicals*, p. 178.

28. Alinsky, *The Cultural Drama*, p. 303.

29. White, Interview, April 30, 1979.

30. Alinsky to Georgie Ann Geyer, June 17, 1964, Alinsky Papers, IAF Institute.

31. Von Hoffman, *Washington Post*, June 17, 1972.

32. John Naisbitt, *Megatrends: Ten New Directions Transforming Our Lives* (New York: Warner Books, 1982), p. 113.

33. Von Hoffman, Interview, December 15, 1978.

34. *New York Times*, September 26, 1982.

35. *New York Times*, January 30, 1983.

36. Alinsky, Interview, 1971.

INDEX

Abrams, Charles, 93
Acheson, Dean, 28
Action for a Better Community
    (ABC), 197
Addams, Jane, 3
Admiral Corporation, 161, 162
AFL-CIO, 73. *See also* Congress of
    Industrial Organizations (CIO)
Alinsky, Benjamin, 1
Alinsky, David, 43, 48–49, 94, 109
Alinsky, Helene, 12; death of, 43, 44,
    53
Alinsky, Jean, divorce from, 243;
    illness of, 100–101, 186; letters
    to, from Rome, 118–119;
    marriage of, to Saul, 92; in
    Southern California, 69, 110
Alinsky, Kathryn, 43, 45, 109
Alinsky, Sarah, 1
Alinsky, Saul, as agitator, 256;
    aloneness of, 253–255; birth and
    early life of, 1–5; college
    education of, 5–9; death of,
    247–248; and churches, 258–260,
    267; corporate world and,
    263–265; as cynic, 250–251;
    government and, 260–263;
    marriages of, 12, 92, 243;
    personal characteristics,
    266–267; philosophical
    meanderings of, 252–253
American Council of Race
    Relations, 36, 37, 39
American Friends Service
    Committee, 39

American Lutheran Council, 141
American Prison Association, 11
Anaconda Copper, 90
Anderson, Patrick, 196
Apostolic Church of God (Chicago),
    138, 146, 157
Arizona, 72
Armour Company, 14
Armourdale (Kansas), 25–26, 27
Armourdale Community Council,
    25–26, 27
Arvin camp, 38
Asia, 243–249; East Asian Christian
    Conference, 243
Association of Community
    Councils, 162
Atlanta (Georgia), 57
Atwell, Fr. Henry, 188
Austin (Chicago). *See* West Town
    project

"Baby Skid Row," 153
Back of the Yards Neighborhood
    Council, 13–24; Agnes Meyers
    on, in *Washington Post*, 54;
    Grand Boulevard alliance with,
    112; Jefferson's "wards" and,
    33; objective of, 23; programs
    of, 21; University of Chicago
    and, 95; youth committee of, 22
Bakersfield, 62
Baumann, John, 270
Baumgartner, Leona, 94, 98, 102
Bay Area, IAF Training Institute
    in, 232, 234, 236

293

Bean Concert, 217
Becker, Stephen, 250
Benedict, Rev. Donald, 168
Bennett, Joan, 29
Bevel, James, 182
Bethlehem Steel Corporation, 88
Beverly Hills Hotel, 42
Beynon, Rev. Lee, 210–211
Birmingham (Alabama), 57
Blacks. See Rochester (New York);
    Southwest Chicago; Woodlawn
    project
Blackstone Hotel (Chicago), 83, 160
Blakeley, Rev. Ulysses B., 137, 140,
    144, 146, 154
Board for Fundamental Education,
    206
Board for Urban Ministry (BUM),
    180–191, 210–211; break with
    FIGHT, 224
"Bobbsey Twins," 84
Bogart, Humphrey, 29
Booth, Heather, 270
Bourbon-Bussets, Count Jacques,
    114
Boyer, Monsignor Carlo, 117
Braverman, Harry, 41, 42, 44
Brazier, Rev. Arthur, 138, 146,
    156–157
Brenner, Henry, 202
Brideshead Revisited, 30
Brown vs. Board of Education, 79
Bowren, L.A. May Fletcher, 35
Boyle Heights (East Los Angeles),
    39, 40, 44
B'nai B'rith, 36
Buckholz, Marjorie, 101, 104
Budd, Britton I., 24
Buettner, Bert, 200
BUILD Organization, 229
Bulkeley, Christy C., 253
Burch, Glen, 68, 69
Burgess, Ernest K., 6, 7, 9, 13
Burke, Monsignor Edward M., 122
Butte (Montana), 37, 89
Butte Citizen's Project (BCP), 90

California, 72. See also Community
    Service Organization (CSO);
    Southern California; United
    Farm Workers; and specific
    locations
California, University of, at Davis,
    68
California Federation of Civic
    Unity, 49
Calixico, 72
Cap and Gown, 7
Campaign for Human
    Development, 270. See also
    National Conference of
    Catholic Charities
Capone, Al, 7–9
Capone gang, 4, 7–9, 10
Cardinale, Monsignor Igino, 119
Cardinal's Conservation Committee
    (Chicago), 77, 136, 138
Caritas International, 117
Carmel, 69, 110
Carmichael, Stokley, 198, 215
Carpenter, Dan, Chelsea project
    and, 100–102; Hudson Guild
    settlement house and, 94; New
    York Foundation proposal of,
    97–99; Penn Station South and,
    104–105, 107
Catholic Charities, of Buffalo, 86,
    88; of Chicago, 111, 113; in
    Montana, 90; of New York, 100.
    See also National Conference of
    Catholic Charities
Catholic Charities Review, The, 96
Catholic Committee for Urban
    Ministry (CCUM), 235
Catholic University of America
    (Washington, D.C.), 75
Catholic Youth Organization
    (CYO), 17
Central West Neighborhood
    Organization, 80, 81
Chambers, Edward, Eastman Kodak
    and, 223; FIGHT Organization,
    191–193, 201, 202, 209–210;

FIGHT-Kodak proxy campaign, 217, 222; IAF Alinsky Institute, 271–273; IAF Training Institute, 229, 230, 232, 234, 236–237, 238; in Lackawanna, 87–89; in Rochester, New York, 176; Southern Chicago project, 124, 127, 129, 130–131, 165; Woodlawn project and, 159
Chandler, Rev. Edgar, 167
Chandler, Rev. Martin, 223
Chandler, Marvin, 184, 189, 207, 208
Chatham Community Council, 161
Chavez, Abilizio "Abe," 69
Chavez, Cesar, Community Service Organizations (CSOs) and, 61–65, 71–72, 165; farm workers and, 170–173, 230; resignation of, 172. See also United Farm Workers
Chelsea Citizen Participation Project, 100
Chelsea Committee for Neighborhood Development, 97
Chelsea Community Council, 95, 102, 104–107, 120
Chelsea memorandum, 105–106
Chelsea proposal, 97–99
Chicago, 109–131; Back of the Yards Neighborhood Council, 19–24; Englewood, 168; Golden Age of Community Organization in, 159, 165–170; Grand Boulevard organization, 112–113; Hyde Park Urban Renewal Project, 120–121; Lawndale, 233; Northwest Community Council, 162–165; Northwest Community Organization (NCO), 159–165; Richard J. Daley, 137, 150, 153–154, 155; South Side, 82; Southwest, 122–131; West Town, 160–165; Woodlawn project, 134–136, 145–159, 173

Chicago, Catholic Archdiocese of, 76–77, 166–170; Hyde Park Urban Renewal Project, 120–121; Office of Urban Affairs, 120, 159–160, 233; Southwest Chicago project, 122–131; Woodlawn project, 138, 142, 144–145. See also Cody, Archbishop John; Meyer, Cardinal Albert; Sheil, Bishop Bernard J. ("Bernie"); Stritch, Cardinal Samuel
Chicago, Presbytery of, 138–141
Chicago, University of, school of urban sociology, 5–9, 32; Schwartzhaupt Foundation and, 59; Settlement House, 95; urban renewal project of, 134, 135, 144, 145–146, 152–154, 156
Chicago Area Project (CAP), 13, 15, 20
Chicago Board of Education, 150–152
Chicago Daily News, 158
Chicago Land Clearance Commission, 144. See also Woodlawn project
Chicago Plan Commission, 145–146
"Chicago School" of urban sociology, 5–9, 32
Chicago Sunday Sun-Times, 187
Christian Century, The, on Reinhold Niebuhr, 258; on Southwest Chicago Project, 127–128, 129, 132; on Woodlawn project, 141–144, 148
"Christmas Massacre," 210
Christopher Movement, 86
Church Federation of Greater Chicago, 167–168
Cincotta, Gale, 270
Citizens Against Pollution (CAP), 238
Citizens Committee for Children, 102
Citizen's Federation of Lackawanna (CFL), 88, 89

"Citizen Participation Project
Prepared by the Hudson Guild,
A," 97
Civic Unity Councils, 39
Clapp, Gordon, 115, 120
Cleaver, Eldridge, 198
Cleveland (Ohio), 34, 38, 60
Cody, Archbishop John, 233, 258
Committee on Education for
American Citizenship, 59
"Committee To Keep Alinsky Out
of New York," 95
Communism, 58, 73, 117, 119;
Senator Joseph McCarthy,
57–58, 113
Community Chest/United Fund,
190, 196, 204. See also United
Fund
Community Service Organization
(CSO), 41–44, 61–72; Cesar
Chavez and, 61–65, 71–72, 165;
farm workers and, 170–173;
Fred Ross and, 49, 53
Congress of Industrial Organization
(CIO), 14–17, 23–24, 36, 45, 47,
73, 257
Congress of Racial Equality
(CORE), Freedom Riders,
134–136
Cooke, Monsignor Vincent, 113
Coughlin, Father Charles E., 55
Council on Religion and Race, 168
Crisis in Black and White, 173–175,
182, 185, 199
"Crisis in the Cities," 234
Cudahy Company, 14

Daley, Richard J., Hyde Park
Urban Renewal Project,
120–121; Woodlawn project
and, 137, 150, 153–155
D'Aurizio, Fr. Joseph, 184, 185
Davis Square Park, 16–18, 20–21, 22
Dawson, William, 149, 155–156
December 20 Agreement, 207, 208,
215, 220

DeGaulle, Charles, 30
Dell' Acqua, Monsignor Angelo,
117–118
Democracy in America, 33
Despres, Leon, 145
deWolfe, Elsie (Lady Mendl), 35
Donovan, William J. ("Wild Bill"),
28
Doremus, Warren, 191
Douglas, H. Paul, 180
Douglas, Helen Gahagan, 29, 37
Douglas, Melvyn, 29
Dreamland Ballroom, 7
Dunn, Father Robert T., 102–108
Dust Bowl migrations, 37
Duveneck, Josephine, 61
Dziewulski, Edward, 163

East Asian Christian Conference,
243
East Los Angeles, 39–45
Eastman Kodak, 201–228; Bishop
Fulton J. Sheen and, 211–217;
Louis K. Eilers, 208, 210, 214,
221, 223; Franklyn D.R.
Florence, 202–210, 214–220;
John Mulder, 206–208, 221–222;
proxy battle with FIGHT,
217–222, 263–264; William S.
Vaughn, 203–205, 207, 213,
220–221, 225. See also FIGHT
(Freedom, Integration, God,
Honor, Today)
Education for American
Citizenship, Committee on, 59
Educationals, 66, 68–71
Edelstein, Julius, 97
Egan, Monsignor John J., attraction
of Saul to, 259; ecumenical
efforts of, 165–170; firing of, by
Cardinal Cody, 258; as IAF
intern, 111; IAF Training
Institute, 231–232, 234; IFCO,
235; Lawndale (Chicago), 333;
Northwest Community
Organization, 159–165; in

Office of Urban Affairs, 123;
Southwest Chicago project,
120–121, 123, 125–126; before
U.S. Commission on Civil
Rights, 125–126; Woodlawn
Latin American Committee
and, 82–83; Woodlawn project,
138, 141, 145
Eilers, Louis K., 208, 210, 214, 221,
223
Eisenhower, Dwight, 72
Elliott, John Lovejoy, 97
Emil Schwartzhaupt Foundation,
56. *See also* Schwartzhaupt
Foundation
El Paso (Texas), 57
Englewood (Chicago), 168
Evans, William C., 200

Fanfani, Amintore, 117–118
Farm Security Administration, 37,
38
Farrell, Fr. Martin, 136–137; TWO
and, 155, 156, 169; Woodlawn
Pastors' Alliance and, 140, 144,
146
Federal Housing Authority, 104
Federation of Churches. *See*
Rochester Council of Churches
Fernandez-White, Jessica, 255
Fey, Harold, 141–142
Field, Marshall, III, Armourdale
and, 25, 26; death of, 120; IAF
and, 34–35, 54, 113; personal
support of Alinsky by, 44, 92
Field, Ruth, 92
Field Foundation, 24
FIGHT (*Freedom, Integration, God,
Honor, Today*), 191–198;
Eastman Kodak and, 201–228;
Employment Committee, 203;
end of, 225; Housing
Committee, 196–197; Job
Training Center, 214; Poverty
Committee, 197; Youth
Committee, 197

FIGHT conventions, first, 193–195;
second, 201, 202–203; third, 222;
fifth, 225
FIGHTON, Inc., 223
First Presbyterian Church
(Chicago), 137
Fisher, Father Adrian, O.F.M., 77
Flemington, Focus on, 218
Florence, Reverend Franklyn D.R.,
179, 182–183; Bishop Sheen and,
211; defeat of, 225–227; Eastman
Kodak and, 202–210, 214–220;
FIGHT Organization and, 191,
195, 197–198; Urban League
and, 190
Flower City, 176, 178. *See also*
Rochester, New York
"Focus on Flemington," 218
Ford Foundation, 56, 58, 111, 118
Foreshore Development Authority,
245
"42 Gang," 10–11, 19
Fortune, 73, 74, 143
Freedom Ride of TWO, 149–150,
157, 160
Freedom Riders (CORE), Chicago
rally of, 134–136
Fresno (California), 173
"Friends of Fight," Eastman Kodak-
FIGHT proxy fight, 218, 220;
FIGHTON Inc. and, 223;
newsletter, 211; organization of,
194, 199–201, 241
Friends Service Committee, 49, 61
Friendship House, 87
Fruitvale, 85
Fund for Adult Education, 68
Fund for the Republic, 111

Gallagher, Monsignor Raymond, 91
Gannett Company, Inc., 212, 215
Gaudette, Kay, 161, 162
Gaudette, Thomas, Northwest
Community Organization
(NCO) and, 165; West Town

project, 161–165, 230–231; work
of, after Alinsky's death, 270
General Theological Seminary, 103
George, Bryant, 139–140, 142, 167
Gerling, Curt, 195, 199
Gerzik, Jake "Greasy Thumb," 4
Geyer, Georgie Ann, 266
Giancana, Momo Salvatore ("Sam"),
10
Gifford, Bernard J., 225–227
Gleeson, Monsignor Patrick J., 124
Goldberg, Arthur, 4
Golden Age of Community
Organization in Chicago, 159,
165–170
Goodman, Benjamin ("Benny"), 4
Graham, Donald, 54
Graham, Jean, 51, 52. See also
Alinsky, Jean
Graham, Mrs. (Jean's mother), 52
Grand Boulevard organization,
112–113
Grapes of Wrath, The 37
Great Depression, 7, 24, 46–47, 261
Greater Woodlawn Pastors Alliance,
144, 146, 148
Guthrie, Woodie, 38

Hanford, 62, 70
Harmon, Richard, BUILD
Organization and, 229; IAF
Training Institute and, 237,
238; TWO and, 165
Harrington, Monsignor D.B., 90
"Harvest of Shame," 171
Hauser, Philip M., 4, 187
Hegel, Georg Wilhelm, 252
Helstein, Rachel, 43, 44
Helstein Ralph, personal support of
Alinsky by, 43–44, 48–49;
United Packinghouse Workers
of America (UPWA) and,
170–171
Heverly, Craig, 163, 164
Hewes, Lawrence S., 38
Hill, Rev. George, 188

Hillcrest Country Club, 42
Hillel, Rabbi, 4
Hispanic community, 110–111
Hollywood High School, 5
Hollywood Tennis Club, 5
Holy Cross Church (Chicago), 136
House Un-American Activities
Committee (HUAC), 57–58, 133
Hudson Guild settlement house, 94,
97, 98, 100–102, 105
Huerta, Dolores, CSO's and, 71,
171–173; United Farm Workers
of America and, 173, 230;
Women's Educationals and, 165
Hughes, Rev. Richard N., 179, 184
Hull-House, 3
Hunt, Lester, on Alinsky as
philosopher, 252; Chelsea
project and, 100, 105; as college
teacher, 231; on Crisis in Black
and White, 174; hiring of, 84; in
Lackawanna, 89–90; resignation
of, from IAF, 165; in South side
of Chicago, 111
Hunterdon County High School,
220
Hutchins, Robert Maynard, as Ford
Foundation director; 56, 58,
111; as University of Chicago
president, 32
Hyde Park, 109–110
Hyde Park Urban Renewal Project,
120–121

Illinois State Penitentiary (Joliet),
11–12
Illinois Synod of the United
Lutheran Church, 138–139
Imperial Valley, 62
Indiana Dunes, 43
Industrial Area Foundation (IAF),
Alinsky Institute, 270, 271, 274;
Annual Reports, 166, 168;
funds, 24, 34, 37, 45, 56, 89;
international consulting
operation, 246–247; New York

advisory committee, 102; Training Institute, 229–238; trustees, 24, 53–54

Inner City Board, 179–180. *See also* Rochester Council of Churches

Institute for Juvenile Research (IJR), 9, 13, 19, 20, 23

Institute of Citizenship (Kansas City University), 66

International Ladies Garment Workers Union (ILGWU), 103–104

Interreligious Council on Urban Affairs, 235

Interreligious Foundation for Community Organization (IFCO), 234–235

Italy, 114–119

Japan, 246

Jefferson, Thomas, 32–33, 67, 254, 258

John L. Lewis: An Unauthorized Biography, 45, 47, 53, 239

John XXIII (Pope), 115, 117, 258

Johnson, Henry, 28–29

Joint Office for Urban Ministry, 224

Joliet (Illinois), 11–12

Jones, Casey, 55

Jones, Ronald, 191

Jungle, The, 14

Kansas City (Kansas), 25, 26, 59, 72

Kansas City (Missouri), 176

Kansas State University, 67

Kearney, Bishop James E., 191

Kelley, Edward J., 22

Kennedy, John F., 133

Kennedy, Robert F., 101, 219, 263

Kifner, John, 214, 229, 248

King, Martin Luther, Jr., 112, 133, 235

King's General, The, 30

Kloetzl, Rev. Walter, 128, 138–139, 141, 163

Knights of St. John, 146

Korea, 51

Ku Klux Klan, 134, 135

Lackawanna (New York), 85–89, 111; Citizens' Federation of (CFL), 88, 89

Lackawanna Neighborhood Cooperative Committee (LNCC), 86, 87, 88

Lamb, Frank, 177

Lash, Trude, 102

Lawndale (Chicago), 233

League for Industrial Democracy, 133. *See also* Students for a Democratic Society (SDS)

Leber, Rev. Charles T., Jr., 137, 140, 141–142, 144

Lehman, Herbert H., 92, 93, 97, 98

Leinbach, Richard, 200

Levi, Julian, 145, 146, 152

Levine, Rabbi Allan, 200

Levy, Adele Rosenwald, 54, 92

Lewis, John L., organizing skill of, 47, 73, 257; and New Deal, 46; personal support of Alinsky by, 44; as president of CIO, 14, 18

Lewis, Kathryn, 24

Lewis, Terry, 51, 52

Lexington Hotel (Chicago), 8

Lincoln Heights, 44

Lindenberg, Sidney, 183

"Little Oxford," 103

Long, Paul, Jr., 183, 184, 199, 200

Los Angeles (California), 34–37, 112; Boyle Heights, 39, 40, 44; East, 39–45

Los Angeles, Catholic Archdiocese of, 36

Lutheran Church, 141; National Lutheran Council, 128; Woodlawn project, 138–139

Lynd, Staughton, 237

McCarthy, Joseph, 57–58, 113

McCrory, John B., 200

McGee, Rev. Robert, 146, 156
McGhee, Paul, 94–97, 98, 100–102, 104
McGinnis, Irene, 243
McGucken, Bishop Joseph T., 40
McMahon, Monsignor John, 122–124, 131
McWilliams, Carey, 35, 41
Macy, Harriet ("Happy"), 52, 53–54, 56, 92, 93
Macy, Valentine ("Val"), 44, 52, 54, 92, 93
Madera, 62
Madison, James, 33, 156, 254
Malcolm X, 182
Manila, 244–245
March, Herbert, 16, 18
Maritain, Jacques, description of Alinsky by, 260; Ford Foundation and, 56, 58–59; personal support of Alinsky by, 44, 49–50, 92; *Reveille for Radicals*, reaction to, 30; *Rules for Radicals*, reaction to, 253; at Vatican, 30, 114–115
Maritain, Raissa, 92
Maroon, The, 152
Marshall Field & Company, 23–24, 30
Martin, Louis, 200
"Martin Luther" (film), 122
Marx, Rabbi Robert, 235
Massina, "Little Dumas," 10–11
Mater et Magistra, 258
Mayer, Milton, 53
Mayne, Calvin, 190
Meegan, Joseph, 16–17, 20, 165, 248
Megatrends, 268–270
Mendl, Lady (Elsie de Wolfe), 35
Menuez, D. Barry, 127, 165, 231
Mexican-Americans. *See* Community Service Organization (CSO); Southern California; United Farm Workers
Meyer, Agnes, Back of the Yards Council, 54–56; personal support of Alinsky by, 44, 92

Meyer, Albert G. Cardinal, 115–116; NCO convention (1964), 169; Southwest Chicago project, 123–124, 126; West Town project, 161; Woodlawn project, 142, 144–145, 155
Meyer, Eugene, 54, 55
Meyer, Katherine, 54
Midas International Company, 233–234
Midwest Academy, 270
Miller, Mike, 270
Miller, Paul, 212, 215
Miller, Richard P., 196
Mills, C. Wright, 133–134
Mine, Mill and Smelters Union, 90
Minidoka (Idaho), 38
Mitchell, Constance, 184
Montana, 29, 57
Monterey (California), 69, 110
Montini, Archbishop Giovanni, 114. *See also* Paul VI (Pope)
Moore, Clement Clarke, 103
Mott, Stewart, 180
Moynihan, Daniel Patrick, 222, 248, 263
Mulder, John, 206–208, 221–222
Mundelein, George W. Cardinal, 17
Murphy, Tom, 87–88
Murrow, Edward R., 171

NAACP, 70
Naisbitt, John, 268–270
Nation, The, 30
National Community Service Organization (NCSO) Inc., 62, 66, 71–72; farm workers and, 170–173
National Conference of Catholic Charities (NCCC), networking power of, 74–76; O'Grady's first address to, 259; St. Louis meeting of, 78–80. *See also* Catholic Charities; O'Grady, Monsignor John

National Farm Workers
Association, 173
National Lutheran Council, 128
National Urban League, 190
Newark (New Jersey), 57
New Deal, 46, 261
New Left, The, 134
New Orleans, 57
New Republic, 214
New York City, 91–108; Hudson
Guild settlement house, 94,
97–98, 100–102, 105; Penn
Station South, 104–105. *See also*
entries under Chelsea
New York City Youth Board, 102
New York Foundation, 92, 94, 96,
97–98, 100
New York Post, 93
New York Times, 101, 212, 214
New York University, 95
New World, 120
Niebuhr, Reinhold, 258
Northeast Mothers Improvement
Committee, 177
Northwest Community Council,
162–165
Northwest Community
Organization (NCO), 159–165

Oakland project, 69
Office of Strategic Services, (OSS),
28
O'Grady, Monsignor John, 72–89; as
director of NCCC, 60;
Cardinal's Conservation
Committee and, 136; *Catholic
Charities Review* editorials, 96;
ecumenical vision of, 167;
executive secretary of NCCC,
53; funding of Chelsea project,
91–93, 100; introduction of
Alinsky to Cardinal Meyer,
115–116; Lackawanna project,
111; resignation of, from
NCCC, 120; in Southern
California, 63–64

Omaha (Nebraska), 34, 57, 72, 74–75
Omaha Community Council, 36
Organization for the Southwest
Community, 127–131, 139; Home
Loan Fund, 129; Home Show,
130; Real Estate Practices
Committee, 129–130
Ostrow, Seniel, 42
Oxnard (California), 171

Paley, William S., 4
Paris, 114
Park, Robert Ezra, 6, 9, 19, 32
Pastors' Conservation Council, 77
Pattern Project, 166
Paul VI (Pope), 258
Peabody, Stuyvesant, 24
Penn Station South, 104–107
Pennsylvania, University of, 12
"People-Oriented Approach to
Urban Renewal and Planning,
A," 153
People's Organizations, 32, 33
Peter's Backyard, 87
Phelosof, Ben, 200
Philadelphia, 57
Philippines, 244–246
Pirrello, Mario, 183
Pittsburgh, 57
Pollock, Jackson, 52
Presbyterian Board of National
Missions, 137, 145
Princeton University, 49
Prohibition, 8
Provisional Organization for the
Southwest Community (POSC),
124, 125, 126–127
"Proxies for People" program,
263–265
Puerto Rican community, 82, 93,
105, 111

Ramage, Rev. David, 167
Reed, Scott, 270
Reuther, Walter, 55

Reveille for Radicals, 29–34, 36, 37,
    43–45, 67, 96, 137, 166, 174, 199,
    239, 240, 244, 257
Rickover, Hyman, 4
Ridgeway, James, 214
Rieser, Leonard, 57, 116, 130
Ritter, Archbishop Joseph E., 78, 79
Roberts, Chalmers, 55
Robinson, Hubbell, 52
Rochester (New York), 168–169,
    176–228; Bishop Fulton J.
    Sheen, 211–217; Eastman Kodak
    negotiations, 201–228; FIGHT
    organization, 191–198, 201–228;
    Friends of FIGHT, 199–201;
    invitation to IAF, 183–191; riots
    of 1964, 176–183
Rochester, Catholic Diocese of,
    185–186; Bishop Fulton J.
    Sheen, 211–217; Bishop James
    E. Kearney, 191
Rochester Area Ministers
    Conference (RAMC), 189
Rochester *Catholic Courier-Journal,*
    188
Rochester Council of Churches,
    Board of Urban Ministry
    (BUM), 180–191, 210–211;
    FIGHT and, 210, 215, 224; 1964
    riots and, 177
Rochester *Democratic & Chronicle,*
    187, 208, 212
Rochester *Times-Union,* 191, 212
Rockefeller, John D., III, 59
Rockefeller, Nelson A., 177
Rockefeller Foundation, 59, 234
Rome project, 114–119
Roosevelt, Eleanor, 97
Roosevelt, Franklin D., 46, 261
Rosen, Theodore, 12, 24
Rosenwald, Julius, 59
Rosenwald Fund, 57
Ross, Fred, 34–39; CSO organizing
    by, 43–44, 53, 60–65, 68, 70–72;
    farm workers and, 170–173, 230
Roybal, Eduardo, 40

Royko, Mike, 248
Rules for Radicals, 239–242, 252, 253
Rutgers University, 60

Sacramento, 62, 71
St. Columbas Church (New York),
    102
St. Cyril's Church (Chicago), 135
St. John Cantius Church (Chicago),
    164
Salinas, 62, 69
"Sal Si Puedes," 61
San Antonio, 57
San Bernardino, 62
San Diego, 57
San Joaquin Valley, 62
San Jose, 60, 61, 66, 69, 70
*Saul D. Alinsky: An Unauthorized
    Autobiography,* 247
"Saul-Paul" letters, 95
Schlesinger, Arthur, Jr., 48
Schuster, George N., 115
Schwartzhaupt, Emil, 59
Schwartzhaupt Foundation,
    Alinsky's proposal to, 59–61;
    Butte project, 89; Carl
    Tjerandsen and, 67; Central
    West St. Louis project, 80–81;
    Chelsea Citizen Participation
    Project, 100; CSOs and, 59–61,
    65, 71; Lackawanna project, 87;
    Leonard M. Rieser and, 57;
    Woodlawn project, 144, 145
Scott, Rev. Raymond, 227
Sealy Mattress Company, 42
Sears, Roebuck, and Company, 54,
    59
Selvas, Ernie, 90
Shaw, Clifford R., 9–13, 15, 19–20
Shaw, G. Howland, John D.
    Rockefeller, III and, 59;
    national organizing campaign
    and, 57; as original IAF
    Trustee, 24; as treasurer of
    NCCC, 74–75; War Bond
    rallies, 28

Shay's Rebellion (1786), 32
Sheen, Bishop Fulton J., 211–217
Sheil, Bishop Bernard J. ("Bernie"),
    Agnes Meyer and, 56–57; Back
    of the Yards Council and,
    17–18; break with Alinsky, 56,
    113; CSO funding and, 41,
    44–46; IAF establishment by,
    23–24
Sherman, Gordon, 233–234
Shriver, Sargent, 262
Shuster, George N., 248, 260
Sibley, Georgiana, 177, 181
Sibley, Mrs. Harper, Sr. (Georgiana
    Sibley), 216
Siciliano, H. Richard, 184
Silberman, Charles, *Crisis in Black
    and White*, 173–175; vs. Philip
    M. Hauser, 186–189; Woodlawn
    project and, 143, 158
Simpkins, Canon St. Julian, 184
Sinclair, Upton, 14
Sleepy Lagoon murder trial, 41
Smith, Alfred E., 32
Smugtown-USA, 199. *See also*
    Rochester (New York)
Soledad, 69
South St. Paul (Minnesota), 26–27,
    57, 72
Southern California, 29, 34–37. *See
    also* Community Service
    Organization (CSO)
Southern Christian Leadership
    Movement (SCLC), 182–183,
    235
Southmoor Hotel (Woodlawn), 151,
    155
Spellman, Cardinal Francis, 56
Square Deal, 147, 149
Steinbeck, John, 37
Step-Up program, 201, 202
Stevenson, Adlai, 51
Stiefel, Babette, 48–49
Still, Douglas, 167, 235, 236
St. Louis (Missouri), 80–81
Stockton (California), 70–71

Stone, Robert, 184
Strassner, Kawlyn, 237
Stritch, Samuel Cardinal, death of,
    115; ecumenical attitude of,
    121–122, 167; Grand Boulevard
    project and, 113; Monsignor
    O'Grady and, 76–77; Near
    North Side project and,
    110–111; Rome meeting of, with
    Alinsky, 115; Sheil's dislike of,
    56; Southwest Chicago project
    and, 123; Woodlawn project
    and, 83–84
Student Non-Violent Coordinating
    Committee (SNCC), 133
Students for a Democratic Society,
    (SDS), 132
Swift meat packing company, 14, 56
Szabo, Monsignor Julius J., 86

Tabankin, Margery, 239
Tardini, Cardinal Domenico, 116
Temporary Woodlawn Committee,
    134
Temporary Woodlawn
    Organization (TWO), black
    voter registration campaign,
    149–150; convention of,
    155–158; defections from,
    148–149; institution of, 146;
    public schools campaign,
    150–152; Square Deal campaign,
    147, 149; urban renewal
    campaign, 145–146, 152–154, 156
Tennis, Eugene, 180, 181, 183, 218
Third Presbyterian Church
    (Rochester), 182, 199
Third Ward Urban Renewal
    program, 195, 197
Third World, 245–246
Thrasher, Fredrich M., 10
Till, Emmett, 135
Time, 18
Tjerandsen, Carl, Butte Citizens
    Project and, 91; Chelsea project
    and, 100, 101, 104; Citizen's

Federation of Lackawanna (CFL) and, 88–89; CSO educationals and, 70, 171, 172; executive secretary of Schwartzhaupt Foundation, 59; at Institute of Citizenship at Kansas State University, 66–67; St. Louis project and, 80–81

Tobias, Richard, 188
Tocqueville, Alexis de, 33, 254
Todd, George, 184, 234, 248
Tormey, Fr. Richard T., 188
Trapp, Shel, 270
Truman, Harry S., 55

Unitarian-Universalists Association, 218
United Cannery, Agricultural Packing and Allied Workers of America (UCAPAWA), 38
United Farm Workers of America, 173, 230. See also Chavez, Cesar; Huerta, Dolores; Southern California
United Fund, 79, 82. See also Community Chest/United Fund
United Mine Workers, 46
United Neighborhood Houses, 95
United Packinghouse Workers of America (UPWA), 43, 170, 171
United Presbyterian Church, Board of National Missions, 243
United Woodlawn Conference, 148
United Woodlawn Project, 146
Urbanization Committee of the United Church of Christ, 168

Valdez, Luis, 41
Vatican, 114–122
Vaughn, William S., 203, 204, 205, 207, 213, 220, 221, 225
Villemas, Joe, 124
von Hoffman, Nicholas, on Alinsky, 258, 268; Cardinal Stritch and, 110, 113; FIGHT-Kodak and,

214; Freedom Riders rally, 134–136; Hyde Park Urban Renewal Project, 120–121; on *John L. Lewis*, 47; Lackawanna project, 85–89; Near North Side project, 110–111; resignation of, 158–159; Southwest Chicago, 124, 127; *Washington Post* reporter, 186, 230; Woodlawn project, 82–85, 136, 144, 145–150, 156–158, 160, 165

Wagner, Robert F., 94, 104
Walker, Lucius, Jr., 235–236
Wallace, Henry, 55
Wallis, W. Allen, 215, 216
Wanger, Walter, 29, 37
War Bond rallies, 28–29
"War on Poverty," 262
War Relocation Authority, 38
Washington Post, 54, 55, 95
"We Shall Overcome," 135–136
West Town, 160–165
WHAM, 188
WHEC-TV, 191
Whelan, Ralph, 102
White, Herbert D., on Alinsky, 251, 266; FIGHT-Kodak struggle, 217, 224; Friends of FIGHT, 200; invitation to IAF and, 183–185, 190; Rochester riot of 1964 and, 180–181
White, Jessica, 270
White, Theodore H., 133
Willis, Benjamin, 151, 157
"Willis Must Go" campaign, 151, 157
Willkie, Wendell, 46
Wilson, Charles, 56, 74
Wilson Company, 14
Winnebago Indian burial sites, 6
Winter, Gibson, 127
Wirth, Louis, 36, 37, 56, 59
Woodlawn Block Club Council, 146

Woodlawn Businessmen's
    Association, 147, 148, 153
Woodlawn Latin American
    Committee, 83
Woodlawn Organization, 154–159.
    See also Temporary Woodlawn
    Organization; Woodlawn
    project
Woodlawn (Chicago) project, church
    support/conflict over, 136–145;
    CORE Freedom Riders rally,
    132–136; Greater Woodlawn
    Pastors' Alliance, 144, 146, 148.
    See also Temporary Woodlawn
    Organization (TWO)

World War II, 28–29
Wozniak, Monsignor William, 84, 85
Wurth, Estelle, 200

Xerox Corporation, 18, 201–202, 223

Young, Andrew, 182
Young Christian Workers (YCW),
    82

Zartman, L. Story, 222
"Zoot Suit," 41
ZOTO (Zone One Tondo
    Organization), 245